Contents

Credits

Special thanks go to the artists and studios that permitted their work to be included in this book.

Skulls depicted in Figures 4.3, 4.4, and 4.5 are provided by:
Orin Adcox
Producer and 3D Artist
Virginia Serious Game Institute
George Mason University
https://orinadcox.com

Cartoon Termite Hero depicted in Figures 6.19, 6.51, 6.52, 6.53, 6.56, 6.58, 6.60, 6.61, 6.63, and 6.69 is provided by:
Amro Awad
Zealous Interactive

Spider Minion depicted in Figures 6.19, 6.46, 6.47, 6.62, 6.63, 6.71, 6.73, 6.61, 6.63, and 6.69 is provided by:
Lil Pupinduy
https://www.artstation.com/lil_pupinduy
https://www.unrealengine.com/marketplace/en-US/profile/Lilpupinduy

Introduction

Welcome game developers and mathematicians!

This book exists to help you learn mathematical concepts commonly used in the wonderful world of game development.

About the Author(s)

Jacob Enfield is a research faculty member at George Mason University where he teaches game development in the Computer Game Design program and conducts research at the Virginia Serious Game Institute. Jacob has worked professionally as an educational game developer and has taught a wide range of subjects including computer science, game development, virtual reality, machine learning, artificial intelligence, and mathematics.

In writing this book, contributions were made by several of the author's emerging personas.

Ms. Pi is a high school math teacher who is always looking for ways to get her students excited about math. She is super excited about sharing this book and just cannot help but offer her own math tidbits.

Noah Itall is a self-proclaimed Unity expert. His sarcasm and passive aggressiveness are often expressed when he knows a "better" way to do things.

Bugs Flanders proudly claims the title of computer nerd. He enjoys figuring out every line of code and is good at fixing scripts that do not work as intended or that do not work at all. Fortunately, Bugs also enjoys sharing his debugging strategies.

Gabriella Green prefers to be called ***GG***, which is actually short for her screen name *Gamer Girl*. She is full of ideas for how games might be designed to be more fun.

DOI: 10.1201/9781032701431-1

About the Book

Math becomes relevant and dare I say "fun" when you apply it to real-world problems.

With that in mind…

The first two chapters provide the fundamental concepts needed to understand examples and activities provided throughout the remainder of this book. Chapter 1 offers an overview of the Unity Game Engine. Chapter 2 offers a primer on computer programming with C#.

Most of the remaining chapters introduce a mathematical concept and demonstrate how it applies to the real-world challenge of game development. These chapters have the following structure:

1. The **Introduction** briefly describes a game development (i.e., *game dev*) challenge.

2. **The Math** section provides a lesson over the math concepts that will be needed.

 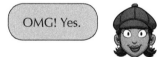 I can help with this!

3. In the **Application** section, a custom game project will be provided, giving you a context to apply the math concepts learned to solve game dev challenges.

Probably not as good as games I've made, but I suppose I'll take a look.

4. The **Challenges** section provides an opportunity to allow you to further modify (*mod*) the game.

OMG! Yes. Challenges may focus on art, design, math, and, of course, coding!

5. The **Achievements** section summarizes and reflects on what was learned and accomplished in the chapter.

6. The **Exercises** section provides problems, sometimes within a game dev context, for learners to practice applying the math concepts covered in the chapter. Answers to exercise problems are provided at the end of the book.

As in the real-life application of mathematics, the solution to a game dev challenge may require the combined use of several different domains, including algebra, geometry, trigonometry, and calculus. Therefore, this book will not cover a single domain in depth. Instead, this book will touch on the relevant concepts from all of these domains.

 And yes, I make comments on my own writing.

Prerequisite Knowledge

To understand the mathematics presented in this book, you should be comfortable with algebra. Familiarity with trigonometry and vector mathematics would be helpful but not required.

 Those are some of the topics you will be learning in this book!

Experience with the Unity Game Engine is **not** required. Chapter 1 provides a light introduction to Unity that covers the features and processes that will be needed to work with the project files and complete the activities and challenges presented in the book. For those who are proficient in using Unity, you may still want to skim through the chapter to ensure that you are prepared for the remaining chapters.

 You think you know something about Unity that I don't. *[scoffs and sneers]*

Computer programming experience is **not** required. Chapter 2 provides a primer for the programming concepts that are needed to understand the lessons, activities, and challenges presented in this book. For those who have programming experience, you may still want to review Chapter 2 to become familiar with the C# language and writing code within the context of the Unity Game Engine.

 A refresher never hurts… and I bet there are some gaps in my coding knowledge.   I have never coded. This should be interesting.

PROJECT FILES

This book is designed for the reader to work on projects included with each chapter. These projects may be downloaded from https://www.routledge.com/9780367527716.

 Be sure to unzip the files after downloading.

INSTRUCTOR RESOURCES

Project files of completed activities, solutions to select challenges and exercises, and other supplementary resources are available to instructors using this book. Requests for instructor resources can be made at https://www.routledge.com/9780367527716.

1

Unity Fundamentals

Why Unity?

Sometimes game programmers start from scratch. They pick up a programming language and just start writing code to create a game world, add gravity to objects, check for collisions between objects, and so on. Other times developers will use code *libraries* that have been written by others to provide much of the functionality developers need to quickly create a game. Very often, game developers use *game engines* that not only offer a large library of code for common functionality needed in games but also provide a visual interface for building the games.

The Unity 3D game engine (Unity) is one of many game engines on the market. Unity was selected for this book because it is popular and widely used in the game industry. Also, it's free to use!

 Technically, *Unity Personal* is free. *Unity Professional* is not. Content from this book will work in either version.

Downloading and Installing Unity

Unity may be downloaded from unity.com/download.

The first step is to download and install Unity Hub. Unity Hub allows you to download and manage different versions of Unity. After launching Unity Hub, click on the **Installs** tab to view all versions of Unity that have been installed and to **ADD** new versions.

FIGURE 1.1 Installs tab of Unity Hub.

While the projects and examples in this book will likely work with many past and future versions, the version of Unity used for this book was 2021.3.25f1. This is a version that has long-term support (LTS). It is recommended that you use the same version or the latest LTS version available. It is recommended to download Unity with *Documentation* and *Visual Studio* by default which is adequate for the projects in this book.

DOI: 10.1201/9781032701431-2

Once Unity is installed, you can open it in the same way you open any program. However, it is better practice to open Unity through Unity Hub. From the **Projects** tab, click on a project from the list or create a **NEW** project. From the **Open** dropdown, you can make existing projects, such as those projects included with this book, appear in the list.

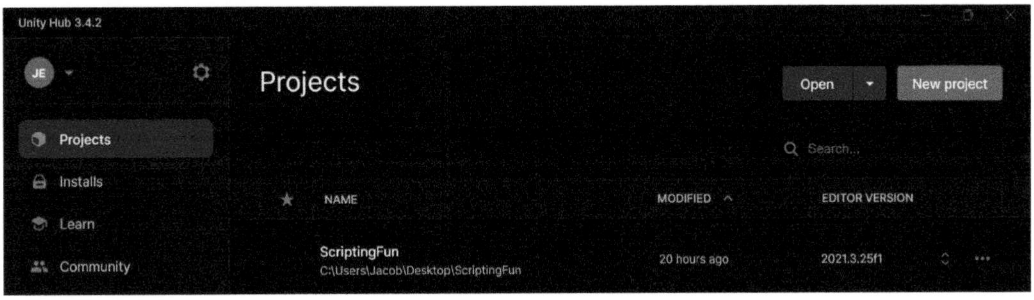

FIGURE 1.2   Projects tab of Unity Hub.

The Unity Interface

When creating a **NEW** Unity project, select the **3D** option, enter a project name, and choose a desired location to save the project files.

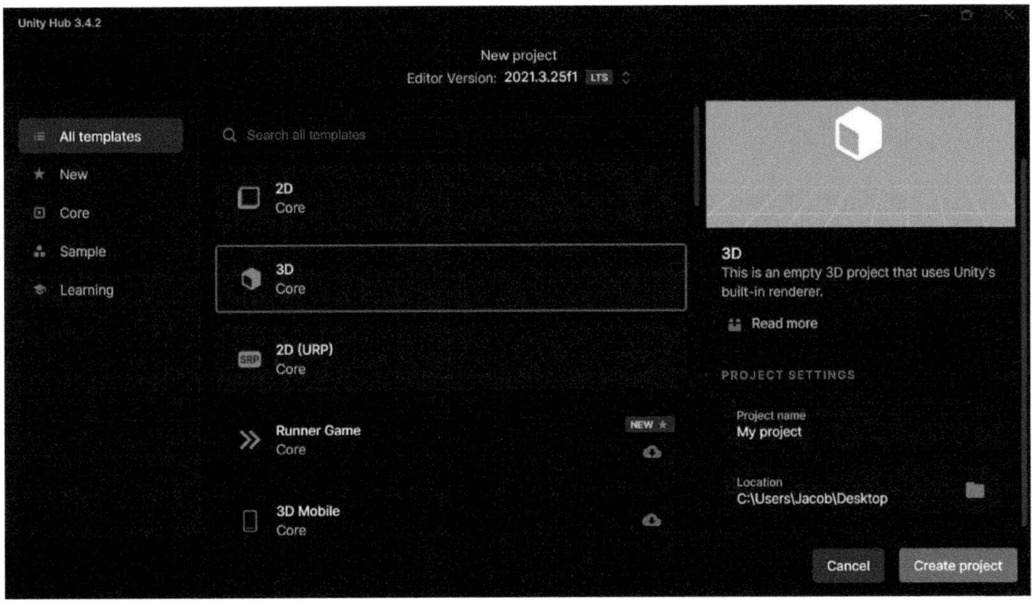

FIGURE 1.3   New Project in Unity Hub.

After you click the **Create project** button, a loading bar will appear while the project is being set up.

After loading, your project will open in Unity.

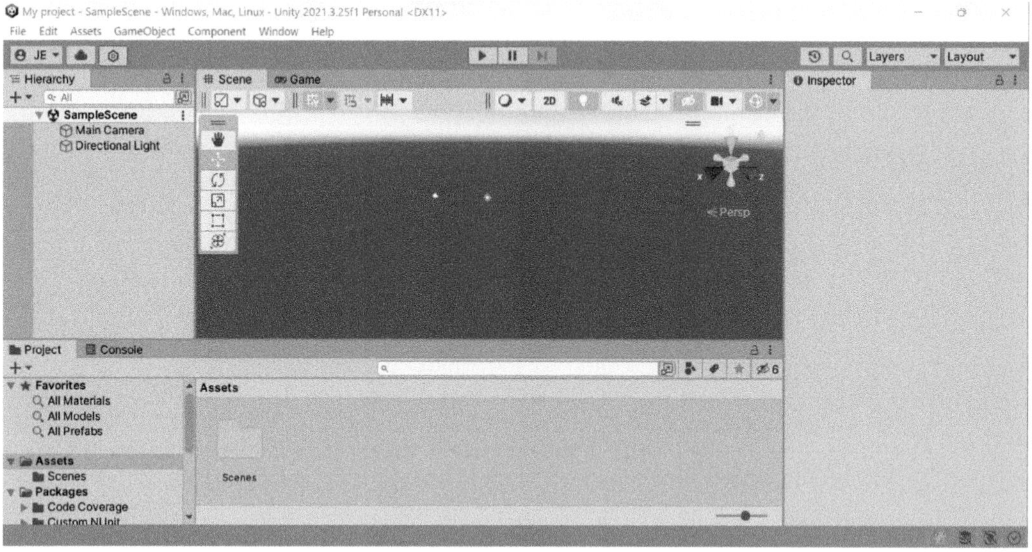

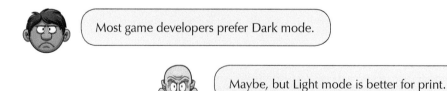

FIGURE 1.4   New Project open in Unity.

By default, newer versions of Unity use the Dark theme. If you want to be more consistent with the images in this book, change to the Light theme through the Preferences located under the Edit menu.

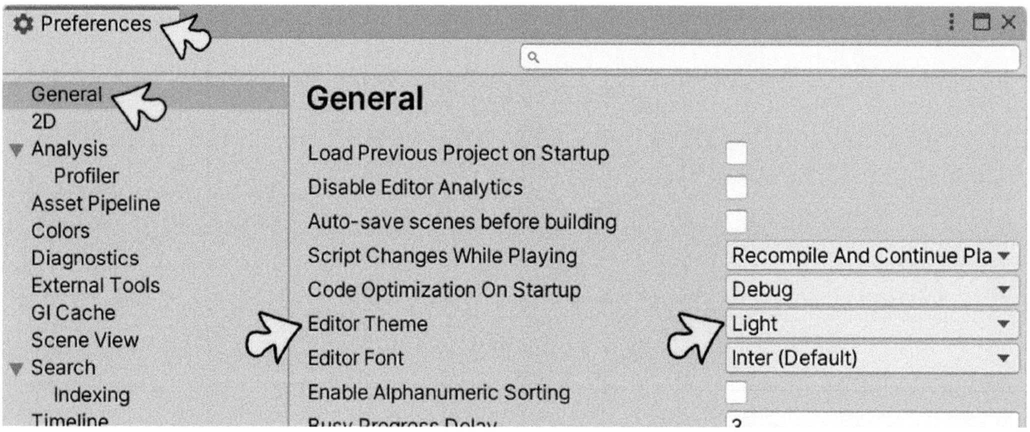

FIGURE 1.5   Preferences Window to change Editor Theme.

Most game developers prefer Dark mode.

Maybe, but Light mode is better for print.

Within Unity, you can open, close, move, dock, and undock windows to achieve a layout that is conducive to your general workflow or to a specific task.

There are several layouts provided by Unity in the **Layout** dropdown menu located at the top-right of the Unity user interface (UI).

You can always select **Default** to return to the default layout. The Default layout is used throughout most of the book.

 I prefer my own custom layout. You can use the Layout menu to save a layout and to open layouts you have previously saved.

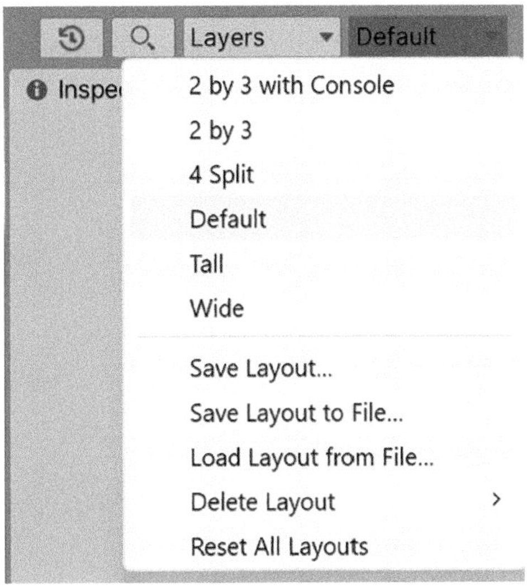

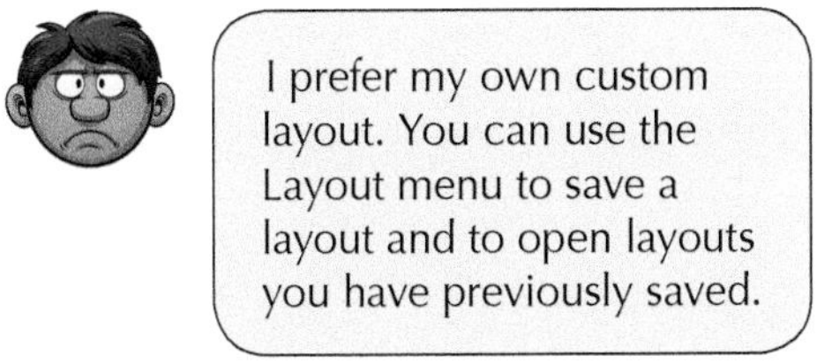

FIGURE 1.6   Layout dropdown options.

Look at the UI elements and windows that are visible in the Default layout.

The *Hierarchy Window* displays a list of all *GameObjects* in the currently open *Scene*.

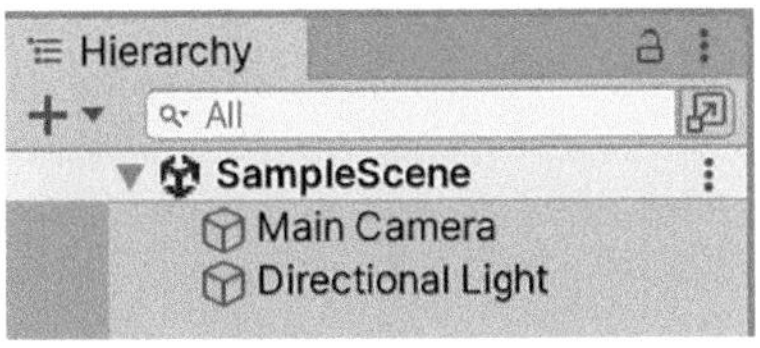

A new project starts with one scene named SampleScene which includes two GameObjects—a *Main Camera* and a *Directional Light*.

The Main Camera provides a view of the game world to the player. The Directional Light lights up the scene so the player is not in the dark.

FIGURE 1.7   Hierarchy Window.

The *Scene Window* displays what is in the scene.

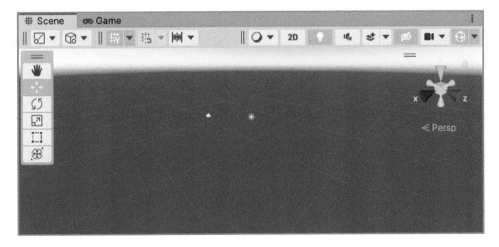

FIGURE 1.8   Scene Window.

The Directional Light has no actual size, but its location is indicated by a sun *gizmo*. Similarly, the camera gizmo indicates the location of the Main Camera which also has no size. Gizmos are visible during editing, but not when the game is running. The blue horizon in the scene is the default *sky box*.

At the top of the Scene Window, there are several buttons that you will find useful. Hover over the buttons for a brief description of what each is used for.

Clicking on an object in the Hierarchy selects it in the Scene as well. When the Main Camera is selected, faint lines appear to indicate the camera's field of view—what can be seen through the camera. The view of the camera is shown through a *Camera Preview* at the bottom-right of the Scene Window.

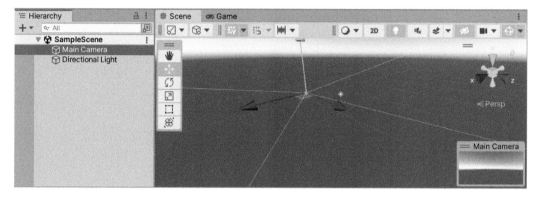
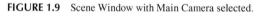

FIGURE 1.9   Scene Window with Main Camera selected.

Clicking within a Window gives that window *focus*. A blue line appears over the tab of the window which currently has focus. Keys pressed on the keyboard may cause different behaviors depending on which window has focus. For instance, pressing the arrow keys while the Scene Window has focus causes a different behavior than pressing the arrow keys when the Hierarchy Window has focus.

In the default layout, the **Game Window** is in the same set of windows as the Scene Window. Click on the Game tab to switch to the Game Window. The Game Window displays the game through the Main Camera. Unity will automatically switch to the Game Window when the game is played.

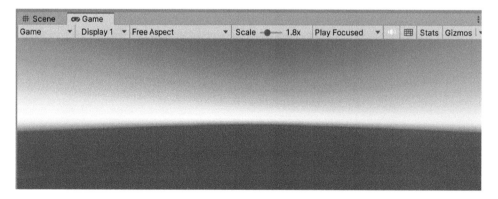

FIGURE 1.10   Game Window.

If you are ever unable to click on objects in the scene to select and edit them, you likely have the Game Window open instead of the Scene Window.

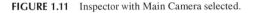

FIGURE 1.11   Inspector with Main Camera selected.

The ***Inspector Window*** shows the name of the currently selected GameObject and its components. If no GameObject is selected, the Inspector window is empty.

The checkbox next to the GameObject's name can be used to toggle the GameObject on and off. This is sometimes useful when you want to temporarily remove an object from the scene without deleting it from the hierarchy.

Components of a GameObject can also be toggled on and off if there is a checkbox next to the component name. The Transform component has no such checkbox, so it may not be toggled off.

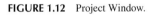

FIGURE 1.12   Project Window.

The **Project Window** provides a view of all files that are saved in the project regardless of whether or not they are being used in the currently open scene.

New projects have an *Assets* folder to save game assets such as textures, materials, 3D models, sprites, audio files, and scripts. The *Scenes* folder within the *Assets* folder contains the default *SampleScene* file.

The files you see in the Project Window reflect the files as they are saved on your computer. The project window will reflect changes made in the File Explorer (Windows) or Finder (Mac), and vice versa.

As the number of files in the project grows, you may want the folder and file icons to be smaller, or even to be displayed in a *list view*. You can do this by moving the slider at the bottom-right to the far left.

FIGURE 1.13   Project Window in List View.

The **Play button** is located at the top center of the Unity interface. Pressing Play will automatically display the Game Window and begin running your game within Unity.

FIGURE 1.14   Play Button.

Pressing the same play button again will stop the game.

Be sure to stop the game before editing. Changes made to the properties of a GameObject while the game is running will **not** be saved.

GameObjects and Components

Everything listed in the Hierarchy Window is a *GameObject*, each made up of components. Click on the *Main Camera* to view its components in the Inspector Window.

❶ Inspector							🔒 ⋮
📦	✓	**Main Camera**				Static	▼
	Tag	MainCamera	▼	Layer	Default		▼
▼ ⤬	**Transform**					❓ ⇄ ⋮	
Position		X	0	Y	1	Z	-10
Rotation		X	0	Y	0	Z	0
Scale		⬡ X	1	Y	1	Z	1
▶ ▣ ✓	**Camera**					❓ ⇄ ⋮	
🎧 ✓	**Audio Listener**					❓ ⇄ ⋮	
			Add Component				

This GameObject has a *name* of "Main Camera" and a *tag* of "MainCamera". The name and tag of a GameObject can be used by scripts to access the GameObject.

The Main Camera has three *components*—a Transform, a Camera, and an Audio Listener. Use the triangles to the left of each component name to expand and collapse the *properties* of the components.

FIGURE 1.15   Inspector showing Main Camera while Camera component is collapsed.

Components are the building blocks of GameObjects.

Notice the Camera Preview appears and disappears in the Scene as the *Camera* component is expanded and collapsed.

The only component that exists for all GameObjects is the *Transform*. This is why there is no checkbox next to the Transform to allow it to be toggled off. A Transform consists of a *Position*, *Rotation*, and *Scale*, each defined by three properties (x, y, and z).

The initial values of properties when the game begins can be set in the Inspector Window using checkboxes, text fields, and other UI elements. You can often change values more quickly by clicking on the label of the property (not the value itself) and dragging left or right. Try this method to change the X property of the Main Camera's position. As you drag left or right, you should see the value change while the Main Camera moves within the Scene view.

Primitive Shapes

The Main Camera and Directional Light have no physical manifestation within the game, so they have no size. GameObjects that have no size do not appear during gameplay, even if their values for their scale change. Other GameObjects do have a visual manifestation. For instance, Unity provides GameObjects with preset components to allow you to quickly add 3D shapes.

Add a GameObject that will appear in your game.

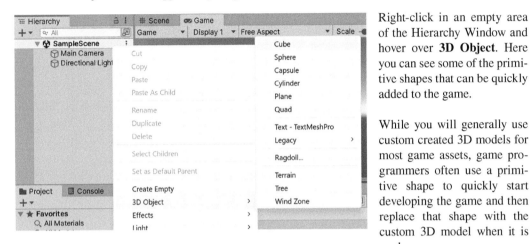

Right-click in an empty area of the Hierarchy Window and hover over **3D Object**. Here you can see some of the primitive shapes that can be quickly added to the game.

While you will generally use custom created 3D models for most game assets, game programmers often use a primitive shape to quickly start developing the game and then replace that shape with the custom 3D model when it is ready.

FIGURE 1.16   List of primitive 3D Objects.

This practice, called *white boxing*, is also useful for rapid prototyping. You can start testing your game concept to ensure it is fun before spending all the time needed to create beautiful 3D models and animations.

From the *3D Object* sub-menu, click on **Cube** to add a cube to the scene.

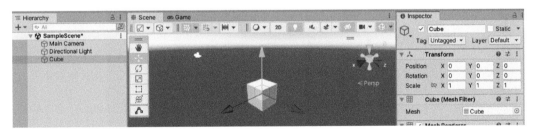

FIGURE 1.17   Selected cube visible in Hierarchy, Scene, and Inspector.

The Cube appears in the Hierarchy and Scene windows. With the cube selected, its components appear in the Inspector Window. Arrows appear around the cube if the Move Tool, which will be discussed in the next section, is selected.

The name of the cube can be changed in the Inspector Window to "Player", or any other name that describes what the GameObject is intended to represent. Naming GameObjects when you create them is highly encouraged to ensure that specific GameObjects can easily be found within the Hierarchy Window. This is important as the number of GameObjects in the Scene grows.

Giving meaningful names to GameObjects is also helpful when writing code that needs to access those objects by name.

Components can be added or removed from the Cube to change its appearance or behavior. For now, take a look at the components that come already attached to the default Cube.

The **Cube (Mesh Filter)** component represents the physical form of the object. Meshes are made up of triangles in 3D space. For instance, one side of a cube could be defined by two triangles.

As a cube consists of six sides, 12 triangles are needed for a mesh that defines a cube.

The **Mesh Renderer** is used to render, or draw, the mesh by showing the faces of all the triangles. Think of the Mesh Renderer as the surface or skin of a GameObject.

The **Box Collider** is used to determine whether or not the GameObject is colliding with other GameObjects. By default, the Box Collider is the same shape as the cube.

With the Box Collider expanded and enabled, toggle off the Mesh Renderer to see the edges of the cube without the mesh.

Be sure to re-enable the Mesh Renderer so the cube will be visible when it is deselected and when the game is played.

Colliders do not have to be the same size or shape as the GameObject they are attached to. In fact, one GameObject can have multiple colliders or have no colliders at all. For example, the Main Camera and Directional Light do not have colliders because they are not intended to collide with other objects in the game.

FIGURE 1.18 Cube components in the Inspector Window.

The **Default-Material** defines what material will be used when rendering the mesh. The default material in Unity can be changed, though it is gray initially.

Navigating the Scene and Manipulating GameObjects

Some of the most important skills in game development are the ability to move about a scene and manipulate GameObjects within a scene to design a level. Try out some of the methods listed below.

When the Scene Window has focus, the left and right arrow keys allow you to pan to the left and right of the scene, while the up and down arrow keys allow you to zoom toward or away from the center of the scene view.

Right-click and drag in the Scene Window to rotate the view. This keeps the camera in the same position as you look around. Think of this as standing in one place in the scene while turning your head to look around.

Scroll up and down to zoom toward and away from the center of the scene view.

While holding the Alt key down on a PC or the Option key on a MAC, right-click and drag in the Scene Window to zoom toward or away from the location of your cursor.

Double-click on any GameObject in the Hierarchy to zoom to that object and give it focus.

Double-click on a GameObject in the Hierarchy Window or click on the object in the Scene Window to give it focus. Then, while pressing down the Alt key on a PC or the Option key on a MAC, click and drag to orbit around the GameObject.

In the default view, the **Tools** are docked in the top left corner of the Scene Window. These tools are used to navigate the scene and manipulate objects. Hover over the buttons to see the name of each tool.

The top row of letters of a typical QWERTY keyboard serves as shortcuts for quickly switching between the tools. The keys are in sequence with the icons, with **Q** activating the View Tool, **W** activating the Move Tool, **E** activating the Rotate Tool, **R** activating the Scale Tool, **T** activating the Rect Tool, and **Y** activating the Transform Tool.

Additional Tools may appear when various types of objects are selected. For instance, the Edit Bounding Volume tool appears when a Cube is selected.

FIGURE 1.19 Tools.

With the **View Tool** selected, click within the Scene Window and drag to *pan* the view of the scene. Panning the scene does not move any objects in your scene; it simply changes your view of the scene.

With the **Move Tool** selected, click on any GameObject to move it. Clicking directly on the arrows that appear on the selected object and dragging will allow you to move the object along a single axis.

When you click on an arrow and move the object along an axis, the corresponding value for the object's position updates in the Inspector Window.

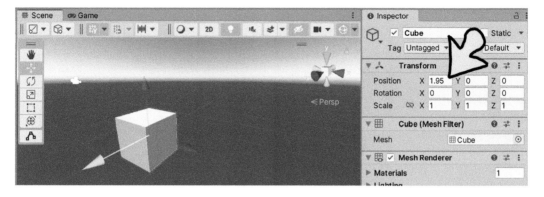

FIGURE 1.20   The Cube's position changes in the Inspector as it is moved along an axis.

You can also click where the three arrows meet to move the GameObject without being restrained along a single axis, though this can make it difficult to place objects as intended within a 3D space.

With the **Rotate Tool** selected, click on any object to rotate it. Clicking directly on the circular lines that appear around the selected object and dragging will allow you to rotate the object along a single axis.

When you click within the circular lines instead of clicking directly on them, the rotation will not be restrained to a single axis. Again, as you rotate GameObjects in the Scene Window, the rotation values should automatically update in the Inspector Window.

With the **Scale Tool** selected, click on an object that has a physical representation in the game, such as the Cube, to resize the object. Clicking directly on one of the three outer blocks that appear around the selected object and dragging will allow you to scale the object along a single axis.

Often you will want to scale an object while constraining its proportions to avoid stretching it in one direction more than another. This is especially true when using 3D models instead of primitive shapes. To scale the object on all three axes at the same time, click on the center block and drag.

The **Rect Tool** can be used to move, resize, and rotate objects. This tool is most useful when working with UI elements and 2D layouts and sprites.

The **Transform Tool** combines the Move, Rotate, and Scale tools.

Like most software, Unity uses many shortcut keys to provide more efficient methods to complete tasks. You can learn many of these shortcuts from the drop-down menus.

For instance, you can see that the shortcuts for common **Edit** functionality are consistent with most other creative software, including *Ctrl X* to cut, *Ctrl C* to copy, and *Ctrl V* to paste.

The *Ctrl Z* shortcut is frequently useful to undo a change and can be pressed multiple times to undo several changes.

Edit		
Undo Move Cube(1.95, 0.00, 0.00)		Ctrl+Z
Redo		Ctrl+Y
Undo History		Ctrl+U
Select All		Ctrl+A
Deselect All		Shift+D
Select Children		Shift+C
Select Prefab Root		Ctrl+Shift+R
Invert Selection		Ctrl+I
Cut		Ctrl+X
Copy		Ctrl+C
Paste		Ctrl+V
Paste As Child		Ctrl+Shift+V
Duplicate		Ctrl+D
Rename		
Delete		
Frame Selected		F
Lock View to Selected		Shift+F

FIGURE 1.21 Edit Menu with shortcuts displayed.

Saving

An asterisk next to the scene name in the Hierarchy Window indicates that the scene has not been saved since the last change.

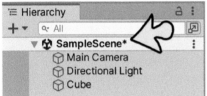

FIGURE 1.22 Asterisk in Hierarchy indicating unsaved changes to the scene.

The asterisk will disappear when the scene is saved and will re-appear when another action occurs.

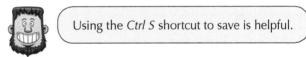

Using the *Ctrl S* shortcut to save is helpful.

Activity: Falling Balls and Animal House

It's time to jump in and get started.

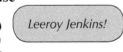

Leeroy Jenkins!

?

This activity will step you through how to complete a very common task—adding a new component to an existing GameObject—to help you become more comfortable with Unity. When finished, your GameObject will be subject to gravity and other forces!

First, you will need the *Falling Balls* project files for this activity. Instructions for downloading the project files used in this book are provided in the Introduction.

Once the project files are downloaded and unzipped, use Unity Hub to open the Falling Balls project. After the project launches in Unity, locate and open the Scene01 scene.

With the scene open and the Main Camera selected, you should see that only one of the three balls is visible through the Camera Preview. That is ok because we want the balls to fall into view when the game begins.

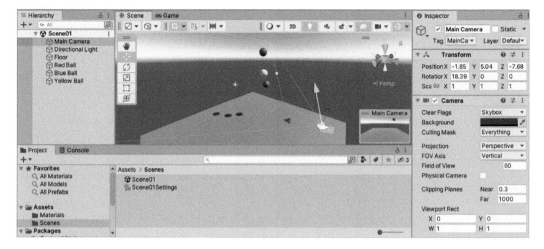

FIGURE 1.23   Falling Balls project open in Unity with Main Camera selected.

A cube was used to create the floor, and spheres were added for the balls. Notice in the Hierarchy Window that the GameObjects were given meaningful names such as "Floor" and "Red Ball". This is good practice to ensure the scene remains manageable for you and other developers on your team.

Notice in the Project Window that a *Materials* folder has been added within the *Assets* folder. Materials were added to the GameObjects to give them color. Additionally, a Physics Material was added to the floor to control how much colliding objects would bounce off it.

Press the Play button to test the game. You should notice that none of the balls fall. How sad. Press the Play button again to stop the game.

Given that Unity has a physics engine, you may wonder why gravity is not automatically being applied to the GameObjects in our scene. This is because not all GameObjects should be affected by gravity and other forces. For example, we do not want the Floor to fall due to gravity or to move when other GameObjects collide with it.

In Unity, applying physics to a GameObject is as simple as adding a *Rigidbody* component.

With the Red Ball selected, click on the *Add Component* button in the Inspector Window.

You can quickly find components by typing the name of the component into the search field. Typing in "rig" narrows the search result list to only a few options.

Click on *Rigidbody* to add this component to the Red Ball.

FIGURE 1.24   Options displayed while typing into Add Component search bar.

Repeat this step for the yellow and blue balls so that there is a Rigidbody on each.

Rigidbody	
Mass	1
Drag	0
Angular Drag	0.05
Use Gravity	✓
Is Kinematic	☐
Interpolate	None ▼
Collision Detection	Discrete ▼
▶ Constraints	
▶ Info	

FIGURE 1.25 Rigidbody component displayed in the Inspector.

A Rigidbody component should now be visible in the Inspector Window when any of the balls are selected.

Notice that the *mass* for each has a default value of 1.

Game Engines reflect the physics of the natural world, so objects fall at the same speed regardless of mass, and objects with greater mass are more resistant to external forces such as collisions with other objects.

Press the Play button again to test the game. You should now see the balls fall, collide with each other, and roll away. Notice the blue ball rolls off the floor before the red ball. Press the Play button again to stop the game.

You can see the properties of a GameObject change while the game is running. For example, if you select the Red Ball before playing the game, you will be able to see its position and rotation values changing in the Inspector Window as the ball moves.

Leave this project open as it will be needed for your first challenge!

Challenges

1. Further modify the Falling Balls project by changing the *mass* property of the Rigidbody components to ensure the red ball rolls off the floor before the blue ball. Do not change the initial position of the balls or any other properties other than the mass.

2. In this challenge, you will need to navigate a scene and manipulate objects to complete a scavenger hunt. From Unity Hub, add and open the Animal House project. Then locate and open the Main scene. In the Hierarchy, expand Furniture, expand Master Bedroom, double-click on Shelves to zoom to them, and use the right-mouse button in the Scene Window to orbit the shelves until you have them squarely in view.

FIGURE 1.26 Shelves within the Animal House project.

The shelves have labels for where various stuffed animals belong. The sheep is already in its proper place. You will need to find the others and return them to their proper place on the shelf.

The challenge is you need to do this with only the Scene Window visible. To view only the Scene Window, press Shift Space while the Scene Window has focus. Using Shift Space allows you to view any window in full screen. Press Shift Space again to return to the current layout.

Use the following hints to find each of the missing animals. Then, move, scale, and rotate each animal to place them in the designated space on the shelf.

pig	Enjoying the beautiful day
rabbit	Dirt don't hurt
kitten	Ready for a nap
elephant	Larger than life
bear	In the forest
monkey	Bumped my head, just like mamma said
penguin	A reprieve on a hot day

Want to practice more while expressing your creativity? Create your own scavenger hunt.

2

Programming Fundamentals

Why Programming?

Adding GameObjects, whether they are primitive shapes or full 3D models, is important in building game worlds. It is equally important to provide behaviors to these GameObjects and give the player the ability to interact with them. Some of these interactions or behaviors can be added with built-in Unity components, such as adding a Rigidbody to an object to allow forces to be applied. However, game developers also need to write code to customize existing behaviors and define new behaviors.

This chapter offers a primer on the computer programming concepts that are common across programming languages—including variables, conditional statements, and functions. Understanding the basic concepts covered in this chapter will prepare you for the mathematics-focused examples and activities in the remaining chapters.

Purpose of Writing Code

Simply, a *computer program* is a list of instructions that directs a computer what to do. Game programming is no different. As computers essentially save and process information, the computer languages used to write computer programs provide a means for instructing the computer to save information (via variables, data types, data structures, etc.) and process information (via conditional statements, operators, functions, etc.).

Editors

Code editing software (e.g., Notepad++, Atom, Sublime Text) is used to write code. These *editors* typically provide features to assist programmers, such as *syntax highlighting* to make code more readable and *code hinting* to make predictive suggestions while writing code. An editor that provides more functionality, such as the ability to compile, execute, and debug code, may be considered an Integrated Development Environment (IDE).

Visual Studio

Visual Studio is a popular IDE that can be used to write programs using a wide range of computer languages. Visual Studio can be downloaded independently or along with Unity, integrates well with the engine, and will be the IDE used throughout this book.

DOI: 10.1201/9781032701431-3

Programming Languages and Syntax

Many computer languages have a wide variety of purposes based on their strengths and weaknesses. Just as natural languages have grammatical rules to define the correct usage of the language, computer languages have *syntax* rules that define how the code must be written. Using proper syntax is important! While humans are very good at understanding languages when grammatical errors are present, computers typically cannot compile or execute scripts that contain any syntax error.

C#

C# (read as "C sharp") is the language used to write scripts within Unity. The syntax for C# is mostly consistent with the syntax for other C-type languages including C, C++, Java, and JavaScript. For example, in all C-type languages, commands end with a semicolon, curly braces are used to group multiple commands together in a *block*, and dot notation is used to access properties and methods of objects.

C# is a *type-safe* language, that is, a variable defined to store data must be defined with the *type* of data that it will store, and this type is immutable (unchangeable). For instance, a variable declared with the *int* keyword may only store integer values while a variable declared with the *float* keyword may only store decimal values.

C# is also case-sensitive. Keywords that have specific meaning in the language such as *int*, *float*, *if*, *else*, *void*, *return*, *public*, and so on must be written in all lowercase. Variable and function names defined in the program are also case-sensitive. A variable named *score* is different than a variable named *SCORE* and a function named *attackEnemies()* is different than a function named *AttackEnemies()*.

The ability for programs written in C# to run on different devices and operating systems aligns well with the Unity Engine, which allows games to be published for various platforms. This DOPE—develop once publish everywhere—approach is one of the benefits of using the Unity game engine.

Create a C# Script

From Unity Hub, create a new project to work along during this lesson.

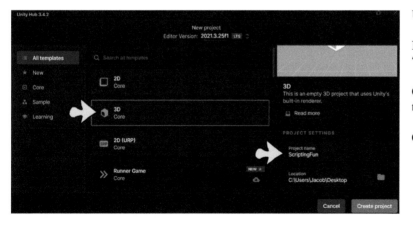

Use the **3D** template.

Name the project "ScriptingFun".

Choose a location for the project to be saved.

Click **Create project**.

FIGURE 2.1   Create project in Unity Hub.

Add a folder to store all scripts.

Assets
■ Scenes
☐ Scripts

Right-click within the *Assets* folder of the Project Window and select *Create > Folder*.

Name the folder "Scripts". Code written for all projects of this book will be saved in a *Scripts* folder.

FIGURE 2.2   Add Scripts Folder.

Create a C# Script

Assets > Scripts
CubeBehaviour

Within the Scripts folder, right-click and select *Create > C# Script*.

Name the script "CubeBehaviour".

FIGURE 2.3   Create C# script.

Edit a C# Script

Double-click the script to open it.

```
CubeBehaviour.cs  ⊕ ✕
C# Miscellaneous Files                    ▾  ⚙ CubeBehaviour
   1    using System.Collections;
   2    using System.Collections.Generic;
   3    using UnityEngine;
   4
   5    public class CubeBehaviour : MonoBehaviour
   6    {
   7        // Start is called before the first frame update
   8        void Start()
   9        {
  10
  11        }
  12
  13        // Update is called once per frame
  14        void Update()
```

What program did your script open in? The script shown here is opened in Visual Studio.

Regardless of the IDE or editor that your script opened in, the filename of *CubeBehaviour.cs* should match the class name of *CubeBehaviour* on line 5 of the script.

FIGURE 2.4   C# script opened in Visual Studio.

If you rename a script after creating it, you must change the class name to match the filename.

Visual Studio integrates well with Unity, allowing the editor to provide information on the C# libraries that Unity is built on.

Trust me. You want to use Visual Studio to edit your code when working with Unity.

It is not enough that your scripts open with Visual Studio.

CubeBehaviour.cs ⊞ ✕

[C#] Miscellaneous Files

If the script did open in Visual Studio, but the "Miscellaneous Files" message appears under the filename, the integration features will not be available.

FIGURE 2.5   Miscellaneous Files message.

Whether your script opened in a different editor or in Visual Studio with the unwanted "Miscellaneous Files" message, you will need to change the default behavior of how scripts are opened from Unity.

⚙ Preferences	⋮ ☐ ✕
🔍	

External Tools

General	External Script Editor	Open by file extension ▾
2D	External Script Editor Ar	✓ Open by file extension
▾ Analysis	Reset argument	Microsoft Visual Studio 2022 [17.4.33110]
Profiler		Microsoft Visual Studio 2019 [16.11.33027]
Asset Pipeline	Image application	
Colors		Browse...
Diagnostics	Revision Control Diff/M	
External Tools	Tool Path	Browse
GI Cache		
Scene View		

Within Unity, select *Edit>Preferences* from the top menu bar.

Select *External Tools.*

Select *Visual Studio* from the *External Script Editor* dropdown menu.

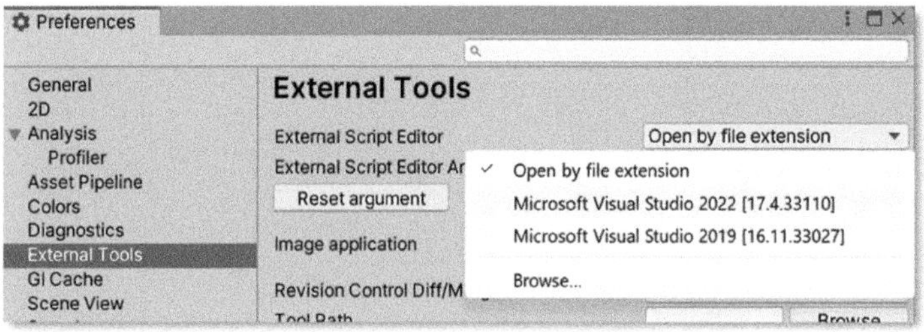

FIGURE 2.6   Set External Script Editor to Visual Studio.

If Visual Studio is not listed as an option, select *Browse* to find the location where you installed Visual Studio on your computer.

Close the Preferences Window after setting Visual Studio as your default editor and close any editors in which your scripts are still open. Then, from the Project Window, double-click the script from within the Scripts folder to open it again.

CubeBehaviour.cs ⊞ ✕

Assembly-CSharp   ▾ ❖ CubeBehaviour

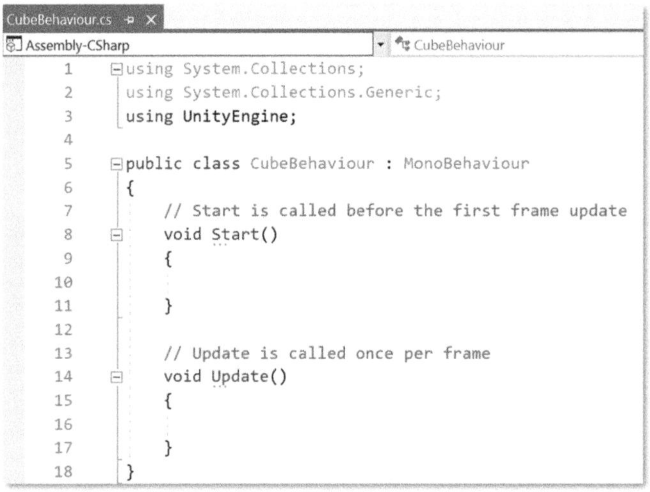

```
 1    using System.Collections;
 2    using System.Collections.Generic;
 3    using UnityEngine;
 4
 5    public class CubeBehaviour : MonoBehaviour
 6    {
 7        // Start is called before the first frame update
 8        void Start()
 9        {
10
11        }
12
13        // Update is called once per frame
14        void Update()
15        {
16
17        }
18    }
```

The *Light* color theme of Visual Studio is used throughout this book. You can change the color theme through the preferences of Visual Studio. Many programmers prefer the *Dark* theme.

The initial code generated when creating a script includes a *class* (CubeBehaviour) that contains two *functions* (Start and Update).

Lines 7 and 13 are *comments* and are ignored when the program executes.

FIGURE 2.7   CubeBehaviour script open in Visual Studio.

As the comments suggest, any code placed within the Start method (between the curly braces on lines 9 and 11) will execute before the first frame. This means that code written here will execute only once—when the game begins with the script attached to a GameObject in the initial scene or when a GameObject that has this script attached dynamically enters the scene during gameplay.

As the next comment suggests, any code placed within the Update will execute repeatedly. If the game is running at a frame rate of 60 fps (frames per second), this code will be executed 60 times every second, assuming the script is attached to a GameObject in the current scene.

Start and *Update* are two of the many functions included for all GameObjects that are automatically called by the engine as the game runs. *Start* and *Update* are so frequently used that they are provided immediately when a new script is created. In fact, the comments seem unnecessary given how well known these functions are to Unity developers.

```
5     public class CubeBehaviour : MonoBehaviour
6     {
7         void Start()
8         {
9             print("Hello World!");
10        }
11
12        void Update()
13        {
14            print("I am still breathing.");
15        }
16    }
```

Delete the comments if you do not find them helpful.

Add a command within the *Start* method to print a message to the Console. The "Hello World!" message is the classic first program for new programmers.

Add a command within the *Update* method to print a different message to the Console.

FIGURE 2.8   Script with updated code.

This script may seem simple, but there is a great deal of room for error. Remember that C# is case-sensitive and that commands, including the print statements, must end in a semicolon. The syntax highlighting can be helpful in finding errors. The keywords are in a different color than the text within quotes, which represent a *string* of characters. The colors used in syntax highlighting are defined by the color theme being used.

Indentation is also helpful in finding errors. While this entire script could technically be written on one line of code, the readability of that code would be very poor. Good indentation involves consistently indenting every new *block* of code. For example, the curly braces on lines 6 and 16 create the block of code that defines the CubeBehaviour class. All commands in this block are indented. Similarly, the curly braces on lines 8 and 10 create the block of all code belonging to the Start method. The code in this block is indented further. Consistent indentation makes it easy to see the pairings of open and closed curly braces. Omitting or misplacing a curly brace is a common error that will prevent your code from compiling or result in unexpected behaviors when executed.

Run a C# Script

Try to run the program you have written. In Visual Studio, select *File > Save* or press *Ctrl S* to save your changes.

Return to Unity and open the console by clicking on the *Console* tab next to the *Project* tab. The output from the print commands that were added to the script should appear in the console.

With the Console visible, press the **Play** button. Did you see any messages appear? Why not?

Hmm… Maybe the script is not running?

FIGURE 2.9 Console with no output.

Remember, files in your project are not necessarily in every scene. In Unity, a script typically needs to be attached to a GameObject in the scene before it will execute.

You could attach the script to any GameObject in the scene, including the default *Main Camera* or the *Directional Light*. Instead, right-click in the Hierarchy Window and select *3D Object>Cube*.

Once the cube is in the scene, there are several ways you can add the CubeBehaviour.cs script to it, including using the *Add Component* button in the Inspector, or by dragging the script from the Project Window into the Scene Window and dropping it directly on the Cube.

The script will appear in the Inspector once it has been successfully attached to the Cube.

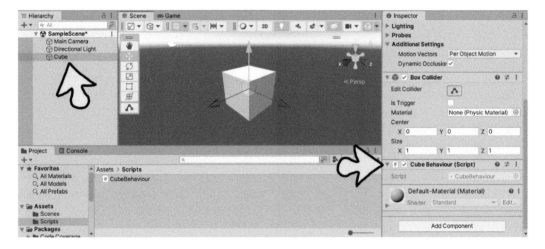

FIGURE 2.10 CubeBehaviour script attached to a Cube.

In the Console window, toggle on the "Clear on Build" and "Clear on Play" buttons so that the old messages, warnings, and errors are cleared from the console every time the Play button is pressed.

At the top-right of the Console Window, the number of messages, warnings, and errors are shown. You can toggle these on and off to filter what is displayed in the Console.

With the messages toggled on, press the Play button again to check that your script runs as expected.

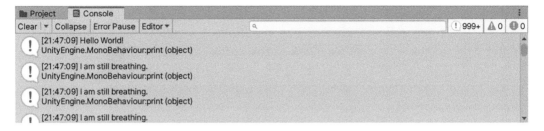

FIGURE 2.11 Console with output displayed during runtime.

The message printed from the *Update* method should repeat continuously. After stopping the game, you can find the message printed by the *Start* method by scrolling to the top of the Console Window.

Notice there is a timestamp next to each message. You can get an idea of the number of frames per second your game is running at by counting the number of messages that are printed in one second, though there are definitely less tedious ways to determine frame rate than this.

Now that you understand how to run a script within Unity, you are ready to learn the fundamental programming concepts needed to understand code discussed later in this book.

Variables and Data Types

Variables are used to store information. Depending on the program requirements, you may need to store a variety of types of data including integers, decimals, text, and so on. In C#, the *type* of data must be specified when a variable is created or *declared*.

For simplicity, remove the *Update* function leaving only the *Start* function that will execute just once.

Modify the code in the Start method as follows.

```
4
5   public class CubeBehaviour : MonoBehaviour
6   {
7       void Start()
8       {
9           int score = 0;
10          float xp = 3.5f;
11
12          print(score);
13      }
14  }
```

1. Declare a variable named *score* that can store integer values and has an initial value of 0.

2. Declare a variable named *xp* that can store decimal values and has an initial value of 3.5f.

3. Print the value that is stored in *score* to the console.

FIGURE 2.12 Script with updated Start method.

This code may seem simple but there is a lot going on. First, on line 9 you are declaring a variable to be of type *int*—meaning it will store an integer—and using the *assignment operator* (the equal sign) to assign an initial value of zero to the variable. Setting an initial value for a variable is called *initializing*.

Similarly, on line 10, *xp* is declared as a variable of type *float*—meaning it will store a decimal—and the assignment operator is initialized to 3.5f.

The squiggly line under the variable name on line 10 indicates a warning. Hovering over the variable name reveals the details of the warning.

```
int score = 0;
float xp = 3.5f;
```

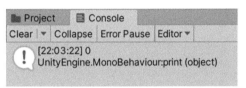

```
print(s
```

[💡 ▾]   [🖈] (local variable) float xp

CS0219: The variable 'xp' is assigned but its value is never used

IDE0059: Unnecessary assignment of a value to 'xp'

Show potential fixes (Alt+Enter or Ctrl+.)

This warning states the variable *xp* is never used. If you were not planning to expand the code further to use this variable, it would be a waste of memory to store the value.

Warning and error messages become easier to read as you gain more programming experience.

FIGURE 2.13   Hovering to see warning message.

📁 Project   📋 Console
Clear ▾ Collapse Error Pause Editor ▾
❗ [22:03:22] 0
UnityEngine.MonoBehaviour:print (object)

If you save your changes in Visual Studio and then press the Play button in Unity, you should see the value of zero printed to the console.

Printing the literal string "score" is different than printing the value of the variable named *score*.

FIGURE 2.14   Console with output during runtime.

```
void Start()
{
    int score = 0;
    float xp = 3.5f;

    print(xp);
}
```

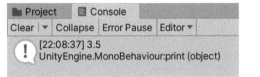

Modify the print statement to print the value of *xp* instead of the value of *score*. The print function is quite versatile in that it can print a variety of data types including string, int, float, and more.

And now the warning moves to indicate that *score* has been declared but never used.

FIGURE 2.15   Printing xp.

📁 Project   📋 Console
Clear ▾ Collapse Error Pause Editor ▾
❗ [22:08:37] 3.5
UnityEngine.MonoBehaviour:print (object)

If you save your changes in Visual Studio and then press the Play button in Unity, you should see the value of 3.5 printed to the console.

Notice the letter *f* that follows the value of 3.5 in the code is not printed to the console.

FIGURE 2.16   Console with output during runtime.

You may wonder why *float* is the type used for variables storing decimal values instead of something more meaningful like *decimal*. You may also wonder why the letter *f* is attached at the end of values assigned to variables of type float. The explanation for both of these curiosities is that there are two different data types in C# (and many other languages) that can store decimal values—*float* and *double*.

A *float* refers to a floating-point value. Just imagine an integer with a decimal point that can float forward or backward within the digits. A variable of type float (i.e., a *float*) requires 4 bytes of memory and can store approximately 6 to 9 digits, depending on the operating system the program is running on.

A *double* can be used to store decimal values with greater precision. A variable of type double (i.e., a *double*) requires 8 bytes of memory ("double" the memory of a float) enabling it to store 15 to 17 digits.

 While the added precision provided by doubles is sometimes needed, often the precision afforded by floats is sufficient and therefore preferred to use less memory.

In C#, a decimal value not followed by an f is a double, while a decimal value followed by an f is a float.

Other types exist for variables that store non-numeric data. For instance, variables of type **bool** store *Boolean* values of *true* and *false*. Variables of type **char** store a single character such as 'a', 'B', '$' and '4'. Variables of type **string** store a series of characters, such as "Hector", "Games are fun!", and "007".

Conditional Statements and Boolean Operators

Conditional statements are used frequently in programming when the program must determine what to do based on the current value of one or more variables. Consider the following code.

```
7    void Start()
8    {
9        string firstName = "Mario";
10
11       if(firstName == "mario")
12       {
13           print("Where is Luigi?");
14       }
15   }
16
```

 Code snippets in this book may show only modified code. Pay attention to line numbers.

For instance, the first three lines of this script are not shown because they contain the same unchanged *using directives* from the earlier versions of the script.

FIGURE 2.17 Script with updated Start method.

This code executes once when the Cube which the script is attached to enters the scene, in this case when the game begins and the scene loads. The variable *firstName* is of type string and is initialized to the value of "Mario" using the assignment operator—a single equal sign.

Line 11 is a conditional statement used to determine if the related code block (lines 12 to 14) will execute or not. The condition that is checked is inside the parenthesis that follows the *if* keyword. In this case, the condition resolves to false because the value of *firstName* does not equal "mario"—the lowercase character 'm' is not the same as the uppercase character 'M'.

Notice the double equal sign is used within the conditional statement instead of a single equal sign. This is because the double equal is a Boolean operator used for comparisons while the single equal sign is the assignment operator used to change the value of a variable.

 It is a common mistake to use a single equal sign when writing a conditional statement.

```
Project    Console
Clear  ▼  Collapse  Error Pause  Editor ▼
  ❗  [22:24:27] Where is Luigi?
      UnityEngine.MonoBehaviour:print (object)
```

Change the string in line 11 to "Mario" and run the program to ensure that the message is now being printed to the console.

FIGURE 2.18   Console with output.

Else statements are often appended after an if block to define code that should execute when the condition fails.

```
 7    ⊟       void Start()
 8            {
 9                string firstName = "Sonic";
10
11    ⊟           if(firstName == "Mario")
12                {
13                    print("Where is Luigi?");
14                }
15    ⊟           else
16                {
17                    print("Who are you?");
18                }
19
20                print("Goodbye");
21            }
22
```

The *else* statement should come immediately after the end of the *if* block.

When this code runs, the conditional statement should evaluate to false, causing the code in the else block to execute and print "Who are you?" to the console.

The "Goodbye" message will print regardless of whether the condition is true or not because it is not part of the conditional statement.

FIGURE 2.19   Updated Start method using else.

There are many Boolean operators other than the double equal sign that may be used within conditional statements, including < for "less than" and > for "greater than". Conditional statements may also chain together multiple conditions using the double ampersand operator for "and" and the double pipe operator for "or".

The pipe, or lbar, can be added by pressing the backslash key while the shift key is down.

Consider the following.

```
 7    ⊟       void Start()
 8            {
 9                int speed = 10;
10
11    ⊟           if(speed > 5 && speed <= 10)
12                {
13                    print("Good driving!");
14                }
15            }
```

Here, using the **&&** operator, both conditions must be true for the entire condition to be true. That is, *speed* must be greater than 5 **AND** *speed* must be less than or equal to 10 for the entire condition to be true. If either condition is false, the entire condition is false.

In this case, both conditions are true so the message will be printed to the console.

FIGURE 2.20   Updated condition using the && operator.

```
7    void Start()
8    {
9        int speed = 10;
10
11       if(speed <= 5 || speed > 10)
12       {
13           print("Bad driving!");
14       }
15   }
```

Here, using the || operator, the entire condition is true if *speed* is less than or equal to 5 **OR** *speed* is greater than 10. If either condition is true, the entire condition is true.

In this case, neither condition is true so the message will not be printed to the console.

FIGURE 2.21 Updated condition using the || operator.

The **not** and **not equal** operators are also frequently used within conditional statements.

```
7    void Start()
8    {
9        int score = 8;
10
11       if(! (score == 3))
12       {
13           print("The score is not 3.");
14       }
15   }
```

The **not** operator—the exclamation mark—negates a Boolean value. That is, it changes any value of *true* to *false* and any value of *false* to *true*.

Line 11 may be read as "if not score is equal to 3".

FIGURE 2.22 Updated condition using the ! Operator.

```
7    void Start()
8    {
9        int score = 8;
10
11       if(score != 3)
12       {
13           print("The score is not 3.");
14       }
15   }
```

The **not equal** operator—the exclamation followed immediately by the equal sign—provides a more elegant way to write the same line of code.

Now line 11 may be read as "if score is not equal to 3".

FIGURE 2.23 Updated condition using the != operator.

I wonder if there is ever a good reason to use the not operator.

I like where your head's at. I'll discuss that in a moment.

Consider the use of Boolean variables within conditional statements.

```
 7      void Start()
 8      {
 9          bool hasKey = false;
10
11          if(hasKey == true)
12          {
13              print("The door opens!");
14          }
15      }
16  }
```

Here, the *hasKey* variable is defined as a *bool* so it may store only values of true and false.

While it is logical that the variable be initialized in the Start method, the conditional statement would make more sense elsewhere—at the moment the player tries to open the door.

FIGURE 2.24   Updated condition using the == operator.

The conditional statement on line 11 is redundant and may be written more elegantly.

```
11      if(hasKey)
12      {
13          print("The door opens!");
14      }
15  }
```

Now, the value of *hasKey* is immediately used to determine if the conditional statement succeeds or fails.

This approach requires less code and improves readability as long as the Boolean variable is well named.

FIGURE 2.25   Updated condition using Boolean variable.

The same shortcut applies when checking if a Boolean value is false.

```
 7      void Start()
 8      {
 9          bool hasKey = false;
10
11          if(hasKey != true) print("You need a key to enter.");
12
13          if (hasKey == false) print("You need a key to enter.");
14
15          if (! hasKey) print("You need a key to enter.");
16      }
17  }
```

FIGURE 2.26   Alternate methods for writing the same condition.

The three conditional statements in this code segment are equivalent, but the statement on line 15 is preferred by most experienced programmers.

Notice the conditions of the *if* statements are followed immediately by a command instead of a block of code wrapped with curly braces. This is possible when only a single command is to be executed as a result of the condition being true. Curly braces are only necessary if multiple commands need to be executed.

I prefer to always use curly braces. It improves readability and makes it easy to add more commands to a conditional block later on.

Variable Scope

All variables defined in examples up to this point have been *local* variables. That is, they were declared within a function—such as the *Start* or *Update* function—and so could only be used within the function in which they were declared. Local variables have limited *scope*. Additionally, each time the function runs, the local variables are declared again using new memory locations and with new initial values. The values stored from previous executions of the function are not accessible by subsequent executions.

Often, you will need to use *class variables* with a greater scope. Class variables are accessible by all functions defined in the class—including the *Start* and *Update* functions—and retain their values when functions finish executing.

Consider a script that increases the value of *numSpacePressed* every time the space bar is pressed.

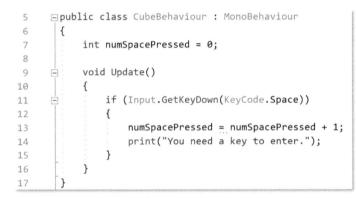

```
5    public class CubeBehaviour : MonoBehaviour
6    {
7        int numSpacePressed = 0;
8
9        void Update()
10       {
11           if (Input.GetKeyDown(KeyCode.Space))
12           {
13               numSpacePressed = numSpacePressed + 1;
14               print("You need a key to enter.");
15           }
16       }
17   }
```

Here, the *numSpacePressed* variable is a class variable because it is declared within the CubeBehaviour class but outside of any function.

As a *class variable, numSpacePressed* may be used by all functions defined in the class. It also means that the value of the variable is retained even when a function finishes executing.

FIGURE 2.27   Use of the + operator within the Update method.

Typically, the class variables are defined above the class functions.

Mathematical Operators

A powerful feature of variables is that their values can change or "vary". A variable named score of type *int* may begin with a value of 0 and then change to any other integer value while the program runs. In addition to using the = operator to assign a new value to a variable, several mathematical operators exist for changing existing numeric values.

Look more closely at the conditional statement from the previous code snippet. Line 11 utilizes the *Input.GetKeyDown* function that is provided with the Unity core library. This function returns true when the key specified is pressed.

In the *Update* method, which runs repeatedly every frame, the value of *numSpacePressed* is increased using the + operator when the space bar is pressed down. Line 13 can be read as "let numSpacePressed equal the current value of numSpacePressed plus one more".

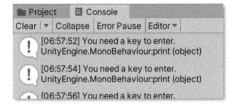

FIGURE 2.28 Console with output.

Running this script should result in the value of numSpacePressed increasing and being printed to the console every time the spacebar is pressed.

The += operator can be used to accomplish the same thing in a more concise manner.

```
13                    numSpacePressed += 1;
```

FIGURE 2.29 Use of the += operator.

Now line 13 can be read as "increase the value of numSpacePressed by 1".

The += operator allows you to increase a numeric variable by any value. However, to increase by exactly one, there is an even more concise method.

```
13                    numSpacePressed ++;
```

FIGURE 2.30 Use of the ++ operator.

The ++ operator was introduced because of how often programmers need to increase the value of a variable by one. Writing += 1 is just too much extra effort!

Just as the +, ++, and += operators are used to increase numeric values, the -, -=, and -- operators exist for decreasing numeric values. Other common math operators include the asterisk for multiplication and the forward slash for division.

Overloading Operators

Operators may be overloaded. For instance, the + operator has been overloaded in C# to behave differently when placed between strings. The behavior of combining the two strings together into one string is called *concatenation*. For example, concatenation is often used within print statements.

```
string firstName = "Bart ";
print("Hello there " + firstName);
```

You can also create new operators for custom data types.

For example, in Unity, a Vector3 is an object that contains three float values. In fact, the *position* and *scale* of every Transform are stored as Vector3 objects.

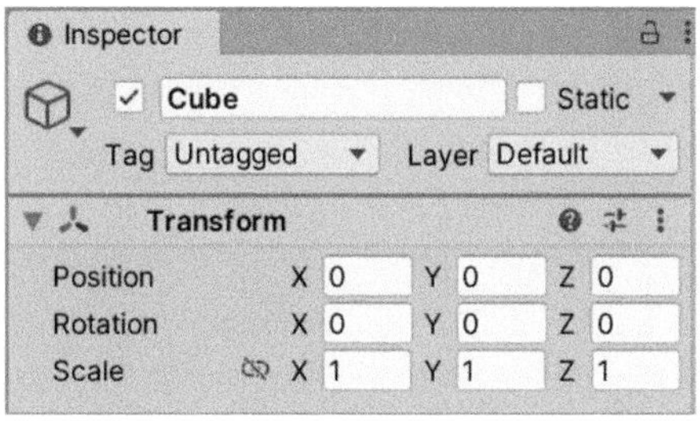

FIGURE 2.31   Transform of Cube.

There is no default behavior for adding or subtracting Vector3 objects in C#. In fact, there is no default Vector3 object in C#. Unity has provided the Vector3 *struct* so that Vector3 objects may be created, and operators have been overloaded so that Vector3 objects may be added and subtracted.

Consider the following script that increases and decreases the size of the cube when the up and down arrow keys are pressed.

```
5    public class CubeBehaviour : MonoBehaviour
6    {
7        Vector3 deltaScale = new (0.02f, 0.02f, 0.02f);
8
9        void Update()
10       {
11           if (Input.GetKey(KeyCode.UpArrow))
12           {
13               transform.localScale += deltaScale;
14           }
15
16           if (Input.GetKey(KeyCode.DownArrow))
17           {
18               transform.localScale -= deltaScale;
19           }
20       }
21   }
```

The conditional statements utilize the *Input.GetKey* function that is provided with the Unity core library. Unlike the *Input.GetKeyDown* function previously demonstrated, this function returns true if the key specified is currently being held down.

FIGURE 2.32   Script with a class property and modified Update method.

Run the code and hold down the up and down arrows to cause the cube to grow and shrink.

Line 7 of the script defines the class variable *deltaScale* of type Vector3. Vector3 is not a primitive type (such as int, float, and bool). Instead, Vector3 is a type provided by Unity that may be used to create Vector3 objects consisting of three float values. The *new* keyword is used to create a new *instance* of Vector3 with the initial float values specified.

The *delta* in the variable name refers to the Greek letter Δ and is commonly used in mathematics to mean "change in". The *deltaScale* variable therefore represents the "change in scale" that will be made on the cube in each frame in which the up or down arrow is held down. Due to how the += operator was overridden for Vector3 objects, adding *deltaScale* to the scale vector of any object will increase that object's size on the *x*, *y*, and *z* axis by 0.02.

Lines 13 and 18 use *deltaScale* to increase and decrease the cube from its current size. The *transform.localScale* property references the Vector3 object for the cube's scale. In line 13, the values in *deltaScale* are added to the current *x*, *y*, and *z* values of the cube's scale using the **+=** operator. You can see the scale values change in the inspector as the cube grows and shrinks.

Access Modifiers

Variables declared within a class but outside of any function are called *properties*. Properties without an access modifier default to *private*. Private properties may only be accessed by code that is written within the class they are defined. Adding the *public* access modifier to a property allows it to be accessed by code written within other classes.

On line 7, add the public keyword in front of the declaration of the *deltaScale* variable.

```
7          public Vector3 deltaScale = new (0.02f, 0.02f, 0.02f);
```

FIGURE 2.33   Use of the public access modifier on a class property.

Now the variable may be accessed and modified by code written inside of other classes, not just the functions written inside the CubeBehavior class.

Typically, you want properties to be private so that code outside of the class cannot access them. This practice of *data encapsulation* ensures that the values of an object are not changed by another object that do not have access to them. In Object-Oriented Programming, it is recommended to avoid the use of public properties and instead utilize public methods (functions) that allow other classes to indirectly access and modify private properties. In this book though, public properties will be used to avoid the additional code that would be needed to strictly adhere to the principle of data encapsulation.

Property Visibility

Save the code and return to Unity. You may need to wait a few seconds for the Inspector Window to update, but you should see your public variable appear under your script name.

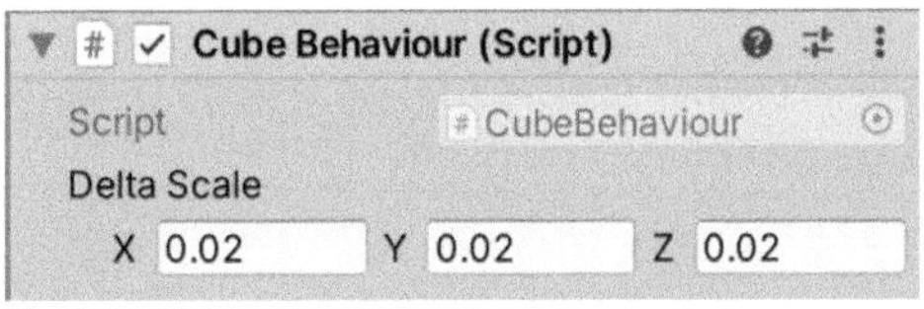

Notice the variable is named *deltaScale* but is displayed in the Inspector Window as "Delta Scale". Unity displays variable names in this way for readability. Rest assured that they refer to the same variable.

FIGURE 2.34   Script attached to Cube in Inspector.

To be consistent with other programmers and Unity conventions, use the camel-case naming convention where all variable names begin in lowercase and use uppercase letters to begin each subsequent word within the variable name. For example, a variable to store a player's first name could be *firstName* in code and would then appear as "First Name" in the Inspector Window.

The default behavior of Unity is to display public properties in the Inspector and hide private properties. However, it is possible to show private properties or hide public properties by using the *HideInInspector* and *SerializeField* attributes.

```
// hide a public property          // show a private property

[HideInInspector]                  [SerializeField]
public int x;                      private int x;
```

Consider the benefits of having properties that appear in the Inspector Window. The values in the Inspector Window which provide the initial values for the properties may then be set differently for each GameObject the script is attached to, and this can be done without editing the code.

For example, you might have three enemies with a public speed property defined in an EnemyBehavior script. The initial speed values for the enemies could be set in the editor.

Alternative Solutions

When programming, it is usually worthwhile to consider all options for adding functionality or solving a problem. For instance, if we wanted the same scale for the *x*, *y*, and *z* values so the object could not be stretched more in one direction than another, only a single value for setting the deltaScale would be needed. Consider the following changes.

```
5    public class CubeBehaviour : MonoBehaviour
6    {
7        public float speed = 0.02f;
8        Vector3 deltaScale;
9
10       void Start()
11       {
12           deltaScale = new (speed, speed, speed);
13       }
14
15       void Update()
```

FIGURE 2.35 Updated script with public float and private Vector3.

On line 7, *scaleSpeed* is declared as a public float and given a default value. On line 8, *deltaScale* is declared as a class variable so it may be used in both the *Start* and *Update* methods, but it is not made public. Within the *Start* method, *deltaScale* is initialized to a new Vector3 with float values for *x*, *y*, and *z* all set to the same value of *scaleSpeed*.

Save the code and return to Unity. The Inspector should update to show only the *scaleSpeed* property with its default value. The initial value can be changed prior to playing the game.

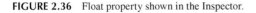

FIGURE 2.36 Float property shown in the Inspector.

Functions

While class variables (i.e., properties) are useful for storing <u>data</u>, class functions (i.e., methods) are used to group together all the commands that will complete an <u>action</u>. For example, the *print* function is used to print text to the console.

Programmers are not limited to functions that are provided to them. They may create their own functions to complete any action they wish. Consider the following code.

```
 5    public class CubeBehaviour : MonoBehaviour
 6    {
 7        void Start()
 8        {
 9            PrintPasswords();
10        }
11
12        void PrintPasswords()
13        {
14            print("12345");
15            print("password");
16            print("T33WT");
17        }
18    }
```

On lines 12 through 17, the custom *PrintPasswords* method is defined. This function definition provides the list of commands that should execute when the function is *called*.

Line 9 is a function call. Without a function call, the code in the function definition would never execute.

FIGURE 2.37   Updated script with a call to a custom method.

Unity automatically calls some functions without the need of writing a function call. This is how the *Start* and *Update* methods get called.

There are many reasons why functions are useful. They provide more readable code by condensing many commands into a single function call with a meaningful name. Functions also reduce code redundancy. Imagine you needed to print the passwords several times through your program. If the commands were not in a function, you would have to repeat the print statements several times. This approach could be tedious if many commands need to be repeated. Additionally, maintaining the code would become more difficult as changes to the commands would need to be made in several places. If the commands are in a function, you may call that function as many times as needed from different places in your code, and any changes to the commands would be made in one place.

Notice the word void preceding the function name on line 12. This indicates the type of value that will be returned by the function. A function with a return type of *void* will return nothing.

Sometimes you want a function to return a value. Consider the following code.

```
5     public class CubeBehaviour : MonoBehaviour
6     {
7         void Start()
8         {
9             int x = Sum();
10            print(x);
11        }
12
13        private int Sum()
14        {
15            return 15 + 237;
16        }
17    }
```

On line 13, the custom method named *Sum* is defined with *int* as the type of value that should be returned.

On line 15, an integer value (the sum of 15 and 237) is returned using the *return* keyword. The return is typically placed in the last line of a function.

FIGURE 2.38 A value returned by a method.

While methods are private by default, I like how this was explicitly stated for the Sum method. The Start method is also private even though the private keyword was not used.

On line 9, the function call is made, and the return value is stored in the variable *x*. The value of *x* is then printed out on line 10.

The return value of a function can be stored into a variable for later use as per the previous example or used immediately without storing the value as shown here.

```
print(Sum());
```

For function definitions and function calls in C#, the name of the function is always followed by parenthesis. Sometimes the parentheses contain parameters (i.e., values to be sent to the function), and other times the parentheses are left empty with no parameters.

Functions can receive data via parameters and return data via a return value. Let's expand the Sum function to make it more useful.

```
7         void Start()
8         {
9             int x = Sum(15, 237);
10            print(x);
11        }
12
13        private int Sum(int a, int b)
14        {
15            return a + b;
16        }
```

On line 13, the function is now defined to expect any two values of type *int* which will be stored in local variables *a* and *b*. The sum of these two values is returned on line 15.

The function call on line 9 must now include two integers as parameters.

The function is much more useful now because it can be used to add any two integers.

FIGURE 2.39 Passing arguments to a custom method.

This example was unnecessary as the plus operator accomplishes the same behavior. However, the code serves as a very simple example of how values could be passed to a function.

Consider an example you might see in a game. You may call *DealDamage()* to deal damage to the player. However, with no parameters, you would not be able to specify how much damage should be dealt. It might be more useful to call *DealDamage(4)* to deal 4 damage—or any other amount specified—to the player.

> The flexibility of functions makes coding so much easier!

Given how frequently randomness is used in games, let's look at the *Random.Range* function.

```
 5   public class CubeBehaviour : MonoBehaviour
 6   {
 7       void Update()
 8       {
 9           if (Input.GetKeyDown(KeyCode.Space))
10           {
11               int x = Random.Range(3, 10);
12               print(x);
13           }
14       }
15   }
```

First, notice the *Update* method is being used instead of the *Start* method so the code will repeat continuously.

In each frame, if the space bar is pressed, lines 11 and 12 are executed.

FIGURE 2.40   Passing ints to the Range method.

The *Range* method of the *Random* class expects two parameters—a minimum value and a maximum value—and returns a randomly generated value that lies between those two values. The definition for the *Range* function is *public* as we are allowed to use it from outside of the *Random* class where it is defined. If you run the code, a new integer value is printed to the console every time the space bar is pressed.

Interestingly, this function has been *overloaded*, meaning there are multiple definitions for the same function name. The function that is used depends on the number and type of parameters that are sent.

Modify line 11 to use the overloaded function that expects float values instead of int values.

```
float x = Random.Range(3f, 10f);
```

Now a different version of the *Range* function is being called, one that takes two float values as parameters and returns a float value that lies between them.

FIGURE 2.41   Passing floats to Range method.

When you play the game now, pressing the space bar will cause random decimal values, instead of random integer values, to be printed to the console.

That was a lot of information. I think I'll need to review this chapter a few times to wrap my head around the concepts.

Concepts I understand:

- Variables ✓
- Data Types ✓
- Conditional Statements ✓
- Math Operators ✓
- Boolean Operators ✓
- Functions ✓
- Parameters ✓
- Access Modifiers ✓
- Overloading ✓

I especially enjoyed the math operators. I can't wait to get into the more complex math in the upcoming chapters.

There is **so** much more. What about data structures, recursion, and object-oriented programming concepts such as abstraction, polymorphism, encapsulation, and inheritance? I mean, you did not even talk about arrays or loops.

Remember, this chapter is intended to provide a brief overview of the concepts used in the lessons and coding activities of this book. You will see them all applied in actual coding solutions in the next sections of this chapter and in later chapters.

Neither this chapter nor this book is intended to cover all programming concepts. However, some of the topics not covered in this chapter, such as loops and arrays, will be covered later in the book at the moment they are needed.

Activity: Bouncy Box

This activity will utilize two methods of moving an object in the scene to create a game called *Bouncy Box* inspired by the popular game of 2014, *Flappy Bird*. You will learn how to build a 2D game, use *Time.deltaTime*, create Prefabs, build upon an *Empty* GameObject to create a *GameController*, spawn objects in the scene on a timed interval, destroy objects upon collision, and access properties and methods of one script from another script.

Step 1: Setup the project

Create a new 3D Unity project named *BouncyBox*. Locate the default *SampleScene* in the Project Window and rename it *Scene01*. Add a Cube to the scene and rename it *Box*. Add a Rigidbody component to the cube so that it falls when the game is played.

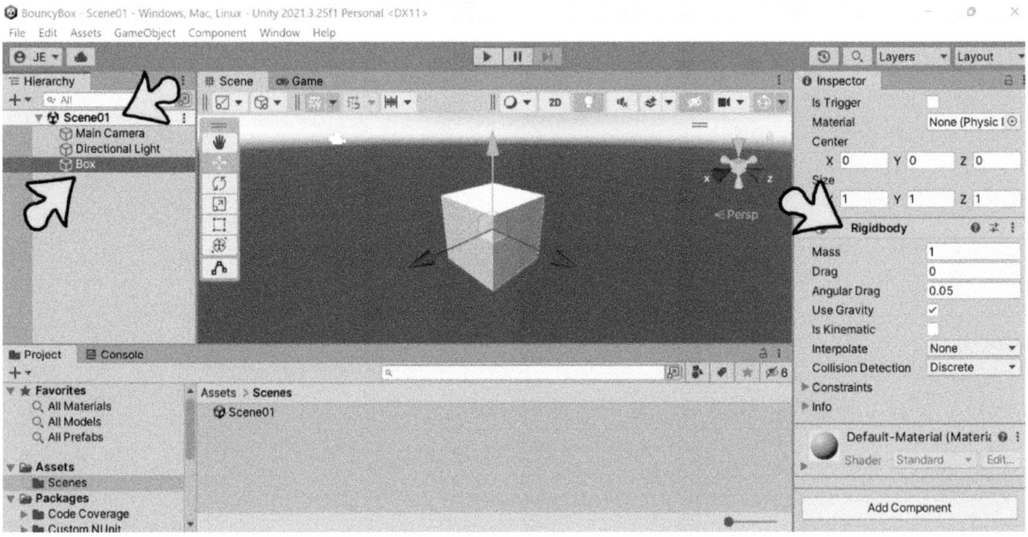

FIGURE 2.42   Open Unity project displaying Scene01, including a cube with an attached Rigidbody.

Step 2: Switch to 2D

With the Main Camera selected, expand the *Camera* component in the Inspector Window.

Select *Solid Color* from the *Clear Flags* drop-down. Click on the eyedropper to the right of the *Background* property to select a dark gray color. Select *Orthographic* from the *Projection* drop-down so the camera will reveal a two-dimensional view instead of a 3D perspective view.

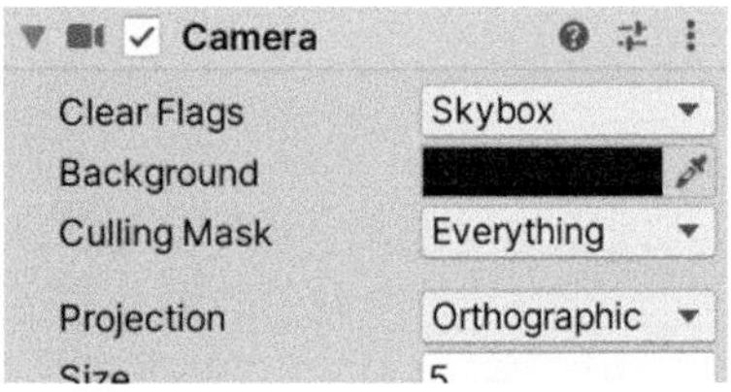

FIGURE 2.43   Camera component.

Make the necessary changes in the Scene Window to reflect more accurately what is seen through the Main Camera. That is, toggle off the Skybox and other effects via the drop-down located at the top of the Scene Window and toggle on the 2D button also at the top of Scene Window. Then, zoom and pan so the Scene view reveals the rectangle formed by the camera.

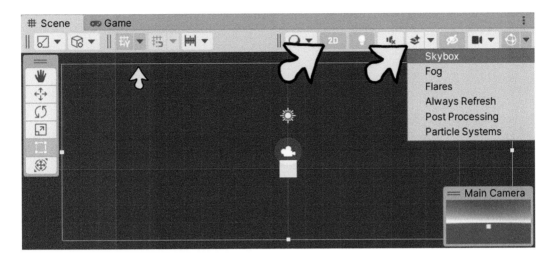

FIGURE 2.44 Scene Window highlighting changes made for a 2D view.

Step 3: Create a bounce ability for the core game mechanic

Create a *Scripts* folder within the *Assets* folder, create a *BoxBehaviour* script in the *Scripts* folder, and attach the script to the *Box* GameObject. Update the code to the following.

```
5    public class BoxBehaviour : MonoBehaviour
6    {
7        public float flapForce = 80;
8        public float health = 100;
9        public float numCoins = 0;
10
11       void Update()
12       {
13           if (Input.GetKeyDown(KeyCode.Space))
14           {
15               GetComponent<Rigidbody>().AddForce(0, flapForce, 0);
16           }
17       }
18   }
```

FIGURE 2.45 BoxBehaviour script to provide bounce mechanic when spacebar is pressed.

After the code is saved, the public properties should appear in the Inspector Window.

You will likely need to increase the *Flap Force* so the bounce is detectable during gameplay when the space bar is pressed.

FIGURE 2.46 Increase flapForce in Inspector.

The *flapForce*, *health*, and *numCoins* properties are defined and initialized in the BoxBehaviour class as these are properties that belong to the box (i.e., the player). In the *Update* method, a code block is set to run anytime the player presses the space bar to apply an upward force to the box. Take a closer look at line 15 of the code which applies the force.

The *GetComponent* function returns the component of the specified type from a specified GameObject.

```
GameObject.GetComponent<Component>()
```

The GameObject is not specified in line 15. When no GameObject is specified, the GameObject used is the GameObject the script is attached to. The command could have been written as:

```
this.gameObject.GetComponent<Rigidbody>().AddForce(0, flapForce, 0);
```

where *this.gameObject* refers to the GameObject that *this* script is attached to—the *Box*.

Once access is gained to the Rigidbody component using the *GetComponent* method, the *AddForce* method of the Rigidbody class is used to add a force with the value of 0 along the *x* axis, the value of *flapForce* along the *y* axis, and the value of 0 along the *z* axis.

 By applying a force only along the *y* axis, the Box will be pushed directly upward.

 Notice the impact of the force is different when the box is falling than when it is already moving upward.

Step 4: Contain the box

Add another cube to the scene and name it *Floor*.

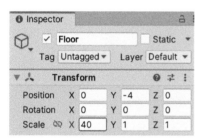

FIGURE 2.47   Transform of Floor.

Change the scale and position of the Floor to serve as a bottom constraint for the box.

Be sure that the *z* value of the Floor's position is set to zero so that the box does not fall in front of or behind it.

Once the floor is in place, the box should fall and come to rest on the floor when the space bar is not being pressed.

In the Hierarchy Window, right-click on the Floor and select *Duplicate*. Rename the *Floor (1)* cube created to *Ceiling*. Move the ceiling upward to serve as the top barrier for the box.

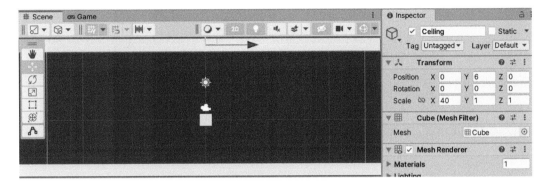

FIGURE 2.48   Transform of Ceiling.

Playing the game now, it may seem as though the box is constrained by the Floor and Ceiling GameObjects. However, you will notice that collisions cause the Box to slightly rotate and if the spacebar is repeatedly pressed, the box will quickly move forward or back on the *z* axis and eventually fly out in front or behind the ceiling.

It is possible to write custom code to solve this issue.

However, Unity provides some components to take care of exactly this type of issue.

In the Update method, you would just need to constantly set the *z* value back to zero, or you could set the rotation values all to zero, or you could do both.

That sounds easier. Let's do that!

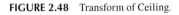

Add a *Rotation Constraint* component to the Box. Within the component, press the *Activate* button so the *Is Active* property is initialized to true.

Click on the arrow next to *Constraint Settings* to expand the section. Under *Sources*, press the plus sign to add a new source to the list. Initially, the value will be empty as indicated by the text "None (Transform)".

The Transform or GameObject placed in this field will be used to constrain the rotation of the Box. That is, the Box will maintain the same rotation values of the GameObject that is used as a source.

Click and drag the *Floor* from the Hierarchy and drop it into the field. Now the Box's rotation will be frozen on the axes which are checked (i.e., the *x*, *y*, and *z* axis).

FIGURE 2.49   Rotation Constraint.

Adding the *Rotation Constraint* component to the Floor or Ceiling would not have the desired effect.

If you make this mistake, click on the three dots to the right of the component's name and select *Remove Component*.

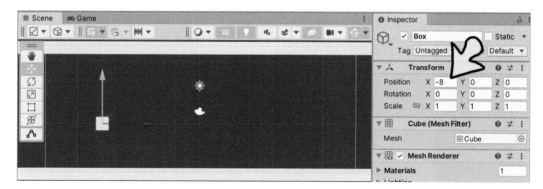

FIGURE 2.50   Remove Component option.

Playing the game now, the box no longer rotates!

However, the *z* value of the box's position still gradually changes and eventually could allow the box to move in front or behind the floor and ceiling. To address this issue, add a *Position Constraint* component to the Box.

Use the Floor as the source of the constraint. Constrain the position only on the *x* and *z* axis by unchecking only the *y* checkbox under "Freeze Position Axes".

When playing the game now, you should see that only the *y* value of the box's position changes.

FIGURE 2.51   Position Constraint.

In later steps, you will be spawning GameObjects that fly into view from the right side of the scene. To ensure the player has time to dodge these objects, move the Box to the left side of the scene.

FIGURE 2.52   Updated Box Position.

Be sure the *x* value you enter for the position does not move the box beyond the view of the camera.

Step 5: Add Color

Create a *Materials* folder in the *Assets* folder of the Project Window. Right-click within the *Materials* folder and select *Create>Material*. Rename the material *boxMat*.

With *boxMat* selected, change the color for the material in the Inspector Window by double-clicking on the color field next to the *Albedo* property. Use the color selector to choose the color for the box.

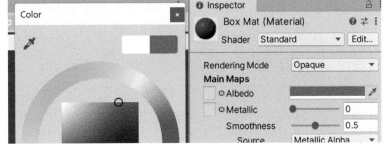

FIGURE 2.53 Color selector used to select pink for Albedo of Box Mat.

 Avoid red and yellow as those colors will be used later for other purposes.

Drag the *boxMat* material from the Project Window into the Scene Window and drop it onto the Box.

 The box should immediately change to the color you selected and the material should appear as a component on the Box visible in the Inspector.

Within the *Materials* folder, create another material named *wallMat*, set the color you want to use for the floor and ceiling, and then drag the *wallMat* onto the *Floor* and *Ceiling* GameObjects.

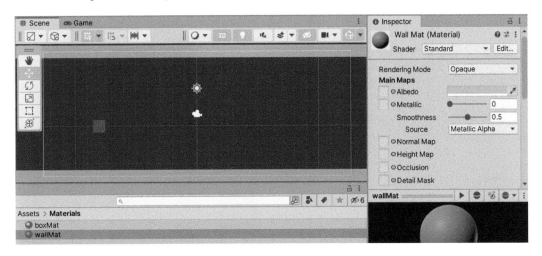

FIGURE 2.54 Color selector used to select light blue for Albedo of Wall Mat.

Step 6: Add a moving Fireball

Fire. Oh my.

This step involves creating fireballs that will move across the screen.

While the Box relied on the physics engine for its movement (i.e., forces being applied to a Rigidbody), the fireballs will instead move via custom code that directly modifies their position values.

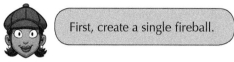

First, create a single fireball.

Create a Sphere in the same manner you created the cubes and name it *Fireball*.

Create a material named *redMat* with a red color and apply it to the Fireball.

Position the Fireball to the right side of the scene outside of the view of the Main Camera.

In the *Scripts* folder, create a new script named *FlyLeft*.

Attach the script to the Fireball.

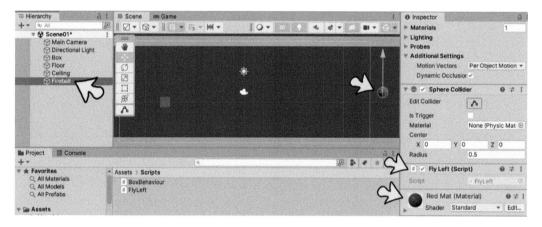

FIGURE 2.55   Unity project showing Fireball with attached FlyLeft script and Red Mat material.

You may wonder why the name *FlyLeft* was used instead of *FireballBehavior*. This is because this script will be used for any objects that need to have the behavior of flying left, not just fireballs.

Right, we could use the same script to make other hazards fly by.

Or we could have power-ups or other desirable items fly by for the player to collect.

Change the FlyLeft code to the following.

```
5    public class FlyLeft : MonoBehaviour
6    {
7        public float minSpeed;
8        public float maxSpeed;
9        float speed;
10
11       void Start()
12       {
13           speed = Random.Range(minSpeed, maxSpeed);
14       }
15
16       void Update()
17       {
18           float deltaX = -1 * speed * Time.deltaTime;
19           Vector3 movement = new (deltaX, 0, 0);
20           transform.position += movement;
21       }
22   }
```

The script provides two public properties so that the minimum and maximum speed of the fireball may be set in the Inspector.

In the Start method, the *speed* is set to a random float value between the minimum and maximum speed. This is not done in the *Update* method because the speed of the Fireball should not change every frame.

In the *Update* method, the Fireball is moved to the left based on the value of *speed*.

FIGURE 2.56   FlyLeft script.

If you play the game now, the Fireball will not fly as expected. This is because no default values were given to *minSpeed* and *maxSpeed*.

If you look at the Script attached to the Fireball in the Inspector, you see that the values for *minSpeed* and *maxSpeed* are both zero. This is the default value for floats when no other value is given.

In the Inspector, set *minSpeed* to 5 and *maxSpeed* to 10.

This should make the Fireball move across the screen at a speed between 5 and 10 units per second.

Play a few times to see the variation in the speed of the Fireball.

FIGURE 2.57   FlyLeft in the Inspector.

If you play a few times, you will see the Box colliding with the Fireball, causing some unwanted behavior. While the Box is mostly constrained, the collision still affects the Box's upward and downward motion.

To fix this, use the checkbox in the Fireball's SphereCollider component to set the *isTrigger* property to true.

When a Collider is set to be a trigger, none of the physical interactions that result when two objects collide will occur.

Now the collider will be used only as a *trigger*, which you will use in a moment to *trigger* an event in code. In the *Bouncy Ball* game that event will be to deal damage to the player.

Before breaking down the code that causes the Fireball to move, a basic understanding of Unity's frame rate is needed. The frame rate in Unity changes based on the complexity of the scene and the processing power of the computer and graphics card that the game is running on.

So, the frame rate in Unity is always changing.

Yea, that's why they call it a variable frame rate.

Consider moving an object one unit to the left of each frame for a full second. If the frame rate is 30 fps (frames per second), the object would move 30 units. However, if the frame rate is running at 60 fps, the object would move 60 units. We need a way to move objects across the screen at the same speed regardless of the variable frame rate.

First, consider how this might be done if the frame rate was a known constant. If the frame rate was 100 fps, the time between frames would be 1/100th of a second and the object would need to move 1/100th of the desired speed each frame.

That would be 1/100 * *speed*.

Or, *timeBetweenFrames* * speed.

If the frame rate was 40 fps, the time between frames would be 1/40th of a second and the object would need to move 1/40th of the desired speed each frame.

That would be 1/40 * *speed*.

Or, *timeBetweenFrames* * speed.

For a variable frame rate, the multiplier needs to continuously change.

That would be 1/*currentFramerate* * speed.

Or, *timeSinceLastFrame* * speed.

This is where *Time.deltaTime* becomes useful. The *deltaTime* property of the *Time* class returns a float value equal to the number of seconds that have passed since the last time the function was called.

So, when placed inside the Update method, *deltaTime* is the "change in time" since the last frame!

You can add a command in your *Update* method and watch the Console as the game runs to test this out.

```
print(Time.deltaTime);
```

In line 18, *deltaTime* is used to determine the value of *deltaX* (i.e., "change in X") that the Fireball needs to move this frame to maintain a consistent speed. The value is further multiplied by -1 so that *deltaX* will be negative, causing the movement to be toward the left instead of the right.

```
16      void Update()
17      {
18          float deltaX = -1 * speed * Time.deltaTime;
19          Vector3 movement = new (deltaX, 0, 0);
20          transform.position += movement;
21      }
```

FIGURE 2.58   Update method of the FlyLeft class.

Programmers new to Unity may try to directly update the *x* value of the Fireball's position with the following command.

```
transform.position.x += deltaX;
```

Unfortunately, the individual values of the position can be read (such as to print out the value) but cannot be changed directly. They are "read only". Therefore, to change the position of a GameObject along one axis, the entire position must be set to a new Vector3 object or by increasing or decreasing by another Vector3 object.

Line 19 defines a Vector3 named *movement* that will represent the amount of movement along the *x*, *y*, and *z* axes that is desired. The *y* and *z* values are set to zero since the Fireball will only be moving on the *x* axis.

Finally, on line 20, the movement vector is added to the Fireball's current position vector. Adding the movement vector to the current position is the result of adding the movement vector's *x* position to the Fireball's current *x* position, the movement vector's *y* position to the Fireball's current *y* position, and the Fireball's current *z* position to the Fireball's current *z* position.

Repeating this code to slightly move the Fireball many times per second creates the illusion of motion!

Step 7: Spawn Fireballs

To spawn fireballs, you will set up a *GameController* that spawns new fireballs at a timed interval. The first step is to turn the Fireball into a Prefab that can be used to generate more fireballs.

Create a folder within the *Assets* folder named *Prefabs*.

Your project should now include folders for Materials, Prefabs, Scenes, and Scripts.

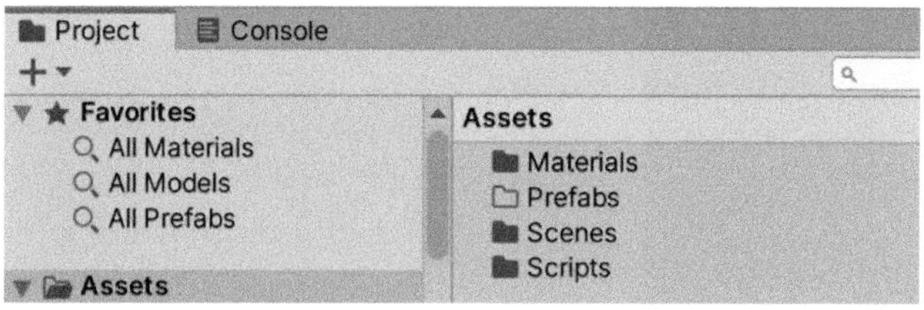

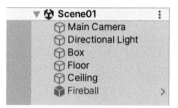

FIGURE 2.59 Current folders within the Assets folder.

Drag the Fireball GameObject from the Hierarchy into the Prefabs folder.

Notice the icon next to the Fireball in the Hierarchy changes to indicate it is an instance of a *prefabricated* GameObject.

Right-click on the Fireball in the Hierarchy and select *Delete*.

FIGURE 2.60 Fireball as a Prefab.

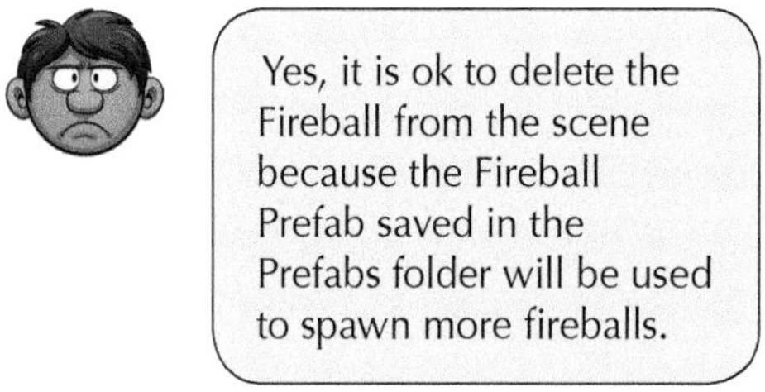

Yes, it is ok to delete the Fireball from the scene because the Fireball Prefab saved in the Prefabs folder will be used to spawn more fireballs.

Set up a GameController as the master controller for the game.

Right-click within the Hierarchy Window and select *Create Empty*.

Change the name of the Empty GameObject to *GameController* and set its position to the origin.

In the Scripts folder, create a new script also named *GameController*.

Then add the GameController script to the GameController GameObject.

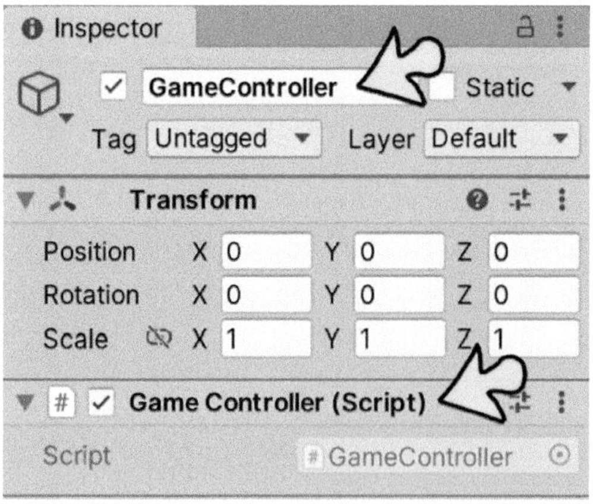

FIGURE 2.61 GameController script attached to the GameController GameObject.

Update the GameController script to the following.

```
5    public class GameController : MonoBehaviour
6    {
7        public float fireballSpawnTime = 3;
8        float fireballTimeElapsed = 0;
9
10       void Update()
11       {
12           fireballTimeElapsed += Time.deltaTime;
13
14           if(fireballTimeElapsed > fireballSpawnTime)
15           {
16               fireballTimeElapsed = 0;
17               print("spawn fireball");
18           }
19       }
20   }
```

FIGURE 2.62 GameController class to print on a set interval.

Play the game with the console open and you should see the message "spawn fireball" printed every few seconds.

The *fireballSpawnTime* is made public so that the value may be changed in the editor. By default, it is set to spawn a new Fireball every 3 seconds.

The *fireballTimeElapsed* tracks the amount of time since the last Fireball was spawned.

The code in the *Update* method is pretty straightforward. In each frame, the *fireballTimeElapsed* is increased by the amount of time that has passed since the method last ran. When the elapsed time exceeds the *fireballSpawnTime*, it is reset to 0 and a message is printed to the console.

Before a Fireball can be spawned, the script must have access to the Fireball prefab.

Add a public property named *fireballPrefab* of type GameObject.

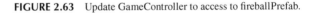

```
5    public class GameController : MonoBehaviour
6    {
7        public GameObject fireballPrefab;
8
9        public float fireballSpawnTime = 3;
10       float fireballTimeElapsed = 0;
```

FIGURE 2.63 Update GameController to access to fireballPrefab.

Save the script and return to Unity to initialize the property within the Inspector Window.

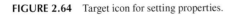

FIGURE 2.64 Target icon for setting properties.

One option to set the property is to click on the target icon on the right side of the *Fireball Prefab* field and then select Fireball from the options.

Now that there is a reference to the Fireball prefab, the GameController script will be able to use that reference to spawn new fireballs.

Update the conditional statement to the following.

```
16              if(fireballTimeElapsed > fireballSpawnTime)
17              {
18                  fireballTimeElapsed = 0;
19
20                  GameObject fireball = Instantiate(fireballPrefab);
21                  float x = fireball.transform.position.x;
22                  float z = fireball.transform.position.z;
23                  float y = Random.Range(-3f, 5f);
24                  fireball.transform.position = new (x, y, z);
25              }
```

FIGURE 2.65   Changes to GameController to spawn fireballs at specified position.

Line 20 is the only line needed to spawn a Fireball. In fact, if a reference to the fireball wasn't needed to randomize the position of the fireball, it could have been spawned with only:

```
Instantiate(fireballPrefab);
```

With that line of code, a new *instance* of Fireball would be created in the scene at the same position specified in the Fireball prefab. With only this line of code, all the Fireballs would begin at the same location.

Line 20 is lengthier because it takes advantage of the Instantiate method's return value (i.e., the GameObject that is created). That value is stored within a local variable named *fireball* so that it may be referenced in the subsequent lines of code.

Lines 21 and 22 store the current *x* and *z* values of the position for the newly created fireball into the local variables *x* and *z*. The *x* and *z* values of the fireball will not be changed.

Line 23 uses the *Random.Range* method to set the value of the local variable *y* to a random float between -3 and 5.

To determine the numbers for your game, drag the Fireball prefab into your scene within Unity to create a new Fireball GameObject. Move it up and down watching the position on the *y* changing in the Inspector Window. Once you have determined the min and max values, delete the Fireball from the Scene and update line 23 to the values appropriate for your game.

Finally, on line 24, the position of the newly created Fireball is set to a new Vector3 object defined by the values of the local variables *x*, *y*, and *z*. You may sometimes see the new keyword followed by the type of object that is being created. In this case, line 24 could have been written as:

```
fireball.transform.position = new Vector3(x, y, z);
```

This more explicit form of creating a new instance of an object specifies the name of the method that is called to create an object. This *constructor* method is unique in that it has the same name as the class it belongs to and returns an object of that type. It is unnecessary only because the compiler knows what constructor to call based on the type of object on the left-hand side of the assignment operator.

When you play the game, you should see new Fireball GameObjects appearing in the Hierarchy Window. As the game continues, the list of fireballs grows. This is concerning! For each new fireball, the required processing power needed to move the fireballs and check for collisions increases. The frame rate will continuously slow, and eventually, the game may crash.

> Clearly, the Fireballs need to be destroyed from the scene after they have left the camera view.

Step 8: Destroy Fireballs

> Where in our scripts should the destroy code be added?

Logically, you would want to check if a fireball has moved off-screen every time its location changes. Because the code for moving the fireball was in the FlyLeft script, you could add the destroy code there.

In FlyLeft.css, add the conditional statement to the *Update* method of the FlyLeft script.

```
18              float deltaX = -1 * speed * Time.deltaTime;
19              Vector3 movement = new (deltaX, 0, 0);
20              transform.position += movement;
21
22              if(transform.position.x < -12)
23              {
24                  Destroy(gameObject);
25              }
```

FIGURE 2.66 Destroy object after it flies out of view.

Remember, *gameObject* (or *this.gameObject*) refers to the GameObject that *this* instance of the FlyLeft script is attached to. In this way, the correct Fireball is destroyed when it moves far enough to the left (i.e., when the *x* value of its position becomes less than -12).

> Again, you can decide how far left to allow your fireballs to go by temporarily adding a Fireball to the scene and looking at its *x* value while it is positioned to the left of the camera's viewable area.

> Play the game to ensure that Fireballs are destroyed from the Hierarchy after they fly out of view.

Step 9: Deal Damage from Collisions

Fireballs should also be destroyed when they collide with the box.

> This is also when the fireball should deal damage.

Your first instinct may be to add code for this in the FlyLeft script since it logically would need to check for collisions every time the fireball is moved. However, it is good to have the FlyLeft script only be responsible for one task (i.e., flying left) so that it may be used on any objects that need the flying behavior without other behaviors specific to fireballs, such as dealing damage.

Fortunately, you can add multiple scripts to the same GameObject.

> So, one script could be for flying left and another for dealing damage. That's helpful.

Create a script named *DamageOnCollision* within the Scripts folder and add it to the Fireball prefab.

> To add the script to the Fireball prefab, click on the Fireball in the Prefabs folder and click the *Open* button in the Inspector. Then click on the *Add Component* button, clear the search bar if needed, click on *Scripts*, and choose "Damage on Collision".

Once the script is attached, update the code to the following.

```
DamageOnCollision.cs  ⊕ ✕   GameController.cs        FlyLeft.cs           BoxBehaviour.cs
Assembly-CSharp                              ▾   DamageOnCollision
   1    using System.Collections;
   2    using System.Collections.Generic;
   3    using UnityEngine;
   4
   5    public class DamageOnCollision : MonoBehaviour
   6    {
   7        private void OnTriggerEnter(Collider other)
   8        {
   9            if(other.tag == "Player")
  10            {
  11                Destroy(gameObject);
  12            }
  13        }
  14    }
```

The *OnTriggerEnter* method is provided by Unity and is executed anytime a Collider on the GameObject the script is attached to comes into contact with a Collider on another GameObject.

The Collider that collided with the Fireball is stored in the variable named *other*. This provides a reference to the other Collider, and the other GameObject, that collided with the Fireball.

FIGURE 2.67   DamageOnCollision class.

Line 9 checks to see if the *other* Collider belongs to any GameObject with a tag of "Player".

> The condition could have been written as:
>
> ```
> if (other.gameObject.tag == "Player")
> ```
>
> and read as:
> "if the other Collider's GameObject is tagged as a Player".

> Both lines of code work because both the Collider and GameObject classes have a tag property that references the same value.

The condition is important because damage should only be dealt when the Fireball collides with the player, not when it collides with other GameObjects such as the floor, ceiling, or other fireballs.

Save the script. However, before this code will behave as intended, the *Box* GameObject needs to be tagged as a *Player*.

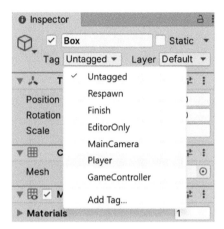

With the Box displayed in the Inspector, choose *Player* from the *Tag* drop-down menu.

Player is one of the default tags provided by Unity. Additional tags can be created using the *Add Tag...* option at the bottom of the drop-down list.

When you play the game now, the fireballs should be destroyed when they collide with the Box (i.e., the Player).

FIGURE 2.68 Tag Box as Player.

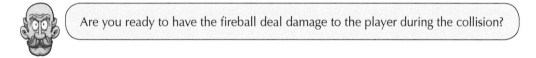

Are you ready to have the fireball deal damage to the player during the collision?

Step 10: Deal damage to the player

Recall that the BoxBehaviour script has a public *health* property. Because the property is public, other classes, including the *DamageOnCollision* class, can access it.

Update the *DamageOnCollision* script to the following.

```
5   public class DamageOnCollision : MonoBehaviour
6   {
7       public float damage = 10;
8
9       private void OnTriggerEnter(Collider other)
10      {
11          if(other.CompareTag("Player"))
12          {
13              other.GetComponent<BoxBehaviour>().health -= damage;
14
15              if(other.GetComponent<BoxBehaviour>().health <= 0)
16              {
17                  Destroy(other.gameObject);
18              }
19
20              Destroy(gameObject);
21          }
22      }
23  }
```

FIGURE 2.69 Implement damage and health to the DamageOnCollision class.

On line 7, the public *damage* property defines the amount of damage *this* object (i.e., the object this script is attached to) will deal to the player upon collision.

Line 11 has been modified to check if the tag of the colliding GameObject is "Player" using the CompareTag method instead of the == operator.

Lines 13 to 18 are also new. Line 13 demonstrates how a script on one GameObject can access the public properties and methods of a script on a different GameObject. In this case, the health property of the BoxBehaviour class (defined in the BoxBehaviour script) which is attached to the Box is reduced by the Fireball's *damage*.

The subsequent conditional statement destroys the other GameObject (i.e., the Box) if its *health* drops to or below zero.

Line 17 destroys the player. Line 20 destroys the fireball.

To test, save the code, select the Box so the value of *health* is visible in the inspector and press Play.

The value of *health* displayed in the Inspector should reduce every time a fireball hits the Box and the player should be destroyed when the health falls to zero.

Step 11: Ending the Game

When the player dies, there is no need to continue spawning new GameObjects. One solution is to disable the GameController when there is no longer a player in the scene.

In the *GameController* class, at the top of the *Update* method, add a conditional statement to detect if the player is no longer in the game.

```
12      void Update()
13      {
14          if(GameObject.FindWithTag("Player") == null)
15          {
16              print("Player destroyed.  Game Over.");
17              this.enabled = false;
18          }
19
20          fireballTimeElapsed += Time.deltaTime;
21
```

FIGURE 2.70 Update GameController class to detect player death.

The *FindWithTag* method returns the GameObjects in the scene which have the specified tag. The value of null is returned if no GameObjects in the scene have the tag. Therefore, this code is simply checking to see if the Box (the only GameObject with the tag of "Player") has been destroyed. If it has, a game over message is printed to the console and *this* script is disabled.

Now when the player dies, the fireballs should stop spawning and the game over message should appear in the console.

Enabling and disabling components, scripts, and entire GameObjects is a powerful tool for Unity developers.

Challenges

Build on the *Bouncy Box* game created in the Application section of this chapter to allow the player to gain coins by colliding with yellow *GoodStuff* GameObjects that move across the screen faster than the Fireballs. The goal for the player is to gain as many coins as possible before their health is depleted.

The following steps should help you complete this challenge.

1. Use a sphere with a yellow material to create a *GoodStuff* GameObject. Be sure to set the Collider to be a trigger.

2. Scale the GoodStuff GameObject down so the GoodStuff is smaller than the fireballs.

Or you could scale the Fireball prefab up.

3. Add the FlyLeft script to the GoodStuff and increase the properties for the min and max speed so that GoodStuff moves faster on average than the fireballs.

Or you could decrease the min and max speed so that the GoodStuff moves slower.

4. Create a Prefab from the GoodStuff and update the GameController to spawn GoodStuff in the same manner that the Fireballs are spawned.
   Here is a portion of the needed code to get you started:

```
5    public class GameController : MonoBehaviour
6    {
7        public GameObject fireballPrefab;
8        public GameObject goodStuffPrefab;
9
10       public float fireballSpawnTime = 3;
11       float fireballTimeElapsed = 0;
12
13       public float goodStuffSpawnTime = 3;
14       float goodStuffTimeElapsed = 0;
```

FIGURE 2.71 Properties of GameController class to implement GoodStuff feature.

Additional code will need to be added to the Update method of the GameController class.

5. Create a *CoinOnCollision* script to provide additional behavior to the GoodStuff. When the GoodStuff collides with the player, it should be destroyed and the value of the *numCoins* property that was previously defined for the BoxBehaviour class should increase by one.

6. Add print statements to provide output to the player, including displaying the player's number of coins each time a coin is collected and displaying the player's health each time damage is dealt.

FIGURE 2.72   Output demonstrating working health and coin mechanics.

Summary

This chapter covered many computer science concepts needed to understand the code presented throughout this book and successfully complete the end-of-chapter activities. Topics included variables, data types, operators, access modifiers, and functions. Other fundamental programming topics, such as loops and arrays, will be covered as needed in later chapters.

The chapter also touched on additional game engine topics such as framerate, colliders, triggers, materials, prefabs, and instantiation. Regarding scripting within Unity, several built-in methods (e.g., Start, Update, OnTriggerEnter, Random.Range, GetComponent, Instantiate, and Destroy) and properties (e.g., deltaTime, position, and tag) were utilized.

Finally, through the *Application* and *Challenges* section, you had the opportunity to build a game from scratch with the Unity Engine. Combined with what was covered in the first chapter, you have just scratched the surface of how to write code and work with a game engine. There is an abundance of resources available for learning more about game programming and game engines as well as many other aspects of game development (e.g., design, writing, audio, art, 3D modeling, and animation). However, the fundamentals of Unity and C# covered in the first two chapters should be sufficient preparation for the topics and activities of this book.

It is time to turn our attention fully to the **Mathematics of Game Development**.

3

Position of Game Objects in 2D | Points on a Coordinate Plane

Introduction

Games require stuff. The game dev challenge of this chapter is to display that stuff in the game at specific locations in a 2D world.

The concepts apply to 3D also.

The Math

Consider an object placed in 2D space.

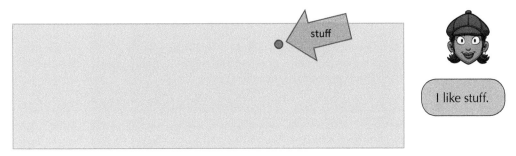

stuff

I like stuff.

FIGURE 3.1 Stuff in 2D space represented by a blue dot.

How can you describe the position of the object?

You could use the handy coordinate plane you learned about in algebra class.

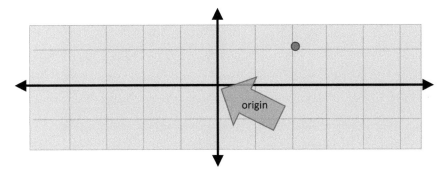

origin

FIGURE 3.2 Coordinate plane overlaid on 2D Space to show the position of Stuff to be at (2, 1).

DOI: 10.1201/9781032701431-4

Recall the horizontal *x*-axis and the vertical *y*-axis of the coordinate plane cross at the origin. The origin is extremely important when plotting points on a coordinate plane. Once we have a point to measure from (the origin), we can specify any other location using the horizontal and vertical distance that location is from the point. The object above is at the coordinates (2, 1) because it is 2 units to the right of the origin and 1 unit above the origin.

Positioning Objects in Games

Consider this alien positioned in 2D space.

FIGURE 3.3   Alien positioned in 2D space.

How can you describe the alien's position?

Again, we need some other position in the game world in which the position of the alien can relate to. We could use a coordinate plane and position everything relative to the origin. In fact, this is exactly how game engines specify the "world" position of game objects.

Alternatively, we could use some other point. A common point to base the position of objects on in 2D web-based games is the top-left corner of the game window. If the alien is 8 units from the left and 2 units from the top, its position could be defined as (8, 2).

FIGURE 3.4   Alien position defined relative to top-left of the window (8 units over and 2 units down).

This positioning method is like plotting points on a coordinate plane, except that the value for the vertical position increases instead of decreases as it moves down.

Even in games that use the traditional coordinate plane to position objects in the game world, the method of positioning from the top-left corner is still frequently used for the user interface (UI) elements that overlay the world.

Pivot Points

Objects *usually* take up space and an area consisting of many points. How then can you specify their position as a single point? That is where pivot points come into play. Here, the pivot point of the alien is on the top of his head, and this point is used to define the alien's position in the game.

FIGURE 3.5   Position as distance from top-left of the window to top-center of alien (8 units over and 2 units down).

Imagine if the alien's pivot point was in the center of his chest. For the alien to be displayed in the same place in the game, the position values would need to be modified accordingly.

FIGURE 3.6   Position as distance from top-left of the window to middle-center of alien (8 units over and 4 units down).

FIGURE 3.7   Alien pivot point at top-center.

FIGURE 3.8   Alien pivot point in middle-center.

The pivot point is also the point that would be used to spin (or pivot) an object around when its rotation value changes.

Typically, the pivot point for objects in web-based games is at the top-left corner of the object.

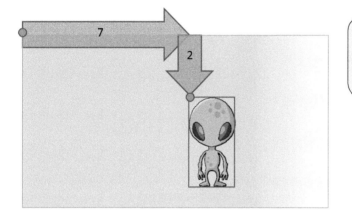

In the Chapter 6 activity, you will see how Unity uses the pivot point as the origin of another coordinate system.

FIGURE 3.9   Top-left corner of alien 7 units over and 2 units down.

Fortunately, most game engines provide support for changing the pivot point, which is often useful.

In most game engines, the origin of the world's coordinate system can be anywhere in the world as determined by where game objects are positioned relative to that origin.

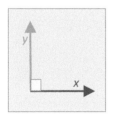

With the origin defined as (0, 0) in 2D games, the first value (x) increases as it moves to the right and decreases as it moves to the left while the second value (y) increases as it moves up and decreases as it moves down.

Unity uses a red arrow to represent the x axis and a green arrow to represent the y axis.

FIGURE 3.10   Colored x and y axes.

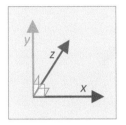

In 3D games, an additional axis is included to represent depth and the origin is defined as (0, 0, 0).

Unity uses a blue arrow to represent the *z* axis.

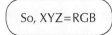
So, XYZ=RGB

Ooh, RGB is the acronym for the additive color model. That will make it easy to remember the colors of each axis.

FIGURE 3.11   Colored *x*, *y*, and *z* axes

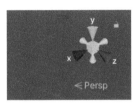

In Unity, the *Scene Gizmo* in the upper-right corner of the Scene Window displays the current orientation from the *Scene Camera* being used to view the scene.

In perspective mode, the Scene Gizmo can be rotated in any direction to change the view while always showing the direction of the axes.

FIGURE 3.12   Scene Gizmo.

When an object in Unity is selected with the move tool, the axis arrows that appear on the object in Scene View may not be consistent with the Scene Gizmo. This is because Unity has a different coordinate system for every GameObject—a topic discussed further in later chapters.

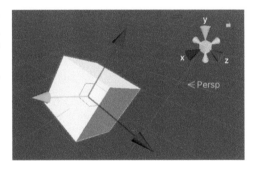

FIGURE 3.13   Cube with different orientation than Scene.

So, the coordinate system for the cube shown is different than the coordinate system of the world in which the cube is placed. Interesting… I am looking forward to learning more about that!

Activity: Platformer

It's time to start placing objects in a game. Follow the steps to complete the activity.

1. Become familiar with the Platformer game.

   Open *Scene01* of the Platformer project from the Chapter 3 project files. The scene has a single empty GameObject named *GameController* which has an attached script also named *GameController*.

   Several of the script's properties are already set in the editor for the existing Prefabs. These Prefabs can be found in the Prefabs folder.

   The *level* property is visible in the inspector to make it easy to switch between levels while developing.

   The *maxFallVelocity* determines the downward velocity that will cause the player to die.

FIGURE 3.14   GameController script attached to GameController GameObject.

When you play the game, you will see more GameObjects appear in the scene.

Expand each GameObject so all children are available to reveal that level 1 consists of two platforms and no enemies.

Use the A and D keys to move and the W key to jump.

The Main Camera is a child of the Player so it will follow the player through the scene.

FIGURE 3.15   Hierarchy expanded during play.

Selecting the *Player* GameObject will reveal the many components attached, including a *SpriteRenderer, Animator, RigidBody2D, BoxCollider2D*, and a script named *PlayerController*.

The PlayerController script includes properties for *jumpForce, maxSpeed*, and *airControl*. You can modify these to get the feel for player movement that you desire.

FIGURE 3.16   PlayerController script.

Looking in the Assets folder of the Project Window, you can get an idea of everything that was used to build the game. Subfolders include Animations, Materials, Prefabs, Scenes, Scripts, and Sprites.

In the *Sprites* folder, you will find the 2D images used in the game. Clicking on the *player-SpriteSheet* you can see the *spritesheet* used for the player character.

 A spritesheet is a single image containing multiple sprites.

Each sprite was created with the pivot point set to the top-left corner of the sprite.

Expanding the *playerSpriteSheet*, you can see a list of the sprites that resulted from *splicing* the spritesheet. These individual sprites make up *frames* of the animation.

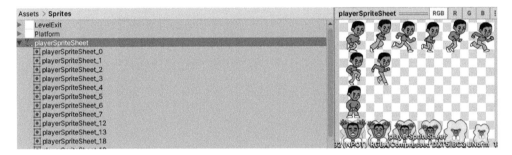

FIGURE 3.17   playerSpriteSheet viewed through the Project Window and Inspector.

The six frames in the first row of the spritesheet make up the run animation. The second row has a frame for the single-frame jumping animation and another frame for the single-frame fall animation. The frame on the third row is for the player's single-frame *idle* state used when the character is standing still, and the last row contains six frames for the die animation.

From these frames, the player animations were created. These can be found inside the Assets → Animations → Player folder.

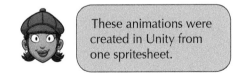 These animations were created in Unity from one spritesheet.

Assets > Animations > **Player**
- Die
- Fall
- Idle
- Jump
- Run

FIGURE 3.18   Player Animations.

The animations are controlled by the *PlayerAnimatorController* which can be found in the Assets → Animations folder. Double-click the *PlayerAnimatorController* to open it in the Animator Window and dock the Animator Window along with the Project and Console windows.

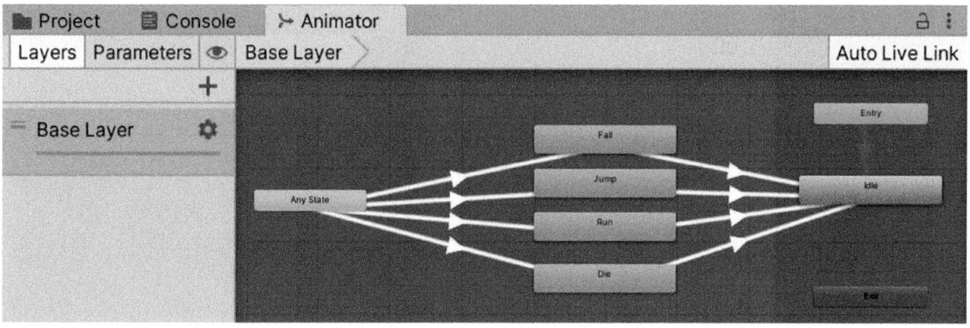

FIGURE 3.19   PlayerAnimatorController shown in the Animator Window.

The parameters defined in the Parameters tab on the left are used to determine which animations should play. The values for these parameters are sent to the animator controller from the PlayerController script. Play the game again with the Animator Window open to see how the animator controller behaves as you move and jump.

Back in the Project Window, you will find the prefabs of the game in the Assets/Prefabs folder.

The icon of a blue cube is an indicator that the items are Prefabs.

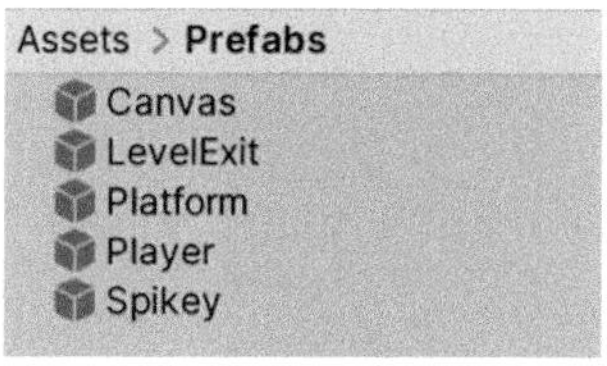

FIGURE 3.20   Prefabs.

Double-click the *Canvas* prefab to open it in the Hierarchy and Scene windows.

The *Canvas* prefab has a child *Text* UI component used to display the current level and game over message.

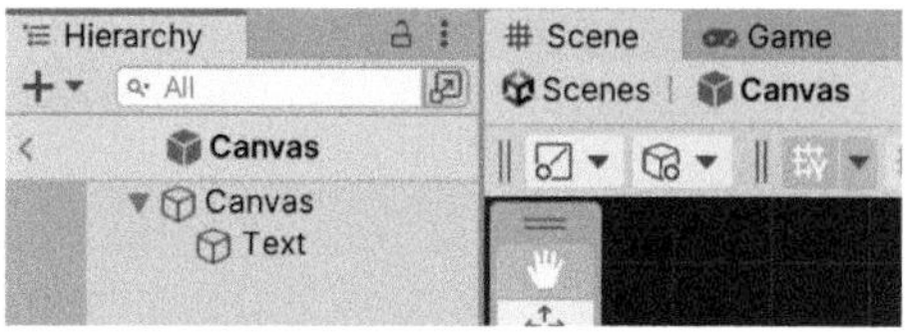

FIGURE 3.21   Canvas Prefab open.

In the Hierarchy Window, click the left-arrow icon next to the *Canvas* Prefab to return to the Scene.

FIGURE 3.22   Exit Prefab icon.

The remaining *LevelExit*, *Platform*, *Player*, and *Spikey* prefabs are added through code to build out levels. Some of these prefabs have a script attached to them to define their behavior.

Locate the four scripts used for the game within the Assets/Scripts folder. You will be modifying the *GameController* script for this activity. This script is attached to the only GameObject initially in the scene and is used to build out the levels and control the game.

While you will not need to make changes to the other scripts, looking over them may strengthen your understanding of programming within Unity.

The *EnemyBehavior* and *LevelExitBehavior* scripts are quite short, but both provide examples of how a script can access the public properties and methods of another script.

Specifically, the EnemyBehavior script calls the *KillPlayer* method of the GameController script; and the LevelExitBehavior script calls the *CompleteLevel* method of the GameController script.

The *PlayerController* script is much longer. It includes code that detects keyboard input and collisions with platforms to determine when to add forces to the player and send values to the player's Animator Controller.

For this activity, you need to be familiar with the *BuildLevel* method of the GameController class.

```
121     private void BuildLevel()
122     {
123         Output("Level " + level);
124
125         if (level == 1)
126         {
127             AddPlatform(-10, -2, 20, 1);
128             AddPlatform(12, -0.5f, 4, 1);
129
130             levelExit.transform.position = new (15, 0.5f);
131         }
132         else if (level == 2)
133         {
134             AddPlatform(-10, -2, 20, 1);
135             AddPlatform(12, -0.5f, 4, 1);
136             AddPlatform(18, 0.5f, 4, 1);
137
138             AddEnemy("Spikey", 5, -1.1f);
139             AddEnemyToPlatform("Spikey", "Platform_1", 19);
140
141             levelExit.transform.position = new (21, 1.5f);
142         }
143     }
```

FIGURE 3.23 BuildLevel method of the GameController class.

This function is called every time the player reaches a new level. Line 123 calls the custom *output* method defined on lines 116–119, updating the UI to indicate to the player what level they are on. Then, depending on which level is being loaded, the platforms and enemies for the level are added to the scene at specified locations, and the LevelExit object that was previously added to the scene is placed at a new location.

Notice, in lines 127 and 128 for example, four values are sent to the *AddPlatform* method in order to create two platforms in the scene.

```
127                     AddPlatform(-10, -2, 20, 1);
```

FIGURE 3.24 Call to the AddPlatform method.

What do these four values represent? Look at the definition of the function to determine this.

```
145       private void AddPlatform(float x, float y, float w, float h)
146       {
```

FIGURE 3.25 Definition of the AddPlatform method.

There are no comments provided above the method to define the purpose of each parameter. However, the property names are useful in determining their purpose. The first two parameters are used to set the position of the platform by specifying the *x* and *y* values of the platform's pivot point—which is the top-left corner of the platform. The second two parameters are used to set the size of the platform, with *w* for the width and *h* for the height.

Enemies are added in level two. However, there are two methods available for adding enemies. The *AddEnemy* method used on line 138 is similar to the *AddPlatform* method.

```
138                AddEnemy("Spikey", 5, -1.1f);
```

FIGURE 3.26 Call to the AddEnemy method.

To add an enemy using this method, the type of enemy and the *x* and *y* coordinates for its position must be sent as arguments.

```
171       private void AddEnemy(string type, float x, float y)
172       {
```

FIGURE 3.27 Definition of the AddEnemy method.

Currently, the only type of enemy in the game is "Spikey" so any other string sent to the function will not create an enemy.

Parameters for width and height are not defined because the size of the enemy is immutable.

The *AddEnemyToPlatform* method used on line 139 works a bit differently.

```
139                    AddEnemyToPlatform("Spikey", "Platform_1", 19);
```

FIGURE 3.28 Call to the AddEnemyToPlatform method.

This method allows you to specify a platform to add the enemy.

As defined on line 154, the type of enemy, the name of the platform, and the horizontal place-ment of the enemy from the left side of the platform are required as arguments.

```
private void AddEnemyToPlatform(string type, string platformName, float x)
{
```

FIGURE 3.29 Definition of the AddEnemyToPlatform method from line 154.

Platforms are automatically named upon their creation following a naming scheme specified in the *AddPlatform* method. The first platform added to a level is named "Platform_1", the second "Platform_2", and so on.

You can see the names of platforms in the hierarchy by expanding the Platforms GameObject while the game is running.

FIGURE 3.30 Platforms GameObject expanded in Hierarchy during runtime.

For proper placement of the enemy on the named platform, the *x* value must fall within a range that relates to the width of the platform. The minimum *x* value of 0 would place the enemy to the far left of the platform, regardless of where that platform is placed in the scene. Also, the *x* value must be less than the width of the platform it is being added.

The highest possible value allowed would place the enemy to the far right of the platform.

2. Build levels

Modify the *BuildLevel* method by adding more platforms and enemies to the first two levels. Make each level require at least 30 seconds to complete.

Also, make the first level easier than the second level.

Most developers would agree that it would be easier to build levels by dragging prefabs into the scene and using the move and scale tools to position and size them than it would be to build a level by writing code. However, game developers do not always have a visual editor to work from. Additionally, methods that spawn platforms and enemies into the scene would be useful for procedurally generated worlds.

Completing tasks in code opens up possibilities for allowing the players to complete those same tasks as a game mechanic.

Right! I could imagine players creating their own platforms during gameplay in the same manner as firing a weapon. This game mechanic could be implemented by calling the *addPlatform* method with the player's position as arguments every time the player presses the space bar or clicks the mouse.

Also, manually entering the coordinates to place elements in the game will help you become comfortable with positioning elements in 2D space and prepare you for the more advanced mathematics lessons of the remaining chapters.

To speed up the process, use graph paper to plan out your entire level in advance. Decide on how many pixels wide and tall each square represents and label the graph axis accordingly. Then shade in squares with various colors to define the locations of platforms, the player starting point, enemies, and the end-of-level while keeping in mind the distance the player will be allowed to jump upward and horizontally.

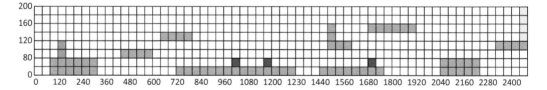

FIGURE 3.31 Platforms and other game objects shaded in on the grid of squares.

In this example, each square is 40 pixels by 40 pixels. The blue player is 40 pixels wide and 80 pixels tall. If the player can jump 140 pixels (3.5 squares) high and 160 pixels (4 squares) horizontally, it should be possible for the player to traverse the green platforms and avoid the red enemies to get to the yellow end of level.

Then, through playtesting, the position of game elements can be adjusted further to ensure the appropriate level of challenge.

For efficient development, change the *level* property of the GameController script in the Inspector Window to the level you are currently working on. This will allow you to test out a level without having to play through all the previous levels first.

Challenges

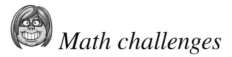 *Math challenges*

Add a third vertical level in which the player must climb upward from platform to platform to complete the level. Be sure to update the *NUM_LEVELS* constant defined in the GameController class to 3 while working.

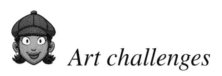 *Art challenges*

1. Change the background color of the Main Camera. Also change the background color of the Scene Window to match by selecting Colors in the project preferences. Preferences are in the Unity menu on Mac and in the Project menu on PC.

2. Change the text color of the UI Text that is part of the Canvas prefab.

3. Change colors or add textures to the Platform and LevelExit prefabs.

4. Modify the playerSpriteSheet to create your own player character with custom animations.

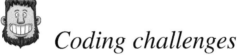 *Coding challenges*

1. Create another *addEnemyToPlatform* which takes only two arguments—the enemy type and platform name—and places the enemy at a random position on the platform.

2. Add a feature that spawns a platform under the player when the space bar is pressed. Modify the game so that players must use this ability to complete levels.

Achievements

In this chapter you:

- Learned how to position objects in a 2D space.
- Acted as a level designer to build out a full level of a platformer game.
- Modified a C# script to add platforms and hazards to a game.

Exercises

1. Find the points labeled on the coordinate plane.

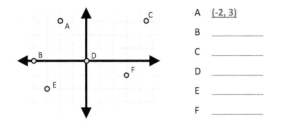

A   (-2, 3)

B   _____

C   _____

D   _____

E   _____

F   _____

FIGURE 3.32   Points A through F plotted on the coordinate plane.

2. Estimate the distance between the points on the coordinate plane.

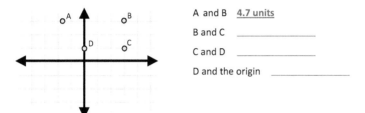

A and B   **4.7 units**

B and C   _____

C and D   _____

D and the origin   _____

FIGURE 3.33   Points A through D plotted on the coordinate plane.

3. What is the distance between points at the given coordinates?

(24, 17) and (6, 17)   **18 units**

(−120, 100) and (−200, 100) _____

(0, −45) and (0, 50) _____

(−70, −320) and (−70, −580) _____

4. A platform with a width of 200 px and a height of 50 px has a position of (100, −20) using the same coordinate system used in the project of this chapter. An enemy has a width of 30 px and a height of 40 px. The platform and the enemy both have pivot points at their top-left corner. What position should the enemy be given to place them the furthest to the right on the platform as possible without any overhang.

4

Distance | Right Triangles, Pythagorean Theorem, and the Distance Formula

---

Introduction

I love triangles; not just because they might represent a piece of pie, cake, or pizza; but for so many "mathy" reasons too. For instance, any polygon can be broken up into triangles.

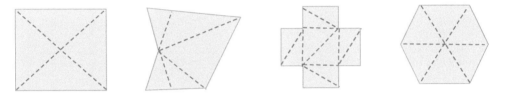

FIGURE 4.1 Various polygons divided into triangles.

If you can work with triangles, you can work with polygons!

In a moment you will see it is often preferred to use as few triangles as possible. Here are the same shapes again each split up into a fewer number of triangles.

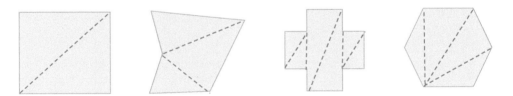

FIGURE 4.2 Various shapes divided into minimal number of triangles.

DOI: 10.1201/9781032701431-5

3D models, which can be used in both 2D and 3D games, are made up of many triangles. The more triangles used, the more realistic the model.

Compare the two models of a skull pictured. The model in front is lower poly and thus has less detail. The model in back is higher poly and thus has greater detail.

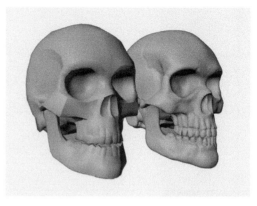

FIGURE 4.3 Low-poly vs high-poly skull models created by Orin Adcox.

Looking at the wireframes that define the 3D models, it is clear the low poly model has far fewer polygons—and thus far fewer triangles—than the higher poly model. In fact, the lower poly model consists of 3,666 triangles, while the higher poly model consists of 69,668 triangles.

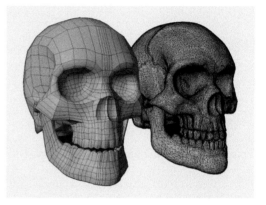

FIGURE 4.4 Wireframes of low-poly vs high-poly skulls created by Orin Adcox.

The quality level may make you believe that high poly is the way to go. However, with a higher polygon count, the processing power needed to draw the models onto the screen increases. In games, models need to be drawn over and over to update the scene. A game that runs at a frame rate of 30 fps would need to redraw the models currently visible in the game 30 times every second.

The game needs to run on hardware that could keep up with this demand.

The processing demands increase as the number of models in your game grows. These are all reasons that a low poly count is often desired for 3D models used for games.

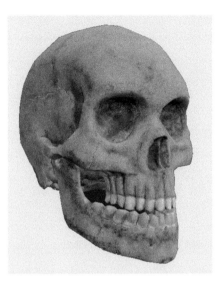

This is especially true when the games are designed for devices with lower processing power, such as smartphones.

It's worth noting that textures may be used to increase the level of detail (lod) on a model without increasing the number of triangles. In Figure 4.5, a texture has been added to the low poly skull.

FIGURE 4.5 Low-poly skull with texture created by Orin Adcox.

Let's look at another example of why our lovable triangles are useful in game development. Triangles allow us to determine the distance between objects in 2D space. In the illustration below, one alien is 30 units to the right and 20 units above the origin. The other alien is 70 units to the right and 35 units above the origin.

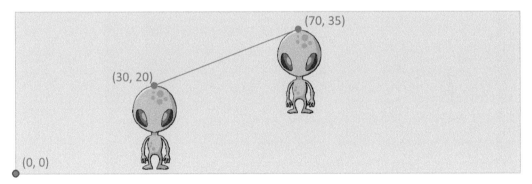

FIGURE 4.6 Line segment between points (30, 20) and (70, 35) connecting two aliens in 2D space.

Why is the distance between game objects important? Here are just a few examples.

- An enemy chases the player only after the player gets close enough to the enemy.
- A grenade deals damage to all players within a given distance from the blast.
- The game object nearest the location of a mouse click is selected.

What does this have to do with triangles?

Great question. I have a feeling we are going to be using the Pythagorean Theorem soon!

Add a couple of lines to the illustration to form a right triangle and label them with meaningful variable names. Note that the Greek letter Δ ("delta") is often used in mathematics to mean "the change in".

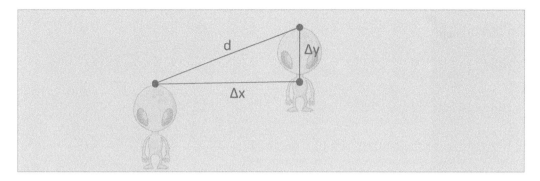

FIGURE 4.7   Line segments added to show change in *x* and change in *y* between the alien positions.

Label the line between the pivot points of the two objects *d* to represent the *distance* you are trying to find. The line labeled Δ*x* ("change in *x*") represents the horizontal distance between the two objects on the *x* axis. The line labeled Δ*y* ("change in *y*") represents the vertical distance between the two objects on the *y* axis.

Recall that a *right triangle* has one angle that is 90 degrees (a *right angle*), the side opposite the right angle is the *hypotenuse*, and the sides that form the right angle are the *legs*.

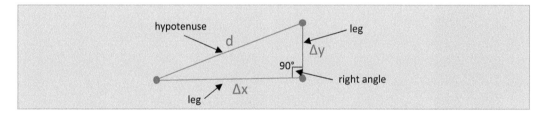

FIGURE 4.8   Labels added to indicate the lines from the hypotenuse and legs of a right triangle.

Any triangle can be broken up into two right triangles.

FIGURE 4.9   A right, acute, and obtuse triangle; each divided into two right triangles.

If you can work with right triangles, you can work with any triangles!

There is a fascinating and well-known relationship between the lengths of the sides of a right triangle. The relationship is described by the Pythagorean Theorem which states that the square of the hypotenuse is equal to the sum of the squares of the legs. That is:

$$a^2 + b^2 = c^2$$

where a and b are the legs of a right triangle and c is the hypotenuse.

Now we have one equation with three variables. If you know the value of two of the variables, you can determine the value of the remaining variable by simply solving the equation for the unknown variable.

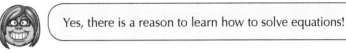 Yes, there is a reason to learn how to solve equations!

In our example, the value of d is unknown, but we can figure out the values for the Δx and the Δy given the position of the two objects.

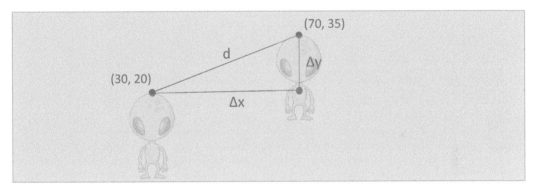

FIGURE 4.10 Coordinates of alien positions added back onto the right triangle.

The values for Δx and Δy depend on the order in which you subtract the x and y values. In the above example, you could get negative or positive results based on the order of subtraction. Compare the two approaches shown here.

The change in the x values is $30-70$.   The change in the x values is $70-30$.

$$\Delta x = -40 \qquad\qquad\qquad \Delta x = 40$$

The change in the y values is $20-35$.   The change in the y values is $35-20$.

$$\Delta y = -15 \qquad\qquad\qquad \Delta y = 15$$

 Either approach works because when you square the values, you will get the same result. For example, 15^2 and $(-15)^2$ both result in the same value of 225.

Regardless of the approach, applying the Pythagorean Theorem gives the same result.

$$\Delta x^2 + \Delta y^2 = d^2$$

$$40^2 + (-15)^2 = d^2 \text{ or } (-40)^2 + 15^2 = d^2$$

$$1600 + 225 = d^2$$

$$1825 = d^2$$

$$d = \pm\sqrt{1825}$$

 Ignore the negative solution to express distance as a positive value.

$$d = \sqrt{1825}$$

$$d \approx 42.72$$

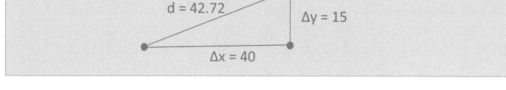

FIGURE 4.11   Calculated distances of each side of the right triangle added to labels.

You should always think about whether your solution makes sense. You can verify the solution by comparing the lengths of the legs, and by knowing the hypotenuse of a right triangle is always the longest side. Yes, 42.72 units appears to be a reasonable distance for the hypotenuse given the lengths of the legs.

You now have a process using the Pythagorean Theorem that will allow you to find the distance between any two points! Life would be even simpler if you could express this in some easy-to-apply formula. Let's start again by plugging our variables into the Pythagorean Theorem.

$$\Delta x^2 + \Delta y^2 = d^2$$

To come up with a generalized formula for finding the distance between two points, we simply need to solve this equation for d.

First, flip the equation to get d on the left side: $d^2 = \Delta x^2 + \Delta y^2$

Take the square root of each side of the equation: $d = \pm\sqrt{\Delta x^2 + \Delta y^2}$

To maintain a positive distance, remove the negative solution: $d = \sqrt{\Delta x^2 + \Delta y^2}$

Finally, you need to express the method for determining the Δx and Δy values. For this purpose, consider (x_1, y_1) to be the position of the first game object and (x_2, y_2) to be the position of the second.

Then, substituting $(x_1 - x_2)$ for Δx and $(y_1 - y_2)$ for Δy, you get the distance formula!

$$d = \sqrt{(x_1 - x_2)^2 + (y_1 - y_2)^2}$$

where d is the distance between points (x_1, y_1) and (x_2, y_2).

You may memorize it, or you may prefer deriving it from the more memorable Pythagorean Theorem when needed. In any case, now you have an easy-to-use formula for determining the distance between two points.

Let's move this conversation into another dimension.

While the x and y coordinates are sufficient for showing positions in 2D space, positions in 3D space require another coordinate for its 3rd dimension. If you consider the x-coordinate defines a point's horizontal position and the y-coordinate defines a point's vertical position, then the z-coordinate could be considered as the depth of the point. That is, the 3rd coordinate defines how far in front or behind the xy-plane the point lies.

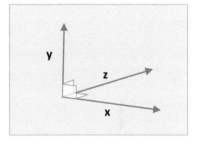

FIGURE 4.12   3D coordinate plane.

Points in 3D can be described by their distance from the origin along each axis. For instance, $(2, -3, 5)$ would describe the point that is 2 units on the x-axis, -3 units on the y-axis, and 5 units on the z-axis.

 I think we are ready to find the distance between points in 3D.

You are quite perceptive!

Consider the distance between points A and B on a coordinate plane.

Visualizing three dimensions on a 2D surface can be difficult. Here, point A is at the origin. It is difficult from this illustration to know the position of B, which may be:

- on the xy-plane with an z component of 0.
- on the yz-plane with an x component of 0.
- on the xz-plane with an y component of 0.
- At a position not on any of the planes formed by the x, y, and z axes. In this case, point B would have non-zero values for the x, y, and z components of its position.

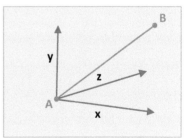

FIGURE 4.13   Segment AB in 3D.

To assist in an accurate visualization of the position of B, point C has been added on the *xz*-plane directly underneath point B to form a right triangle.

The right triangle will also aid us in finding a formula for the distance between points A and B. You can already see the length of BC represents the Δy between points A and B.

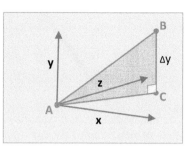

FIGURE 4.14   Right Triangle ACB.

We know the length of one side of the right triangle. If we knew the distance from A to C also, we could use the Pythagorean Theorem to find the distance from A to B.

To find the distance between A and C, a point can be placed along the *x*-axis to form a right triangle on the *xz*-plane. The legs of that right triangle would represent the Δx and Δz between points A and C, as well as between points A and B.

Using the distance formula, the length of $AC = \sqrt{\Delta x^2 + \Delta z^2}$.

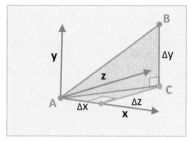

FIGURE 4.15   Δx, Δy, and Δz of AB.

Apply the distance formula again to triangle ABC to find the distance between points A and B.

$$d = \sqrt{\left(\Delta y\right)^2 + \left(\sqrt{\Delta x^2 + \Delta z^2}\right)^2}$$

Simplified, we have a formula for finding the distance between two points.

$$d = \sqrt{\Delta x^2 + \Delta y^2 + \Delta z^2}$$

This formula should look quite familiar. The formula for finding the distance in 3D is just an extension of the formula for finding the distance between points in 2D.

$$d = \sqrt{\left(x_1 - x_2\right)^2 + \left(y_1 - y_2\right)^2 + \left(z_1 - z_2\right)^2}$$

where *d* is the distance between points (x_1, y_1, z_1) and (x_2, y_2, z_2).

Activity: Bombs Away

It's time to apply the distance formula in a game. Follow the steps to complete the activity.

1. Become familiar with the *Bombs Away* game.

    Open *Scene01* of the BombsAway project from Chapter 4 project files. Press the Play button and use the mouse to drop bombs on enemy ships.

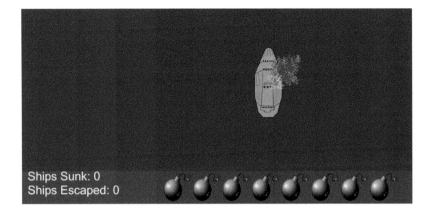

FIGURE 4.16 Explosion on a ship while playing Bombs Away.

Notice that even when you hit a ship, the ship does not sink. That is the bug you will be fixing in this activity!

When the game is working properly, the player will need to sink enough ships to win before too many of them escape. Because it takes some time for the bombs to drop, timing will be most important.

Press the Play button again to stop the game.

Expand the GameObjects in the Hierarchy Window to see what initially makes up the level.

There is a camera, a *GameController*, and a *Canvas* that contains all user-interface (UI) elements. The UI includes a *StatusText* to display the number of ships that have sunk or escaped, a *BombPanel* to show the number of bombs remaining, and a *GameOverPanel* that appears when the game ends.

FIGURE 4.17 Expanded Hierarchy.

2. Find the erroneous code.

Open the *GameController* script and scroll down to find the *ExplosionAt* method.

```
92   ⊟       public void ExplosionAt(Vector3 blastPos)
93           {
94   ⊟           for (int i = ships.transform.childCount-1; i >= 0; i--)
95               {
96                   GameObject ship = ships.transform.GetChild(i).gameObject;
97                   float deltaX = ship.transform.position.x - blastPos.x;
98                   float deltaY = ship.transform.position.y - blastPos.y;
99                   float distance = Mathf.Sqrt(deltaX * deltaX - deltaY * deltaY);
100                  Debug.Log(distance);
101  ⊟               if(distance < blastRadius)
102                  {
103                      Sink(ship);
104                  }
105              }
106          }
```

FIGURE 4.18   ExplosionAt method of the GameController class.

The *ExplosionAt* method is used to check whether or not an explosion hits a ship. The method is called from elsewhere in the program so that it executes at the moment an explosion occurs.

In a moment we will go over the code in more depth, but for now just understand that the method determines whether the ship is hit based on the blast radius of the explosion and the distance the explosion is from the ship.

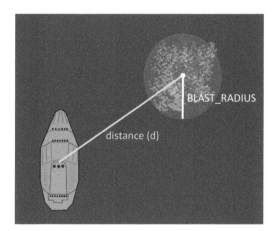

> If the distance from the center of the explosion to the center of the ship (*d*) is less than the blast radius (*BLAST_RADIUS*), the function should return a value of true to indicate there was a hit. Otherwise, the function should return false to indicate there was not a hit.

> Later you will have the opportunity to adjust the blast radius, but it is currently set to 1 unit.

FIGURE 4.19   Ship outside of blast radius.

For some reason, the method *always* returns a value of false, which is why the ships never sink. Your objective is to figure out why and fix it.

3. Debug using the Console

Use the console to help find the error. In addition to displaying warnings and errors, the console can display messages while a program is running. The *Debug.Log* method is used to print information to the console. You can see it has already been added in the *ExplosionAt* method to display the value of *distance* after it is calculated.

```
100                              Debug.Log(distance);
```

FIGURE 4.20   Call to Debug.Log method.

You could update the script to use the *print* method instead of the *Debug.Log* method.

```
100                              print(distance);
```

FIGURE 4.21   Call to print method.

The *print* method simply calls the Debug.Log method. However, because the print method is defined in the *MonoBehaviour* class, it may only be used from within classes that inherit from *MonoBehaviour*. Like most C# scripts written within Unity, the *GameController* class does inherit from *MonoBehaviour* as specified in the class definition.

```
5      public class GameController : MonoBehaviour
```

FIGURE 4.22   Definition of GameController class extending MonoBehaviour.

While a full discussion of inheritance is beyond the scope of this book, it is useful to know that you may always use the *Debug.Log* to print messages to the Console, whereas the *print* method only works if used within a class that extends MonoBehaviour.

Play the game and drop some bombs as close to the ship as possible. What type of values are you getting?

Notice the value of distance printed to the console is often *NaN*. This is short for "not a number".

Also, notice the ship does not sink even if the explosion is very near the ship.

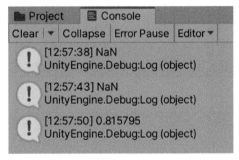

FIGURE 4.23   Console showing distances.

By dropping enough bombs, you may realize that NaN results anytime the change in *y* is greater than the change in *x*.

With this clue and the ability to use the console for debugging, you are almost ready to find the error in this code and fix it.

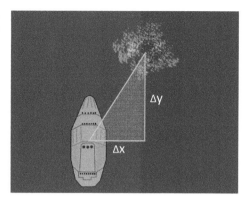

FIGURE 4.24 Right triangle formed with a line between the ship and a blast.

As this book is not focused on learning to program, rest assured that the error is in fact a mathematical error. That is to say, the code is correctly written following the syntax rules of the language but the math being applied is incorrect. Still, it may be helpful to understand the lines of code that make up the *ExplosionAt* function.

```
92    public void ExplosionAt(Vector3 blastPos)
93    {
94        for (int i = ships.transform.childCount-1; i >= 0; i--)
95        {
96            GameObject ship = ships.transform.GetChild(i).gameObject;
97            float deltaX = ship.transform.position.x - blastPos.x;
98            float deltaY = ship.transform.position.y - blastPos.y;
99            float distance = Mathf.Sqrt(deltaX * deltaX - deltaY * deltaY);
100           Debug.Log(distance);
101           if(distance < blastRadius)
102           {
103               Sink(ship);
104           }
105       }
106   }
```

FIGURE 4.25 ExplosionAt method of the GameController class.

The *for* statement on line 94 creates a loop that repeats the code block from lines 95 to 105 for each ship currently in the game. If only one ship is in the game, the code block only executes once. If no ships are in the game, the code block does not execute. Line 96 creates the variable *ship* as a quick reference to the ship that is currently being accessed.

Line 97 defines and initializes the variable *deltaX* (Δx) to be the difference between the *x* value of the explosion's position and the *x* value of the ship's position. Similarly, *deltaY* (Δy) is initialized on line 98 to be the difference between the explosion's *y* value and the ship's *y* value.

Lines 99 and 100 define the variable *distance*, initialize it using the distance formula, and then print that calculated value to the console.

The asterisk (*) is used for multiplication, so *deltaX * deltaX* is equivalent to "Δx times Δx", or $(\Delta x)^2$.

Finally, lines 101–104 direct the ship to sink if the distance calculated is less than the blast radius required for a hit.

Take some time to identify and fix the error.

You may want to compare the distance formula from the chapter to the code.

After making the necessary changes to the code, save the file in the editor and refresh the page to test it out. Once you have successfully "debugged" the program, ships will disappear every time an explosion occurs close enough to a ship, and the "Ships Sunk" score should be updated accordingly.

After you have resolved the error,

1. Reflect as to what mathematical occurrence was causing the erroneous code to calculate distance as NaN.

2. Comment out or delete the *Debug.Log* or *print* command that you were using to debug.

Challenges

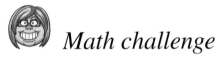

Math challenge

Adjust the volume of explosions so they have a linear relationship with the distance the explosion is from the ship.

The adjustment of the volume can be made in the *ExplosionAt* method of the GameController class, just after the distance is calculated on line 99.

However, to adjust the volume property of the bomb's AudioSource component, you must have access to that component. Unfortunately, neither the GameController class nor the *ExplosionAt* method has access to the bomb that caused the explosion.

One approach to address this is to send the bomb as a parameter to the method instead of only sending the bomb's position. This will give the method access to the entire bomb, including the position of its Transform component and the volume of its AudioSource component.

Taking this approach, you should change the name of the method for clarity. No longer are you saying "explosion at" a given position, but instead "explode" a given bomb. The changes needed for this approach are on the lines indicated in Figure 4.26.

```
public void Explode(GameObject bomb)
{
    for (int i = ships.transform.childCount-1; i >= 0; i--)
    {
        GameObject ship = ships.transform.GetChild(i).gameObject;
        float deltaX = ship.transform.position.x - bomb.transform.position.x;
        float deltaY = ship.transform.position.y - bomb.transform.position.y;
```

FIGURE 4.26   Explode method created by modifying the ExplosionAt method.

After saving the changes made in the *GameController* class, the call to the *ExplosionAt* method in the *BombBehavior* class should now appear as an error.

```
29                        gc.ExplosionAt(transform.position);
```

FIGURE 4.27   Call to ExplosionAt underlined in red indicating an error.

Update this line of code to use the new method name and to pass the GameObject which the script is attached to—the bomb, instead of the position of the bomb.

```
29                        gc.Explode(gameObject);
```

FIGURE 4.28   Error addressed by updating method call.

After saving this change, you should be ready to complete the math challenge back in the GameController script. The first step is to adjust the volume when an explosion occurs.

```
100                        bomb.GetComponent<AudioSource>().volume = 0f;
101                        Debug.Log(distance);
```

FIGURE 4.29   Volume of a bomb's AudioSource set to 0 from within the GameController class.

The code shown here sets the volume to 0. If you play the game to test it out, you should hear no explosions. If you change it to 1f, then you should hear the explosions at 100% volume. Your challenge is to change the constant on the right side of the equal sign to an expression using the value of *distance* so that the explosion is louder when it is near the ship.

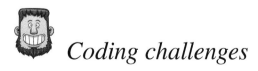

Coding challenges

1. Make *blastRadius* visible in the inspector window and adjust the value until it feels good for your game. The *blastRadius* is a property defined in the *GameController* class.
2. Calculate the amount of damage dealt based on the distance the explosion is from the ship. The closer the blast is to the ship, the higher the damage inflicted. For example:
   - 100% of the max damage should be inflicted when the blast occurs exactly at the center of the ship (when the distance between the blast and the ship is 0).
   - 40% of the max damage should be inflicted when the blast occurs at a distance from the ship that is 60% of the blast radius.
   - No damage should be inflicted when the blast occurs at a distance equal to or beyond the blast radius.

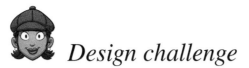

Adjust the values for the following properties until the game is sufficiently challenging:

GameController class

- INITIAL_BOMB_COUNT

- MAX_ESCAPED_SHIPS (*for lose condition*)

- GOAL_SUNKEN_SHIPS (*for win condition*)

ShipBehavior class

- minSpeed

- maxSpeed

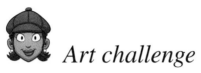

Replace sprites used for the bomb and ship with custom-made sprites.

Achievements

Colliders such as those used in the BouncyBox game of Chapter 1 are very common in game development. CircleColliders use the 2D distance formula and SphereColliders use the 3D distance formula to determine if two colliders are colliding. Consider the math needed to determine if two circles are colliding. You need to know the radius of each circle and the distance between them.

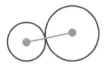

If the distance between the centers of two circles is equal to the sum of their radii, then the circles are in contact.

FIGURE 4.30   Tangent circles.

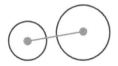

If the distance between the centers of two circles is greater than the sum of their radii, then the circles are not colliding.

FIGURE 4.31   Non-intersecting Circles.

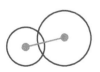

If the distance between the centers of two circles is less than the sum of their radii, then the circles are overlapping.

FIGURE 4.32   Intersecting Circles.

This is just one of many examples of how the distance between points is useful in game development.

You could create a function for finding the distance between two points. It might be defined as:

```
public float getDistance(Vector2 a, Vector2 b);
```

The function would take two positions and use the distance formula to return the distance between those positions. However, there is no need to do this in Unity, because the Vector2 class already provides a *Distance* method that does exactly this.

```
public static float Distance(Vector2 a, Vector2 b);
```

Likewise, when working in 3D, the Vector3 class also provides a Distance method.

```
public static float Distance(Vector3 a, Vector3 b);
```

Learn more about Vector2 and Vector3 classes using the Unity Scripting API:

https://docs.unity3d.com/ScriptReference/Vector2.html
https://docs.unity3d.com/ScriptReference/Vector3.html

Lastly, consider why game developers should know the distance formula even when methods that calculate distance between points already exist.

In this chapter you:

- Learned how the Pythagorean Theorem describes the relationship between the sides of a right triangle.
- Derived the distance formula from the Pythagorean Theorem.
- Applied the Pythagorean Theorem and the distance formula to determine the distance between objects in a 2D game.
- Took on the role of game developer to test and debug code.
- Took on the role of a level designer to adjust the balance of a game to the desired difficulty level.
- Explored the Unity API to learn more about the Vector2 and Vector3 classes.
- Learned how the distance between points is fundamental for algorithms related to collision detection.

Exercises

1. Find the length of the hypotenuse of the right triangle.

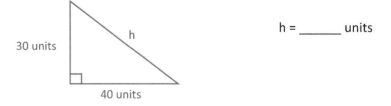

h = _____ units

FIGURE 4.33   Right triangle with legs 30 units and 40 units in length.

2. Find the length of the right triangle's missing leg.

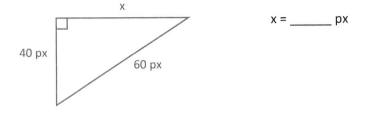

x = _____ px

FIGURE 4.34   Right triangle with one leg 40 pixels and a hypotenuse 60 pixels in length.

3. Find the distance between the points A and B on the coordinate plane.

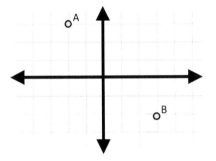

FIGURE 4.35   Points A and B on a coordinate plane.

4. A player at position (−200, −450) is attempting to sneak by an enemy robot at position (0, 500). The robot is able to detect any player within 1,000 units of its location.

   What is the distance between the player and the enemy? _____

   At the current positions, will the robot detect the player? _____

5. The player character in a 3D game is at position (3, 7, −2). A health pack is at position (2, −5, 4).

   How far is the health pack from the player? _____

5

Field of View | Pi and Finding Angles Using SIN, COS, TAN

Introduction

A challenge in many games is in dealing with those pesky enemies. While some enemies may be quite sophisticated, others are a bit indifferent to what is going on around them.

For example, the Little Goombas in *Super Mario Bros.* simply move in one direction until they hit an obstacle and reverse direction, fall off a ledge, or get smashed. Their behavior is the same regardless of what the player is doing.

The challenge increases as enemies get smarter. Sometimes an enemy is on a *patrol* following a pre-defined path. Sometimes an enemy reacts to a player when the player is detected, often chasing the player with malicious intent of causing harm.

How does an enemy "detect" the player? Maybe the enemy becomes aware of the player when they come out of the shadows or makes too much noise. More commonly, the enemy detects the player when the player gets too close.

Fortunately, you learned in Chapter 2 how to determine the distance between two game objects.

Often, the enemy will detect the player only after the player enters the enemy's *field of view* (FOV).

Typically, an enemy's FOV allows them to "see" in the direction they are facing within a specified angle up to a specified distance.

In more advanced implementations, the enemy may have more trouble detecting a player that is in a less visible area of the FOV. Here, the gradient used for the FOV might represent the probability of the red enemy detecting the green player.

FIGURE 5.1 Green dot within red dot's field of view.

DOI: 10.1201/9781032701431-6

In some games, obstacles may impede the field of view allowing the player to avoid detection by hiding behind objects.

FIGURE 5.2   Obstacle in red dot's field of view hiding green dot.

 What math is needed to determine if a player is in the enemy's FOV?

 Great question. In short, the answer is Trigonometry! Let's dive in.

The Math

First, we need to review how to measure angles in degrees. Turning 360 degrees is a full circle. Turning 180 degrees is a half-circle. With a 180 degree turn, you end up facing in the opposite direction. This is why the phrase "make a 180" refers to reversing your direction.

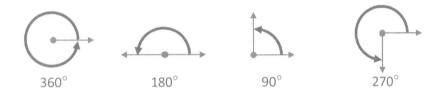

FIGURE 5.3   Various angle rotations shown with initial and ending positions of a ray.

Adding or subtracting 360 degrees changes the number of rotations but results in the same angle between the initial and final directions. The following angle measurements are equivalent.

FIGURE 5.4   Equivalent angle rotations of −105°, 255°, 615°, and 975°.

While measuring angles in degrees is common, it is often useful to measure angles in *radians*.

 Radians is typically the preferred unit for measuring angles in computer programming, including game programming.

To understand radians, it is important to understand circles. Let's start with the common terminology used to describe circles.

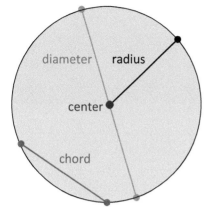

circle - all points on a plane equidistant from a *center* point on the same plane.

radius - distance from the center to any point on the circle

chord - distance from one point of a circle to another.

diameter - distance from one point of a circle to another through the center.

circumference – distance around the circle.

FIGURE 5.5   Elements of a circle labeled.

The first relationship that is quite clear is that the diameter is twice the length of the radius. The other well-known relationship is between the diameter and circumference of a circle. That is, dividing the circumference of any circle by its diameter always results in the same value. This *constant* is universally labeled with the Greek letter π (pi) and has a value of approximately 3.1415.

So, π is defined by the circumference (C) of any perfect circle divided by its diameter (d).

$$\pi = C / d$$

Solve this equation for C to create a formula that can be used to find the circumference of any circle with a known diameter.

$$C = \pi d$$

Because we know the diameter is twice the radius, we could also find the circumference of a circle using the radius instead of the diameter.

$$C = \pi(2r)$$

$$C = \pi d, \quad C = 2\pi r$$

where C is the circumference, r is the radius, and d is the diameter of a perfect circle.

While this equation can be applied to a circle of any size, let's apply it to a circle with a radius of exactly 1 unit to facilitate our discussion of radians.

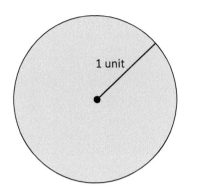

The actual unit used does not matter. That is, we could have a circle with a radius of 1 inch, 1 centimeter, 1 mile, or any other single unit.

With a *unit circle*, the circumference is:

$$C = 2\pi(1)$$

Simplified, that is:

$$C = 2\pi$$

FIGURE 5.6   Unit circle.

So, the distance around a unit circle is 2π (approximately 6.283) units. This is the basis for how to measure angles in radians. The angle measured in radians is equal to the distance along the circumference of the unit circle formed by that angle. A full 360° rotation is 2π radians and the circumference of that circle is 2π units, a 180° rotation is π radians (half of 2π), and the distance around half a unit circle is π units, and so on.

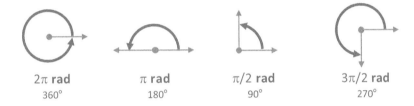

| 2π **rad** | π **rad** | $\pi/2$ **rad** | $3\pi/2$ **rad** |
| 360° | 180° | 90° | 270° |

FIGURE 5.7   Various angle rotations with angles labeled in radians and degrees.

To convert an angle from radians to degrees, multiply by 180 / π.

$$\frac{\pi}{2}\text{rad} * \frac{180}{\pi} = 90 \text{ degrees}$$

To convert an angle from degrees to radians, multiply by π / 180.

$$90 \text{ degrees} * \frac{180}{\pi} = \frac{\pi}{2}\text{rad}$$

$\pi/2$ **rad**
90°

FIGURE 5.8   90° rotation.

Expressing angles as radians will be useful when programming an enemy's field of view. However, we first need a few more tools for finding unknown angles.

Let's return to our beloved right triangles!

From Chapter 4, we know we can use the Pythagorean Theorem to find the length of one side of a right triangle when the lengths of the other two sides are known. However, we also need a way to determine the unknown angles of a right triangle.

Greek letters are commonly used as variable names to represent angles. In the following illustration, the Greek letter *theta* (θ) is used as the measure of an angle that we need to find.

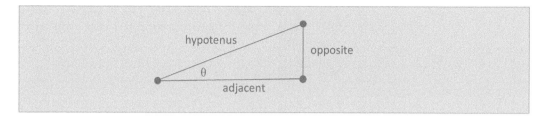

FIGURE 5.9 Right triangle with θ as the smallest angle.

For all right triangles, the *hypotenuse* is the side opposite the right angle.

Also, the hypotenuse is always the longest side.

The other two sides are labeled relative to the angle.

- The *adjacent* side is the leg next to—or adjacent to—the angle θ.
- The *opposite* side is the leg across from—or opposite of—the angle θ.

To find the measure of θ, use the trigonometric functions sine (sin), cosine (cos), and tangent (tan).

For any right triangle,

- The **sine** of an angle is equal to the length of the opposite side divided by the length of the hypotenuse.
- The **cosine** of an angle is equal to the length of the adjacent side divided by the length of the hypotenuse.
- The **tangent** of an angle is equal to the length of the opposite side divided by the length of the adjacent side.

$$\sin \theta = \text{opposite} \,/\, \text{hypotenuse}$$

$$\cos \theta = \text{adjacent} \,/\, \text{hypotenuse}$$

$$\tan \theta = \text{opposite} \,/\, \text{adjacent}$$

where *opposite* is the leg opposite of θ, *adjacent* is the leg adjacent to θ, and *hypotenuse* is the side opposite the right angle.

You could use these formulas with a known angle of a right triangle to find unknown sides.

For instance, consider the following example where one side of a right triangle is known (the hypotenuse is 100 units in length); two angles of the right triangle are known (the right angle and another angle which measures $\pi/6$ radians, or 30 degrees); and the opposite and adjacent sides are unknown.

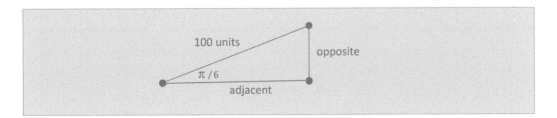

FIGURE 5.10   Right triangle with hypotenuse of 100 units and one angle of π/6 radians.

We could use either the sine or cosine formulas to find the length of the legs as follows.

sin (π/6)=opposite / 100   cos (π/6)=adjacent / 100

Solving for the unknowns we get:

opposite=sin (π/6) * 100   adjacent=cos (π/6) * 100

Use a calculator to find the sin and cos of π/6.

Google search for "calculator" to find this handy calculator.

Be sure your calculator is set to radians.

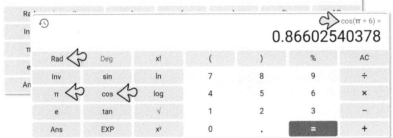

FIGURE 5.11   Calculator showing sin and cos of π/6.

Plugging in the resulting values into our equations, we get:

opposite=0.5 * 100   adjacent≈0.867 * 100

Multiply to finish solving for the unknown lengths of the right triangle.

opposite=50 units   adjacent≈86.7 units

These lengths sound reasonable when compared to the known length of the hypotenuse.

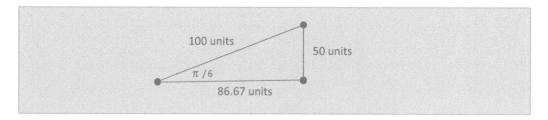

FIGURE 5.12   Same right triangle with newly calculated side lengths added.

Often, more than one length of the right triangle is known and must be used with the sin, cos, and tan formulas to determine an unknown angle.

Let's look at another example.

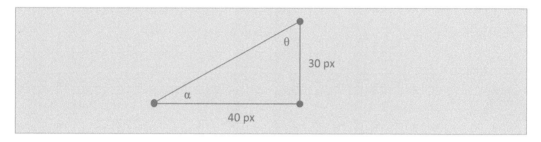

FIGURE 5.13   Right Triangle with 30-pixel side opposite angle α and 40-pixel side opposite angle θ.

This time, the lengths of the legs are known while the angles θ (theta) and α (alpha) that are opposite the legs are unknown. Let's solve for θ first. The side opposite θ is 40 pixels in length and the adjacent side is 30 pixels. The distance formula could be used to determine the hypotenuse, but only two sides are needed to find the unknown angle. The formulas for sine and cosine both use the hypotenuse which is currently unknown, so let's use the tangent formula instead.

$\tan\theta = $ opposite / adjacent

$\tan\theta = 40 / 30$

Select the trigonometric function to use based on the information that is known.

When solving equations, use inverse operations to get the unknown by itself.

For example, division is the inverse of multiplication. The equation **5x=8** could be solved for *x* by dividing both sides by 5.

And subtraction is the inverse of addition. The equation **y+7=2** could be solved for *y* by subtracting 7 from both sides of the equation.

The inverse operations for sin, cos, and tan are:

* inverse sine (arcsin), denoted by $\sin^{-1}$
* inverse cosine (arccos), denoted by $\cos^{-1}$
* inverse tangent (arctan), denoted by $\tan^{-1}$

Using the inverse tangent, you can solve **tan θ=40 / 30** for the unknown angle θ.

$$\tan\theta = 40/30$$

$$\tan^{-1}(\tan\theta) = \tan^{-1}(40/30)$$

$$\theta = \tan^{-1}(40/30)$$

Plugging this into a calculator in radians mode, we find $\theta \approx 0.927$ rad.

arctan(40 ÷ 30) =
0.927295218

Rad	Deg	x!	(	)	%	AC
Inv	sin	ln	7	8	9	÷
π	cos	log	4	5	6	×
e	tan	√	1	2	3	−
Ans	EXP	xʸ	0	.	=	+

FIGURE 5.14   Calculator showing inverse tan of 40/30.

Convert this to degrees by multiplying by 180 / π.

0.927295218 × 180 ÷ π =
53.1301023542

FIGURE 5.15   Calculator showing radian measure multiplied by 180/π.

Because the sum of the angles of every triangle is 180 degrees, we can determine the measure of the remaining unknown angle (α).

$$90° + 53.13° + \alpha = 180°$$

$$143.13° + \alpha = 180°$$

$$\alpha \approx 36.87° \text{ (this is an approximation due to the prior approximation of } \theta)$$

You could have also found α by solving a trig function: $\tan\alpha = 40/30$

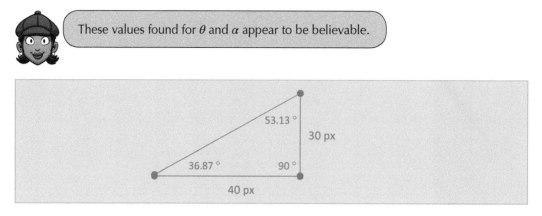

These values found for θ and α appear to be believable.

FIGURE 5.16 Same right triangle with newly calculated angles added.

Using sin, cos, and tan formulas to find unknown angles or sides of right triangles is often useful in mathematics.

They are frequently used by game developers as well. The next section demonstrates one such example.

The mnemonic *soh-cah-toa* is commonly used for remembering the trig formulas.

$$\sin \theta = \frac{o}{h} \qquad \cos \theta = \frac{a}{h} \qquad \tan \theta = \frac{o}{a}$$

Activity: Avoid Detection

The mathematical concepts covered in this chapter are frequently useful in game development. Adding a field of view (fov) to enemies is a fun example.

First, you will need the *Avoid Detection* project files for this activity. Instructions for downloading the project files used in this book are provided in the Introduction.

After unzipping the project, adding it to Unity Hub, and opening the project, open Scene01 and play the game. Use the W or up arrow key to move forward and use the mouse to change direction. Notice the enemies begin to chase the player when they are close to and facing the player. In this activity, you will make a geometric shape to represent the fov for each enemy.

FIGURE 5.17   Enemy field of views displayed while playing.

This is not at all a complete game, but I suppose it does provide a demonstration of the enemy AI that might be used in a game.

I notice the enemy stops chasing and returns to their patrol when the player is no longer in their fov.

When playing the game with the player selected, the *speed* and *health* properties of the player are visible in the Inspector. You should see the player's health diminishing when in contact with an enemy. While there is no way to win the game, the player will be destroyed when their health is depleted.

Take some time to familiarize yourself with the project and code before beginning the activity. First, explore the contents of the game by expanding all GameObjects in the Hierarchy Window.

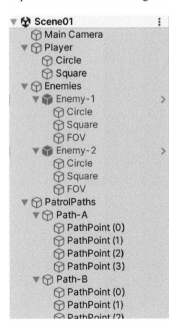

The Main Camera is providing a top-down perspective for the player and currently has a static position—it stays in one place. In one of the challenges for this chapter, you will have the opportunity to make the camera follow the player.

The *Player* is comprised of two primitive sprites—a circle and a square. This "programmer art" is sufficient for the developer to continue working while the artists create character art and animations for the player.

Two enemies can be found within the *Enemies* GameObject. The blue cube icons signify that these are instances of a prefabricated GameObject. Each Enemy prefab consists of two primitive sprites—a circle and a square—and an FOV GameObject which is used for the field of view.

Enemies are programmed to follow a patrol path. Two patrol paths can be found within the *PatrolPaths* GameObject. Patrol paths are defined by a series of path points which guide the enemies along a path.

FIGURE 5.18   Hierarchy Expanded.

With *Enemy-1* selected, you can see an *EnemyBehavior* script is used to define the behavior of enemies.

Enemy-1 is set to follow the *Path-A* patrol path and to chase the *Player* when detected. The *sightAngle* and *sight-Distance* properties define the enemy's FOV.

The *hearingDistance* property defines the distance the enemy will detect the player even when the player is not within the enemy's field of view.

The *dps* property defines the *damage per second* that the enemy deals to the player when attacking (i.e., when in contact with the player). The *attackColor* property defines a color for the enemy while they are attacking. The *walkSpeed* defines the speed of the enemy when on patrol and the *runSpeed* defines the speed of the enemy while chasing the player.

Finally, the *showFOV* property defines whether or not the field of view will be visible during gameplay.

Modify these properties to see how they change the behavior of Enemy-1.

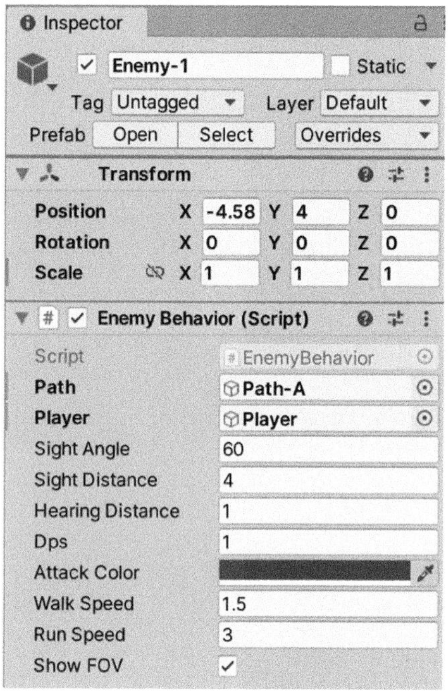

FIGURE 5.19   Enemy-1 in Inspector.

In the Project Window, you can see all assets are organized in sub-folders of the Assets folder. Notice the Scripts folder contains the two scripts used to define the behavior of the player and the enemies. Take a look at these scripts to see how mathematics makes these behaviors possible.

Review the *PlayerController* script first. The script includes only three public properties.

```
5     public class PlayerController : MonoBehaviour
6     {
7         public float speed = 4;
8
9         public const float MAX_HEALTH = 100;
10
11        [Range(1, MAX_HEALTH)]
12        public float health = MAX_HEALTH;
```

FIGURE 5.20   Class and public properties defined on lines 5 through 12 of the PlayerController script.

Notice the *MAX_HEALTH* property is defined as a *const*. Because the value is constant and cannot be changed, Unity does not display the property in the Inspector Window. The *speed* and *health* properties are displayed in the Inspector.

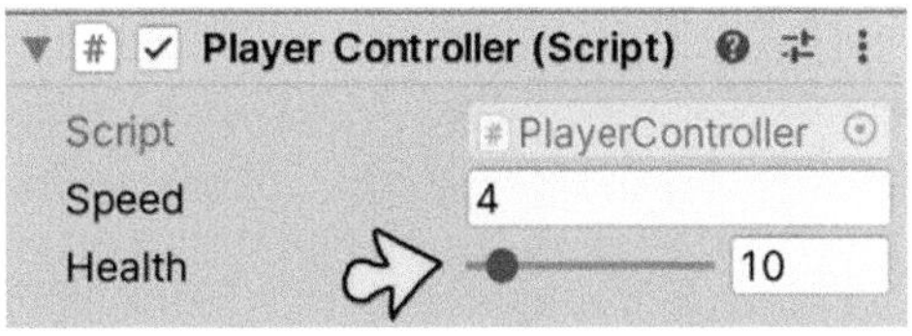

FIGURE 5.21   PlayerController on Player.

Line 11 defines a range of values to restrain the possible values for the health property defined in the following line. Unity provides a slider in the Inspector Window which restricts the value from being set outside of the range of possible values.

On line 12, the default value for health is initialized to the highest value possible. The initial value of health was reduced to 10 for this game in the Inspector Window, making it faster to test the code that executes at the moment the player's health is depleted.

The Update method of the *PlayerController* class moves and rotates the player based on user input.

```
14       void Update()
15       {
16           Vector3 dir = Input.mousePosition - Camera.main.WorldToScreenPoint(transform.position);
17           float angle = Mathf.Atan2(dir.y, dir.x) * Mathf.Rad2Deg;
18           transform.rotation = Quaternion.AngleAxis(angle, Vector3.forward);
19
20           if (Input.GetKey(KeyCode.UpArrow) || Input.GetKey(KeyCode.W))
21           {
22               transform.position += transform.right * Time.deltaTime * speed;
23           }
24       }
```

FIGURE 5.22   Update method defined on lines 14 through 24 of the PlayerController class.

Line 16 determines a vector that defines the direction the player should face based on the current position of the mouse. To understand this line of code, you need to know how Unity stores positions in relation to the game and to the screen.

For both 2D and 3D games in Unity, positions are stored as Vector3 objects. A Vector3 simply stores three float values. When used for a position, a Vector3 stores an *x*, *y*, and *z* value to represent the distance the object is on each axis from the origin of the coordinate system in which it is placed.

The screen position of an object is typically different than its world position. Consider for a moment a game in which the camera follows the player. The player always has the same screen position (i.e., the center of the screen), but the player's position in the world changes with every movement the player makes. On the other hand, a stationary object in the game, such as a tree, would always have the same world position but its screen position would change as the player moved through the world.

While world positions are defined in relation to the center of the game world, screen positions are defined in relation to the bottom left of the screen. Because a screen is always a 2D representation, the depth (*z* value) of a screen position is always 0.

With this understanding, you should be ready to analyze Line 16 of the code.

```
Vector3 dir = Input.mousePosition - Camera.main.WorldToScreenPoint(transform.position);
```

FIGURE 5.23 Line 16 of the PlayerController class.

In Unity, you can get the screen position on the mouse using the *mousePosition* property of the *Input* class. Specifically, *Input.mousePosition* stores the position of the mouse, in pixels, from the bottom left of the screen.

> For instance, a mousePosition with Vector3 values of (3.2, 7.5, 0) would indicate the mouse is 3.2 pixels to the right and 7.5 pixels above the bottom left corner of the screen.

The *Camera.main.WorldToScreenPoint* method transforms a position from world space into screen space. That is, when you send it the world position of an object, it gives you the position on your screen where the object appears. Because *transform.position* refers to the player (i.e., the world position of the GameObject this script is attached to), the *WorldToScreenPoint* function returns the screen position of the player.

Finally, subtracting the screen position of the player from the screen position of the mouse results in a directional vector from the player to the mouse.

> Vectors and vector subtraction will be discussed further in the next chapter.

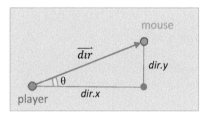

You can draw a right triangle to visualize the *x* and *y* values of the directional vector that results from the subtraction.

> Despite *dir* being a Vector3, only two dimensions are relevant for a 2D game. The *z* property of *dir* has a value of 0.

FIGURE 5.24 Right triangle with a vector as the hypotenuse.

Line 17 calculates the measure of the angle the player would need to face to be looking directly at the mouse location (i.e., θ in Figure 5.24).

```
float angle = Mathf.Atan2(dir.y, dir.x) * Mathf.Rad2Deg;
```

FIGURE 5.25 Line 17 of the PlayerController class.

This is relevant to this chapter's math lesson, so let's break it down. The *Atan2* function of the *Mathf* class returns the arctangent (inverse tangent) in radians using the opposite and adjacent sides of a right triangle provided.

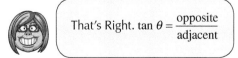

> That's Right. $\tan \theta = \dfrac{\text{opposite}}{\text{adjacent}}$

The Rad2Deg property of the Mathf class is equal to 180/π, so multiplying by *Mathf.Rad2Deg* converts the radian measurement into degrees.

The measure in degrees of *θ* is stored in the local variable *angle*.

However, an angle by itself is not sufficient for describing a direction. Consider the possible positions of the mouse relative to the player that would result in the same measure for *θ*.

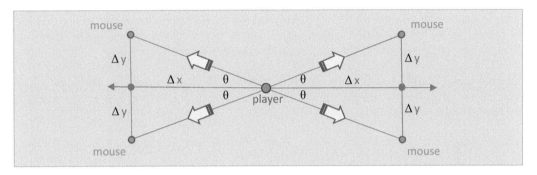

FIGURE 5.26   Right triangles forming the same interior angle symmetrically drawn from the player position.

The large arrows indicate the direction from the player to the mouse.

Each of these possible mouse positions results in the same absolute values for Δ*x* and Δ*y*, and therefore the same measure for *θ* using the formula $\theta = \tan^{-1}(\Delta x / \Delta y)$. Despite having the same value of *θ*, the direction from the player to the mouse is clearly different for all four different mouse positions.

Just as we need a point in 2D space to be able to describe the position of objects, we need a base angle in which all other angles can be described. This game, like most, defines the east-facing direction (right) to be 0 radians.

FIGURE 5.27   Player facing east.

Rotating counter-clockwise from 0 radians (also 0°), an object facing north (up) has a direction of π/2 rad (90°), an object facing west (left) has a direction of π rad (180°), and an object facing south (down) has a direction of 3π/2 rad (270°).

Alternatively, by rotating clockwise from 0 radians in the negative direction, an object facing south (down) could be expressed as −π/2 rad (−90°), an object facing west (left) could be expressed as −π rad (−180°), and an object facing south (down) could be expressed as −3π/2 rad (−270°).

With a measure of 0 radians for the direction of east established, all other directions can now be expressed in relation to 0 rad. This means that θ is the direction from the player's screen position to the mouse's screen position only when the mouse is positioned to the upper right of the player.

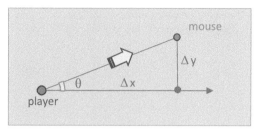

FIGURE 5.28 θ when the mouse is upper right of the player.

With just a little math, the direction from the player to the mouse can be determined for any possible positioning. The angle representing the direction of the vector can be calculated by adding or subtracting the appropriate angle based on which quadrant the mouse lies in relation to the player.

When the mouse is positioned to the lower-left of the player, the player would face the mouse with a direction of $\theta + \pi$, or $\theta - \pi$. Adding or subtracting π rad (180°) from θ is equivalent to turning around to face in the direction opposite of θ.

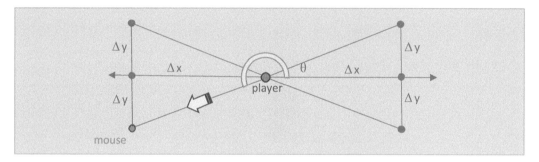

FIGURE 5.29   Angle formed when the mouse is to the bottom left of the player, 180° past θ.

When the mouse is positioned to the upper-left of the player, the player would face the mouse with a direction of $\pi - \theta$. That is, starting from the left-facing direction (π), rotate clockwise by θ.

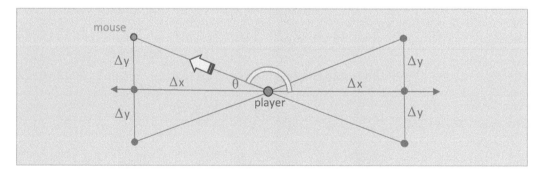

FIGURE 5.30   Angle formed when the mouse is to the top left of the player, 180° minus θ.

The enemy would face the player to the bottom-right with a direction *−θ*.

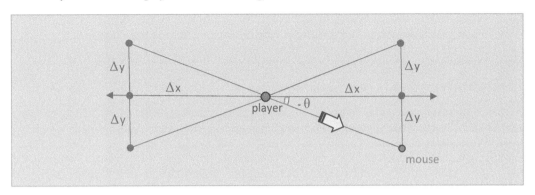

FIGURE 5.31 Angle formed when the mouse is to the bottom right of the player, *−θ*.

Unity's *Mathf* class does provide an *Atan* method which returns the arctangent of a value given. However, we now know that *θ* is not always the angle we are actually looking for. If we used the *Atan* method, additional code would be needed to determine the actual angle based on where the enemy is positioned in relation to the player.

Fortunately, the *Mathf* class also provides the **Atan2** method to handle this bit for us. Take another look at how this method was used in our script.

```
float angle = Mathf.Atan2(dir.y, dir.x) * Mathf.Rad2Deg;
```

FIGURE 5.32 Line 17 of the PlayerController class.

The *Mathf.Atan2* method needs two parameters representing the change in *y* and the change in *x* to correctly calculate the inverse tangent.

 The signs of *dir.y* and *dir.x* (whether they are positive or negative) are used to determine which quadrant the resulting angle should lie.

Once the angle is calculated, it is used in the next line to set the rotation of the player using the *AngleAxis* property of the *Quaternion* class.

```
transform.rotation = Quaternion.AngleAxis(angle, Vector3.forward);
```

FIGURE 5.33 Line 18 of the PlayerController class.

 So, the first few lines of the Update method cause the player to face toward the position of the mouse.

The remaining few lines of the *Update* method move the player forward when the W or up arrow keys are being pressed.

```
if (Input.GetKey(KeyCode.UpArrow) || Input.GetKey(KeyCode.W))
{
    transform.position += transform.right * Time.deltaTime * speed;
}
```

FIGURE 5.34 Lines 20 through 23 of the PlayerController class.

In Unity, the forward direction is on the *z* axis. This might seem natural for 3D games with First Person controls. In a 2D game where the *z* axis is not relevant (assuming the game is designed on the *x-y* plane), the forward direction of a GameObject will not be in the *z* direction. In our game, you can see the *Player* is facing right (in Scene view) when its rotation is 0 (as shown in the Inspector Window). Therefore, the Player in this game can be moved forward by increasing the *x* value of its position. The *transform.right* property, equivalent to the Vector3 (1, 0, 0), is used to move the player forward.

As discussed in Chapter 2, the movement vector should be multiplied by appropriate scalars to adjust for frame rate and the player's speed.

The *TakeDamage* method is the only method other than Update in the PlayerController class.

```
public void TakeDamage(float damage)
{
    if (damage >= health)
    {
        health = 0;
        print("GAME OVER: PLAYER DIED.");

        Time.timeScale = 0;
        Destroy(this.gameObject);
    }
    else
    {
        health -= damage;
    }
}
```

This method is straightforward. The player is destroyed if the damage sent to the method is greater than or equal to the player's current health. Otherwise, the player's health is decreased by the amount of damage specified.

The *TakeDamage* method is called from the EnemyBehavior script when a collision with the player is detected.

FIGURE 5.35 Lines 26 through 40 of the PlayerController class.

The *EnemyBehavior* class is more complex with 16 properties and 9 methods. Only the code relevant to this activity will be discussed here.

The public properties visible in the Inspector were discussed previously. The remaining properties are all private, accessible only to the methods of the EnemyBehavior class.

The *isAttacking* and *pathTargetId* properties are initialized when they are declared. The remaining private properties are initialized in the *Start* method.

The *target* property determines what the enemy will be moving toward. Sometimes this is the player and sometimes it is the next path point in the enemy's patrol path.

```
7     private float speed;
8     private GameObject fov;
9     private bool isAttacking = false;
10
11    private GameObject target;
12    private int pathTargetId = 0;
13    public GameObject path;
14
15    public GameObject player;
16    public float sightAngle = 60f;
17    public float sightDistance = 4f;
18    public float hearingDistance = 1f;
19
20    public float dps = 1f;
21    private Color initialColor;
22    public Color attackColor = Color.red;
23    public float walkSpeed = 1.5f;
24    public float runSpeed = 3f;
25
26    public bool showFOV = true;
```

FIGURE 5.36   Properties of the EnemyBehaviour class.

Most of the code in the Start method creates the Mesh used for the enemy's fov.

Notice when the FOV of an enemy is selected prior to playing the game, the Mesh has no value.

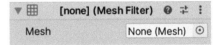

FIGURE 5.37   Mesh Filter of FOV prior to play.

While playing, the value of the Mesh updates.

However, currently, the Mesh is empty. It is a mesh with no vertices.

FIGURE 5.38   Mesh Filter of FOV during play.

I suppose adding vertices is what this activity entails.

You got it. Don't worry though. Much of the code is already written. You will only need to modify a few lines. Afterall, the focus is on math, not programming.

Who said I was worried?

The *fov* property serves as a reference to the FOV game object and is initialized as such on line 32.

```
fov = transform.Find("FOV").gameObject;
```

FIGURE 5.39   Line 32 of the EnemyBehavior class.

Lines 37 to 74 create the mesh based on the enemy's forward direction and *sightAngle*. To complete this code, the *x* and *y* values need to be calculated in the code that is commented out.

```
37          List<Vector3> vertices = new List<Vector3>();
38          List<Vector2> uv = new List<Vector2>();
39          List<int> triangles = new List<int>();
40
41          vertices.Add(new Vector3(0,0,0));
42          uv.Add(new Vector2(0, 0));
43
44          float startAngle = -1 * sightAngle / 2;
45          float endAngle = sightAngle/2;
46          int numArcVertices = 10;
47          float radius = sightDistance / transform.localScale.x;
48          float angle = startAngle;
49          for (int i = 0; i < numArcVertices; i++)
50          {
51              // float x =                    Looks like a job for
52              // float y =                    Trig functions!
53
54              // vertices.Add(new Vector3(x, y, 0));
55              // uv.Add(new Vector2(x, y));
56
57              angle += sightAngle / (numArcVertices - 1);
58          }
59
60          for(int i = 1; i<vertices.Count-1; i++)
61          {
62              triangles.Add(0);            It would probably be
63              triangles.Add(i);           best to understand the
64              triangles.Add(i + 1);       existing code before
65          }                               making changes.
66
67          Mesh mesh = new Mesh();
68          mesh.vertices = vertices.ToArray();
69          mesh.uv = uv.ToArray();
70          mesh.triangles = triangles.ToArray();
71
72          fov.GetComponent<MeshFilter>().mesh = mesh;
73
74          fov.GetComponent<MeshRenderer>().enabled = showFOV;
75      }
```

FIGURE 5.40   Lines 37 through 75 of the EnemyBehavior class.

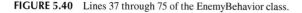

First, a few local variables are declared. The *vertices* variable will reference a list of *Vector3* objects; the *uv* variable will reference a list of *Vector2* objects; and the *triangles* variable will reference a list of integers.

```
37              List<Vector3> vertices = new List<Vector3>();
38              List<Vector2> uv = new List<Vector2>();
39              List<int> triangles = new List<int>();
```

FIGURE 5.41   Lines 37 through 39 of the EnemyBehavior class.

The vertices will include the origin (0, 0, 0) located at the center of the enemy and all other points that are needed to draw the mesh.

Knowing that a mesh is made of triangles, how can an arc representing the field of view be created?

Three vertices, illustrated here with yellow dots, gives a very rudimentary fov. However, with only three vertices the mesh would end up with 3 straight sides and not be very accurate to the arced fov that has been implemented.

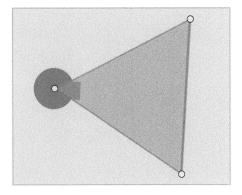

FIGURE 5.42   fov using 3 vertices.

Clearly, more than three vertices will be needed.

A better representation of the fov will result by adding more vertices along the arc.

> I notice three vertices give you one triangle and then each additional vertex created gives an additional triangle.

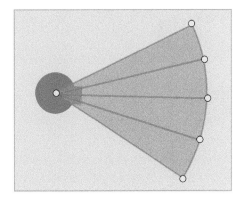

FIGURE 5.43   fov using 6 vertices.

> The more vertices you have, the more curved the arc will be... but also the more triangles your mesh will have. As a game developer, you should improve performance by adding only the number of vertices required to achieve the visual accuracy desired.

> Also, the number of vertices needed depends on the size of the arc. Larger fovs will need more vertices.

The *uv* List holds the same coordinates as the *vertices* List. You can see in the code (on lines 41 and 42, and on lines 55 and 56) that every time a new vertex is added to the *vertices* List it is also added to the *uv* List. The only difference between the Lists is that one is storing the vertices as Vector3 objects and the other is storing them as Vector2 objects. In this way, you can use whichever list type is needed.

The *triangles* List is more interesting and will be discussed in a moment.

The next bit of code adds the origin as the first element of the *vertices* and *uv* Lists.

```
41          vertices.Add(new Vector3(0,0,0));
42          uv.Add(new Vector2(0, 0));
```

FIGURE 5.44   Lines 41 and 42 of the EnemyBehavior class.

An algorithm is needed to determine the positions of the remaining vertices. Local variables are defined and initialized for this purpose.

```
44          float startAngle = -1 * sightAngle / 2;
45          float endAngle = sightAngle/2;
46          int numArcVertices = 10;
47          float radius = sightDistance / transform.localScale.x;
48          float angle = startAngle;
```

FIGURE 5.45   Lines 44 through 48 of the EnemyBehavior class.

As can be seen in the Enemy prefab, the forward-facing direction of the enemy is to the right.

This is when no rotation has been applied on any axis. That is, the rotation of the enemy is (0, 0, 0).

The enemy's field of view should face in the same direction as the enemy.

Because the FOV GameObject is a child of the Enemy, it will already rotate as the enemy rotates.

With right as the forward direction (having a rotation of 0°), the value of sightAngle can be used to determine the *startAngle* and *endAngle*.

For example, assume the *sightAngle* was set in the Inspector to 60 degrees—a good estimate of the fov shown in our example. Then, line 45 would initialize the *endAngle* to half of the *sightAngle* (i.e., 30°) and line 44 would initialize the *startAngle* to the opposite of that (i.e., −30°).

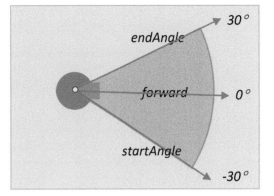

FIGURE 5.46   fov with start and end angles.

Line 46 sets the *numArcVertices* to 10.

For simplicity, there are only five in our example.

The radius of the arc (i.e., the radius of the circle that the arc is a part of) is the distance in which the enemy will be able to see. On line 17, the *sightDistance* is initialized to 4. This is the same value used in the Enemy prefab.

So, why not just use the sightDistance to set the radius?

```
float radius = sightDistance;
```

Consider an Enemy that is doubled in size (i.e., scaled to 2, 2, 2). The children of the Enemy, including the FOV, will also double in size. This is not desired. Only the values of *sightDistance* and *sightAngle* should determine the size of the FOV. Dividing by the amount the enemy is scaled along the *x* axis corrects for this.

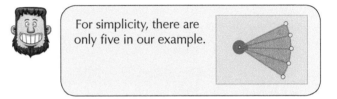

```
47          float radius = sightDistance / transform.localScale.x;
```

FIGURE 5.47   Line 47 of the EnemyBehavior class.

For example, if an Enemy had doubled in width (i.e., the scale of the Enemy on the *x* axis was set to 2), then the radius of the FOV would also double in size. To counter this, the radius is divided by that same value on line 47.

The inverse of multiplying by 2 is dividing by 2.

Finally on line 48, the *angle* variable is set equal to the *startAngle*. The *angle* represents the angle to the vertex currently being calculated and will change each time another vertex needs to be calculated.

Lines 49 through 58 use a *for* loop to repeat a block of code.

```
49          for (int i = 0; i < numArcVertices; i++)
50          {
51              // float x =
52              // float y =
53
54              // vertices.Add(new Vector3(x, y, 0));
55              // uv.Add(new Vector2(x, y));
56
57              angle += sightAngle / (numArcVertices - 1);
58          }
```

FIGURE 5.48   Lines 49 through 58 of the EnemyBehavior class.

Each time the code repeats, a new vertex is added.

 This is the perfect opportunity to learn how for loops work!

The variable *i* is declared and initialized to a value of zero. The value of this variable will change each time the code repeats (i.e., iterates). This variable is known as the *iterator*.

```
for (int i = 0; i < numArcVertices; i++)
```

FIGURE 5.49   Iterator initialization of for loop emphasized.

The following condition determines if the code within the block should be repeated. The code repeats if the condition is true and stops repeating if the condition fails.

```
for (int i = 0; i < numArcVertices; i++)
```

FIGURE 5.50   Condition of for loop emphasized.

The last part of the for loop modifies the iterator. Often, the ++ operator is used to increase the iterator by one.

```
for (int i = 0; i < numArcVertices; i++)
```

FIGURE 5.51   Iterator modification of for loop emphasized.

Consider the case in which the value of *numArcVertices* is 5. The code block (i.e., lines 50 to 58) would repeat 5 times.

- The first iteration (or loop) occurs when i=0.
- The second iteration occurs when i=1.
- The third iteration occurs when i=2.

- The fourth iteration occurs when i=3.
- The fifth iteration occurs when i=4.

When i=5, the condition fails and the code following line 58 begins.

The code that is being repeated needs to create the vertices at the correct positions along the arc. This is achieved on line 57 by changing the *angle* to point toward the next vertex as each iteration finishes.

The *angle* was initialized prior to the loop to equal the *startAngle*. The code commented out will create a vertex on the arc in that direction. Then, the angle will be increased to point toward the next vertex that will be created.

Dividing the *sightAngle* by the *numArcVertices - 1* gives the amount the angle should increase in each iteration.

For example, if the *sightAngle* is 60° and the *numArcVertices* is 5, then the numArcVertices - *1* is 4 (i.e., the number of triangles in the mesh) and the increase would be 15° (i.e., 60°/4).

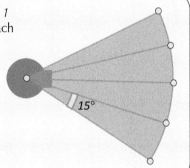

Consider the first time the code block is executed, the vertex at one end of the arc should be created.

The *x* and *y* values for that vertex are needed to create the Vector3 and Vector2 objects to be added to the Lists (see lines 54 and 55).

Trig functions can be used to determine these values. Visualize a right triangle with the *x* and *y* values we need.

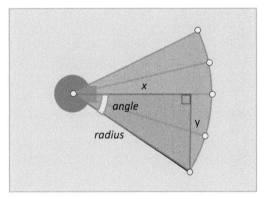

FIGURE 5.52   Right triangle with end vertex.

Use the appropriate Trig functions to find the opposite leg (i.e., *y*) and the adjacent leg (i.e., *x*).

The values for the angle and radius are already known and stored in variables, so we can use them to find the values of *x* and *y*. Since we know the hypotenuse, the sine function can be used to find the opposite side, and the cosine function can be used to find the adjacent side.

cos θ=adjacent / hypotenuse   sin θ=opposite / hypotenuse

Substitute in the variables used in our example.

cos (angle)=x / radius   sin (angle)=y / radius

Convert the angle measurement from degrees to radians by multiplying by π/180.

cos (π/180 * angle)=x / radius   sin (π/180 * angle)=y / radius

Solve both equations to get the needed formulas.

x=cos (π/180 * angle) * radius y=sin (π/180 * angle) * radius

Finally, the missing code on lines 52 and 53 can be added and the code that was commented out can be commented back in.

> The Deg2Rad property of the Mathf class is equal to π/180 so may be used to convert the angle from degrees to radians.

Once done correctly, you should see the fov for each enemy when you run the game!

While finishing lines 51 and 52 completes the activity, some of the challenges in this chapter will require an understanding of the remainder of the code used to create the mesh. Start with the code that executes right after all the vertices have been created.

```
60          for(int i = 1; i<vertices.Count-1; i++)
61          {
62              triangles.Add(0);
63              triangles.Add(i);
64              triangles.Add(i + 1);
65          }
```

FIGURE 5.53   Lines 60 through 65 of the EnemyBehavior class.

A for loop is used again—this time to add integers to the *triangles* List. A triangle is established by three integers which indicate which of the vertices from the vertices List define the triangle.

Take a moment to fully understand this.

In the previous code, the vertex positions were added to the *vertices* Lists in order, starting with the origin.

(0, 0, 0)	(x, y, 0)	(x, y, 0)	(x, y, 0)	(x, y, 0)	(x, y, 0)
0	*1*	*2*	*3*	*4*	*5*

Each vertex has a position in the List (i.e., an index value) that can be used to access it. The first item in the List is at index 0.

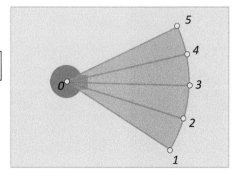

FIGURE 5.54   fov with vertices numbered.

The *triangles* variable stores a List of integers which defines the triangles of the mesh. This Array must have a size which is a multiple of three, with the first three values defining the first triangle, the next three values defining the second triangle, and so on.

In our example, the *triangles* List should have 12 values defining 4 triangles:

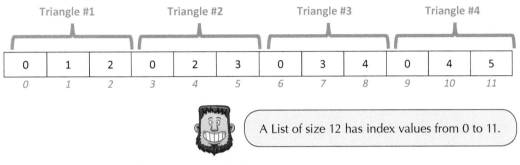

A List of size 12 has index values from 0 to 11.

Consider how the for loop is used to create the List.

```
60          for(int i = 1; i<vertices.Count-1; i++)
```

FIGURE 5.55 Line 60 of the EnemyBehavior class.

In our example, there are six Vector3 positions stored in the vertices List, indexed 0 to 5.

(0, 0, 0)	(x, y, 0)	(x, y, 0)	(x, y, 0)	(x, y, 0)	(x, y, 0)
0	1	2	3	4	5

 The Count property of a List gives the number of elements in the List.

 That is 6 in our example. And because 1 is subtracted from the Count, the conditional part of the for loop evaluates down to i<5.

The loop repeats 4 times, once for each triangle.

When i=1, 2, 3, and 4.

The first vertex of every triangle is the origin that is stored in the *vertices* List at index 0.

```
61          {
62              triangles.Add(0);
63              triangles.Add(i);
64              triangles.Add(i + 1);
65          }
```

FIGURE 5.56 Lines 61 through 65 of the EnemyBehavior class.

In the first iteration when i = 1, the additional two index values added are 1 and 2.

In the 2nd iteration when i = 2, the additional two index values added are 2 and 3.

In the 3rd iteration when i = 3, the additional two index values added are 3 and 4.

In the last iteration when i = 4, the additional two index values added are 4 and 5.

Why do we save index values in the triangles List instead of just directly saving the positions of each vertex for each triangle as Vector3 objects?

Meshes use the same vertices for multiple triangles, storing all the vertices avoids redundancy. After all, integers require less memory than floats—and Vector3 objects contain three float values.

Simply, it requires less memory for storage. This is especially important for high-poly meshes—those consisting of many triangles.

The next bit of the code in the *Start* method uses the Lists that were built to create a mesh.

```
67          Mesh mesh = new Mesh();
68          mesh.vertices = vertices.ToArray();
69          mesh.uv = uv.ToArray();
70          mesh.triangles = triangles.ToArray();
```

FIGURE 5.57   Lines 67 through 70 of the EnemyBehavior class.

First, a new Mesh is created on line 67 and stored in a variable named *mesh*. The Mesh class includes many properties including *vertices*, *uv*, and *triangles*—all Arrays used to define a Mesh. The Lists used in our code were purposely named to match these Mesh property names, but they are different. For instance, *vertices* is a List while *mesh.vertices* is an Array. An Array is very similar to a List but cannot change in size after it is created.

The *List* class has a *ToArray()* method that returns the elements of the List as an Array. This is the method used on lines 68 and 70 to create Arrays from the Lists needed to create the Mesh.

Recall the Lists were stored in local variables defined in the Start method.

When the Start method is finished executing, these variables cease to exist and the memory used to store the values of the Lists is freed up.

The Arrays of the Mesh class have a greater scope and exist as long as the mesh that they belong to exists.

Why did we need the Lists at all?
Why not just add values directly to the Arrays of the mesh?

You cannot change the size of an Array after it is first created. The List allowed us to add one element at a time. Only when we had all of the values did we use them to initialize the Arrays for the Mesh.

The next line of code sets the mesh property of the *MeshFilter* Component to the *mesh* we created.

```
72          fov.GetComponent<MeshFilter>().mesh = mesh;
```

FIGURE 5.58 Line 72 of the EnemyBehavior class.

Remember, before the game begins the mesh property was not set. But the value of the Mesh updates as soon as the game begins. This is due to Line 72!

The last line of code simply enables or disables the Mesh depending on whether the *showFOV* property was set to true or false in the Inspector Window.

```
74          fov.GetComponent<MeshRenderer>().enabled = showFOV;
```

FIGURE 5.59 Line 74 of the EnemyBehavior class.

Be sure the showFOV is toggled on in the Inspector if you want to be able to see the FOV when playing the game.

Challenges

Math and Coding challenge

1. Improve the fov mesh by using the size of the fov to determine the number of vertices to create.

   Recall that our code was written to use 10 vertices to form the arc of the fov.

```
46              int numArcVertices = 10;
```

FIGURE 5.60 Line 46 of the EnemyBehavior class.

Modify this line of code to determine the value based on the sightAngle of the FOV. For instance, a sight angle of 50 might have 5 vertices along the arc forming 4 triangles, while a sight angle of 100 might have 10 arc vertices forming 9 triangles.

2. Modify the Mesh to use an arc to represent the field of view.

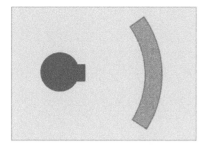

FIGURE 5.61   Arc displayed for fov.

I can imagine dividing the arc up into vertices and triangles.

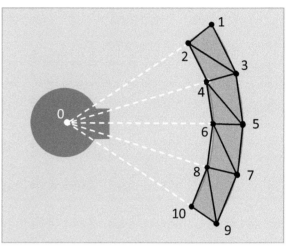

FIGURE 5.62   Arc triangles with labeled vertices.

To achieve the arc using those vertices and triangles, you would first need to store the vertices in the correct order. This would involve storing an extra arc vertex for each angle. You could, for example, add a vertex at 80% of the length of x and y just after adding the vertex at x, y.

You would also need to modify your list of triangles. No longer would each triangle include the vertex at position 0. Instead, the first triangle would include vertices of 1, 2, and 3; the second triangle would include vertices of 2, 3, and 4; and so on.

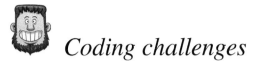

Coding challenges

1. Modify the code so the player is not required to press the W or up arrow key to move. Instead, the player character should always be moving towards the location of the cursor.
2. Put the enemies in communication with each other. Update the code so that if the player character is detected by one of the enemies, all the enemies begin to attack.

Art & Design challenge

Replace programmer art for the player character and enemies with custom art, or with assets downloaded from the Asset Store.

Achievements

Trigonometry is useful for finding unknown angles and distances. The example for this chapter was a 2D game where objects all had the same z value of 0. Consider how the trig functions might be used when finding unknown angles and distances between object place in a 3D space.

In this chapter you:

- Applied the trig functions known by the acronym *soh-cah-toa* to determine unknown sides and angles of right triangles.
- Learned how the *Atan2* method may be used to find the direction from one object in 2D space to another.
- Acted as a game developer to dynamically create a mesh for an enemy's field of view using the *sightAngle* and *sightDistance* specified.

Exercises

1. Find the unknown sides and angles of the right triangle.

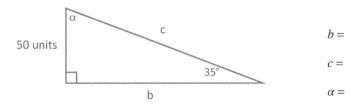

$$b =$$

$$c =$$

$$\alpha =$$

FIGURE 5.63 Right triangle with 35° angle opposite 50-unit leg.

2. Find the unknown sides and angles of the right triangle.

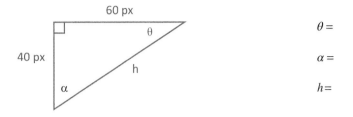

$\theta =$

$\alpha =$

$h=$

FIGURE 5.64   Right triangle with legs of 40 pixels and 60 pixels.

3. Game objects **Mouse** and **Cheese** in a 2D game have position coordinates stored in variables **mouse.X**, **mouse.Y**, **cheese.X**, and **cheese.Y**. The values represent distances measured in pixels.
   a.   What formula would give the distance between the mouse and cheese?
   b.   If the cheese is above and to the left of the mouse, what formula would give the angle the mouse needs to move in to get to the cheese?

4. Game objects **Mouse** and **Cat** in a 2D game have a forward-facing direction stored in variables **Mouse.forward** and **Cat.forward**. These are angles defining the direction they are facing. The variable **directionToMouse** has already been calculated using the *atan2* function to get the direction the cat would need to move to get to the mouse.

   If the cat has a line of sight with a π/3 rad field of view and unlimited sight distance, what condition can be used to determine whether or not the mouse is in the cat's view?

5. Game objects **Mouse** and **Cat** in a 2D game have a forward-facing direction stored in variables **Mouse.forward** and **Cat.forward**. What condition can be used to determine whether or not the cat and mouse are facing in the same direction, give or take π/6 radians?

6

Simulating Physics in a Virtual World | Matrices and Vectors

Introduction

This chapter will introduce vectors as a subset of matrices used widely in game engines to simulate physics. Vectors provide a means of storing physics-type data such as position, size, movement, and velocity. Furthermore, vector operations provide programmers with a simple way to describe interactions within a physical world. This chapter will provide you with a basic understanding of how vectors are used to apply physics within a virtual world, including the <u>what</u> (is a vector), the <u>how</u> (are vector operations performed), and the <u>why</u> (are specific vector operations useful in game programming).

The Math

Vectors are used heavily in game development, physics, and computer programming. However, there can be confusion as to what a vector is in each of these contexts. For instance, a *Euclidean Vector* is defined by a *magnitude* and *direction*. Visualizing a vector, the magnitude m is the length of the vector, and an arrow is used to indicate the vector's direction.

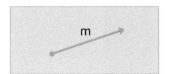

$|m|$ Vertical bars are often used for the notation of magnitudes.

$\|m\|$ Double vertical bars are sometimes used to distinguish magnitudes from the common absolute value notation.

FIGURE 6.1   Vector of length m.

Vectors are often denoted with a half-arrow symbol accent mark over a single letter or by an initial and terminal point.

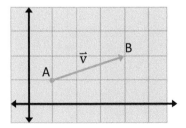

The vector shown may be written as $\vec{v}$ or $\overline{AB}$.

Do not let this fool you into believing that vectors have a position. Remember, vectors have only a magnitude (i.e., length) and a direction (i.e., heading).

FIGURE 6.2 $\overline{AB}$ labeled as $\vec{v}$.

DOI: 10.1201/9781032701431-7

Vectors are equal if they have the same direction and magnitude.

Consider vector $\overline{AB}$ with initial point A at (1, 1) and terminal point B at (4, 2); and vector $\overline{CD}$ with initial point C at (7, 2) and terminal point D at (10, 3).

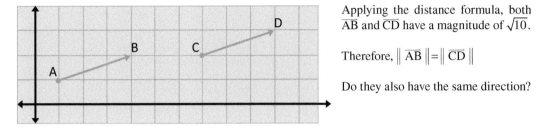

Applying the distance formula, both $\overline{AB}$ and $\overline{CD}$ have a magnitude of $\sqrt{10}$.

Therefore, $\|\overline{AB}\| = \|\overline{CD}\|$

Do they also have the same direction?

FIGURE 6.3   Equal vectors $\overline{AB}$ and $\overline{CD}$.

Recall from Linear Algebra that the slope of a line is equal to the "rise over run" of the line from one point to another. From both A to B and A to C, the rise is 1 and the run is 3. Therefore, the slope of both $\overline{AB}$ and $\overline{CD}$ is 1/3 and they have the same direction.

Because the magnitude and direction are equal, $\overline{AB} = \overline{CD}$.

More generally, a vector is defined as a list of *scalars* (numeric values) and can be visualized as a row or column. Vectors that describe a position or movement in 2D space are comprised of two scalars that describe the position or movement along each axis. Likewise, vectors that describe a position or movement in 3D space are comprised of three scalars.

 The Vector2 and Vector3 classes provided by Unity are intended for this purpose and include many properties and functions for working with vectors.

A *matrix* is a table of scalar values consisting of one or more rows and one or more columns. Therefore, a vector is a special type of matrix consisting of a single row or column.

Scalar	*Vector*	*Matrix*	
3.2	3.2	3.2	7
	5	5	3
	4.4	4.4	0.6

Position and movement are not the only use of vectors. Vectors may be used for many different purposes. For example, vectors may describe the scale of an object defined by how much it is stretched on each axis or the rotation of an object with values indicating the amount of rotation around each axis.

 In Computer Science, *arrays* and vectors are both *data structures* often used to store a group of items in a particular sequence. In many languages, arrays are a static size while a vector can grow and shrink in size as items are added or removed. Additionally, vectors in computer programming can store numeric or non-numeric data.

For game development, common uses of vectors are to store the position, rotation, and scale of game objects. Consider a happy face as an object in a 2D game positioned by its center point.

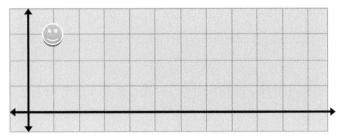

The position of the object is at [1, 3].

Possibly the scale is [0.5, 0.5] to reduce its size to 50% of its original.

Possibly the rotation is [0, 0] so that it retains its original upright orientation.

FIGURE 6.4   Smiley face at (1, 3) on the coordinate plane.

It is also common in game dev to use vectors to move objects. Consider the happy face example.

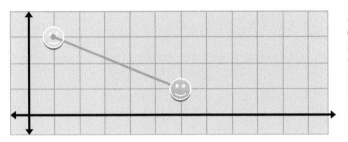

A vector [5, −2] might be used to define the distance the object should move on the *x* and *y* axes. Adding this vector to the object's original position vector of [1, 3] would give it a new position described by the vector [6, 1].

FIGURE 6.5   Vector from (1, 3) to (6, 1).

In this case, the vector is defined in *component form* by the movement along each axis. Later, you will see how the *direction* and *magnitude* can be computed from the component form of a vector.

Adding two vectors is just one example of how matrix mathematics is useful to game developers. There are many other use cases for applying operations on matrices, including vectors.

 Performing operations on matrices is much like trying to make two people fall in love—the operations only work if the matrices are compatible.

Rules for Matrix Mathematics

To add two matrices of the same size, add the numbers in the corresponding positions:

$$\begin{bmatrix} 4 & 5 \\ 6 & 7 \end{bmatrix} + \begin{bmatrix} 2 & 2 \\ 1 & 1 \end{bmatrix} = \begin{bmatrix} 6 & 7 \\ 7 & 8 \end{bmatrix}$$

 Matrices that do not have the same size are incompatible and cannot be added.

Because vectors are matrices, the rules for matrices also apply to vectors.

$$\begin{bmatrix} 1 & 2 & 3 \end{bmatrix} + \begin{bmatrix} 4 & 6 & 8 \end{bmatrix} = \begin{bmatrix} 5 & 8 & 11 \end{bmatrix}$$

> Vector addition is common in game dev. For example, you can add a force (defined as a vector) to an object to change its position (also defined as a vector). This is what was done in the previous example where vector [5, –2] was added to an object's position vector of [1, 3] to get a new position vector of [6, 1].

You can visualize vector addition quite easily in 2D, and with a bit more work in 3D, by drawing the vectors in a coordinate plane.

Consider an object with a position vector of [1, 2] that is to be moved by adding the vector [5, 1]. The new position of [6, 3] is the sum of vectors and may be found visually by placing the initial point of one vector at the endpoint of the other.

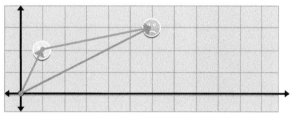

FIGURE 6.6   Vector addition visualized.

> Vector addition may be done on vectors with any number of dimensions, though it is difficult to visualize beyond 3D.

Vectors may be added in any order with the same resulting vector.

[1 2] + [5 1] = [6 3]

[5 1] + [1 2] = [6 3]

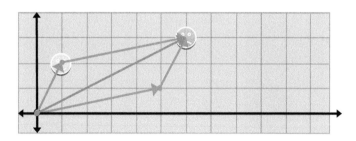

FIGURE 6.7   Commutative property of vector addition visualized.

To subtract matrices of the same size, subtract the numbers in the matching positions:

$$\begin{bmatrix} 4 & 5 \\ 6 & 7 \end{bmatrix} - \begin{bmatrix} 2 & 2 \\ 1 & 1 \end{bmatrix} = \begin{bmatrix} 2 & 3 \\ 5 & 6 \end{bmatrix}$$

The same rule applies to vectors:

$$\begin{bmatrix} 1 \\ 2 \\ 3 \end{bmatrix} - \begin{bmatrix} 4 \\ 6 \\ 8 \end{bmatrix} = \begin{bmatrix} -3 \\ -4 \\ -5 \end{bmatrix}$$

Vector subtraction is commonly used in game dev to determine the vector representing the movement from one object to another.
The order of subtraction matters. For example,
* position B [2 3] – position A [1 1] = vector A to B [1 2]
* position A [1 1] – position B [2 3] = vector B to A [−1 −2]

To transpose a matrix, switch the row and column indices to flip the matrix over its diagonal starting from the top left.

For example, consider the matrix $\begin{bmatrix} 4 & 6 \\ 5 & 7 \end{bmatrix}$. Visualize the diagonal as $\begin{bmatrix} 4 & 5 \\ 6 & 7 \end{bmatrix}$

Transposing this matrix, we see the 5 and 6 values switch places. $\begin{bmatrix} 4 & 6 \\ 5 & 7 \end{bmatrix}$

The same operation can be done on a matrix with dimensions that are not equal.

For example, consider the matrix $\begin{bmatrix} 4 & 5 \\ 6 & 7 \\ 8 & 9 \end{bmatrix}$. Visualize the diagonal as $\begin{bmatrix} 4 & 5 \\ 6 & 7 \\ 8 & 9 \end{bmatrix}$

The transpose of this matrix $\begin{bmatrix} 4 & 6 & 8 \\ 5 & 7 & 9 \end{bmatrix}$ results from flipping the values over the diagonal.

So, the first row becomes the first column, the second row becomes the second column, and so on.

The same rule applies to vectors. The transpose of $\begin{bmatrix} 4 \\ 6 \\ 8 \end{bmatrix}$ is $\begin{bmatrix} 4 & 6 & 8 \end{bmatrix}$.

Sometimes a vector can be transposed to have the same dimensions as another vector. For example, while a 3×1 vector cannot be added to a 1×3 vector, one of the vectors could be transposed so that they have the same dimensions and can then be added.

To normalize a vector, change the magnitude of the vector to 1 while maintaining the same direction.

The result is a *unit vector*—a vector with a magnitude of 1.

Consider a vector v̄ represented by [5, −2] defining the change on the *x* and *y* axes.

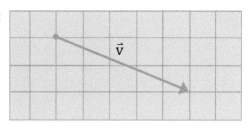

FIGURE 6.8   Vector v̄ with magnitude greater than one.

The normalized vector would have the same direction with a magnitude of 1 unit.

Unit vectors are denoted using the ˄ (i.e., "hat") accent mark. The unit vector û is read as "u hat".

The accent does look like a pointy little hat. So cute. ☺

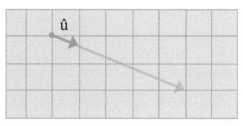

FIGURE 6.9   Unit vector û resulting from normalizing v̄.

The magnitudes of the original and normalized vectors could be viewed as the hypotenuses of two right triangles.

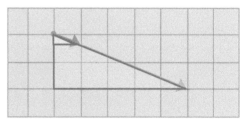

FIGURE 6.10   Similar right triangles formed from vectors û and v̄.

These two right triangles are *similar triangles* because:

> Triangles are similar if the measures of their corresponding angles are equal.

The relationship between the sides of similar triangles will be helpful in our example.

> The *corresponding sides* of similar triangles are in proportion.

This means the ratio of one set of corresponding sides of similar triangles is the same as the ratio between the other sets of corresponding sides.

In our example,

$$\frac{x_1}{x_2} = \frac{y_1}{y_2} = \frac{m_1}{m_2}$$

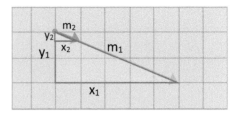

where the sides of the original vector are x_1 for the horizontal length, y_1 for the vertical length, and m_1 for the magnitude; and the sides of the unit vector are x_2 for the horizontal length, y_2 for the vertical length, and m_2 for the magnitude.

FIGURE 6.11 Sides of right triangles formed by vectors of same direction.

Some of these values are known. From the vector $[5, -2]$, we know $x_1 = 5$ and $y_1 = -2$. Also, by definition of a unit vector, we know $m_2 = 1$.

Other values can be calculated. The magnitude of the original vector (m_1) can be calculated using the distance formula to be $\sqrt{29}$ units, or approximately 5.385 units.

Plugging in the known values to our equal ratios,

$$\frac{5}{x_2} = \frac{-2}{y_2} = \frac{\sqrt{29}}{1}$$

You can now calculate x_2 and y_2 of the unit vector.

$$\frac{\sqrt{29}}{1} = \frac{5}{x_2} \text{ and } \frac{\sqrt{29}}{1} = \frac{-2}{y_2}$$

Cross multiply to get: $x_2 \sqrt{29} = 5$ and $y_2 \sqrt{29} = -2$

Divide to solve for x_2 and y_2: $x_2 = \dfrac{5}{\sqrt{29}}$ and $y_2 = \dfrac{-2}{\sqrt{29}}$

The normalized vector of $[5, -2]$ is the unit vector $\left[\dfrac{5}{\sqrt{29}}, \dfrac{-2}{\sqrt{29}} \right]$, or approximately $[0.93, -0.37]$.

 These values should seem reasonable when looking back at the illustration of the unit vector.

So, $\left[\dfrac{5}{\sqrt{29}}, \dfrac{-2}{\sqrt{29}} \right]$ is the result of normalizing $[5, -2]$. In fact, the formula for normalizing any vector is:

$$\bar{v}_n = \frac{\bar{v}}{\| \bar{v} \|}, \text{ where } \bar{v}_n \text{ is } \bar{v} \text{ normalized.}$$

 Directional vectors are typically normalized in game engines to standardize them. More importantly, using the magnitude of 1 for all directional vectors is helpful when applying a scalar, such as a value for speed, to a direction.

Most game engines provide a function for normalizing vectors. In Unity, the *Vector3* and *Vector2* classes each have a *Normalize* method.

The Vector3 and Vector2 classes in Unity provide static properties for common directional vectors. For example, here are the static properties for the Vector3 class.

back	Shorthand for writing Vector3(0, 0, -1).
down	Shorthand for writing Vector3(0, -1, 0).
forward	Shorthand for writing Vector3(0, 0, 1).
left	Shorthand for writing Vector3(-1, 0, 0).
negativeInfinity	Shorthand for writing Vector3(float.NegativeInfinity, float.NegativeInfinity, float.NegativeInfinity).
one	Shorthand for writing Vector3(1, 1, 1).
positiveInfinity	Shorthand for writing Vector3(float.PositiveInfinity, float.PositiveInfinity, float.PositiveInfinity).
right	Shorthand for writing Vector3(1, 0, 0).
up	Shorthand for writing Vector3(0, 1, 0).
zero	Shorthand for writing Vector3(0, 0, 0).

FIGURE 6.12   Static properties of the Vector3 class from the Unity API.

Most of these are unit vectors. For example, Vector3.right is $\begin{bmatrix} 1 & 0 & 0 \end{bmatrix}$ and Vector3.left is $\begin{bmatrix} -1 & 0 & 0 \end{bmatrix}$; both vectors have a magnitude of one but face in opposite directions along the x axis. Vector3.one is an exception. While it describes the direction of $\begin{bmatrix} 1 & 1 & 1 \end{bmatrix}$, this is not a unit vector—it does not have a magnitude of one.

To multiply a matrix by a scalar, multiply each value of the matrix by the scalar:

$$3\begin{bmatrix} 2 & 3 \\ -1 & 0 \end{bmatrix} = \begin{bmatrix} 6 & 9 \\ -3 & 0 \end{bmatrix}$$

This operation is called *scalar multiplication*.

The same rule of scalar multiplication applies to vectors:

$$10\begin{bmatrix} 0.93 & -0.37 \end{bmatrix} = \begin{bmatrix} 9.3 & -3.7 \end{bmatrix}$$

The directional (unit) vector [0.93, −0.37] calculated previously has a magnitude of one.

Multiplying the directional vector by 10 results in the vector [9.3, −3.7] which has a magnitude of 10.

The term scalar is appropriate for describing a multiplier for *scaling* a vector to be shorter or longer.

> In game dev, a scalar value for *speed* is often multiplied by an object's forward-facing direction vector. The resulting vector will have the magnitude equal to the speed and can then be added to the position vector of the object.

To negate a matrix, multiply it by −1:

$$-1 \begin{bmatrix} 2 & 3 \\ -1 & 0 \end{bmatrix} = \begin{bmatrix} -2 & -3 \\ 1 & 0 \end{bmatrix}$$

This rule is equivalent to negating each component of the matrix.

$$\begin{bmatrix} 1 & 0 & -9 \end{bmatrix} \text{ negated is } \begin{bmatrix} -1 & 0 & 9 \end{bmatrix}$$

Negating a directional vector results in a vector of the same magnitude in the opposite direction.

> I could imagine many situations where that would be helpful. For example, consider a game where a vector defines the forward direction of a player, but you want them to have the ability to move backward. The vector for moving backward could be calculated by negating the forward vector.

Recall that order matters when subtracting vectors. For example,

$$\begin{bmatrix} 5 & 1 \end{bmatrix} - \begin{bmatrix} 1 & -2 \end{bmatrix} \neq \begin{bmatrix} 1 & -2 \end{bmatrix} - \begin{bmatrix} 5 & 1 \end{bmatrix}$$

However, subtracting a vector from another vector is the same as adding its opposite. For example,

$$\begin{bmatrix} 5 & 1 \end{bmatrix} - \begin{bmatrix} 1 & -2 \end{bmatrix} = \begin{bmatrix} 5 & 1 \end{bmatrix} + \begin{bmatrix} -1 & 2 \end{bmatrix}$$

> That is true of scalars too. $6 - 7 \neq 7 - 6$, but $6 + -7 = -7 + 6$

> That is kind of obvious since adding and subtracting vectors just requires the adding and subtracting of their scalar components.

After vector subtraction is changed to vector addition, the order no longer matters.

Changing vector addition to vector subtraction might not seem useful since adding and subtracting the scalar components requires about the same amount of effort. However, it is much easier to visualize scalar addition. Consider the $\begin{bmatrix} 5 & 1 \end{bmatrix} - \begin{bmatrix} 1 & -2 \end{bmatrix}$. How would you visualize vector subtraction?

This feels like an accident waiting to happen.

Fortunately, visualizing addition is much easier. Switching to $\begin{bmatrix} 5 & 1 \end{bmatrix} + \begin{bmatrix} -1 & 2 \end{bmatrix}$, we simply need to place the initial point of one of the vectors at the terminal point of another.

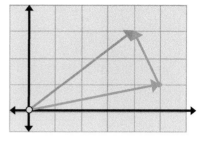

FIGURE 6.13   Visual of [5 1]+[−1 2].

Operations with Position Vectors

Working with vectors becomes much easier when they are described with their initial point at the origin. A *position vector* is any vector with an initial point at the origin. Consider equal vectors $\vec{v}$ and $\vec{w}$ below.

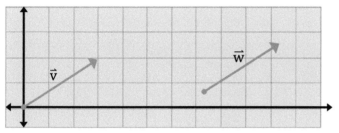

The vectors are equal because they have the same direction and magnitude.

However, $\vec{v}$ is a position vector because it has an initial point at the origin while $\vec{w}$ is not.

FIGURE 6.14   Positional vector $\vec{v}$ on same coordinate plane with equal non-positional vector $\vec{w}$.

Angle brackets are used to denote position vectors. Here, $\vec{v} = \langle 3\ 2 \rangle$ and $\vec{w} = \begin{bmatrix} 3 & 2 \end{bmatrix}$.

The initial and terminal points of $\vec{w}$ are unknown. In fact, [3 2] describes the direction and magnitude of the vector, but not its position.

On the contrary, the position of $\vec{v}$ is known, hence the term "position vector". It has an initial point at (0 0) and a terminal point at (3, 2).

Every point has a unique, one-to-one relationship with a position vector. That is every point is the terminal point for one and only one position vector.

Of course, all of this applies to three-dimensional vectors as well. For example, <2 −4 7> is a position vector with an initial point at the origin and a terminal point at (2, −4, 7).

So, <2 −4 7> is the same as (2, −4, 7)?

Ugh… no. <2 −4 7> is a vector and (2, −4, 7) is a point.

I can see why it might be confusing since the components of the terminal point and positional vector are equal. That is actually what makes position vectors so easy to work with.

However, Noah is right that they are not the same. As a vector, <2 −4 7> defines a direction and a magnitude, not a position. The point (2, −4, 7) describes a position, which has no direction and no magnitude.

Consider again $\begin{bmatrix} 5 & 1 \end{bmatrix} + \begin{bmatrix} -1 & 2 \end{bmatrix} = \begin{bmatrix} 4 & 3 \end{bmatrix}$

This could be visualized as before such that:

- $\begin{bmatrix} 5 & 1 \end{bmatrix}$ is positioned with its initial point at the origin—it is the position vector $\langle 5 \ 1 \rangle$.

- $\begin{bmatrix} -1 & 2 \end{bmatrix}$ is positioned with its initial point at the terminal point of $\langle 5 \ 1 \rangle$, which is (5, 1).

- And $\begin{bmatrix} 4 & 3 \end{bmatrix}$ is positioned with its initial point at the origin—it is the position vector $\langle 4 \ 3 \rangle$.

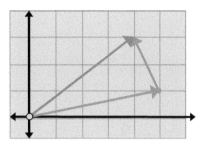

FIGURE 6.15   Vector addition visualized.

This positioning helps our visualization of the vector addition, but remember a vector is defined by only direction and magnitude—not position.

So, you could visualize $\begin{bmatrix} 5 & 1 \end{bmatrix} + \begin{bmatrix} -1 & 2 \end{bmatrix} = \begin{bmatrix} 4 & 3 \end{bmatrix}$ with any position you want.

Vector $\begin{bmatrix} 4 & 3 \end{bmatrix}$ has the same direction and magnitude as the position vector $\langle 4 \ 3 \rangle$, so the vectors are equal.

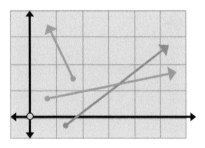

FIGURE 6.16   Vector addition visualized with vectors positioned arbitrarily.

You could also visualize the vector addition using only position vectors.

$\langle 5 \ 1 \rangle + \langle -1 \ 2 \rangle = \langle 4 \ 3 \rangle$

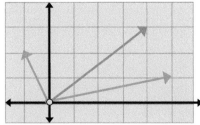

FIGURE 6.17   Vector addition visualized with position vectors.

Using position vectors often simplifies the mathematics used when working with vectors.

For example…

The direction of a 2D vector can be defined by its slope. Recall the slope of a line is equal to its rise over run between any two points on the line.

$$\text{slope} = \frac{\text{rise}}{\text{run}}$$

If the terminal point (x_1, y_1) and initial point (x_2, y_2) are known, the formula may be written as:

$$\text{slope} = \frac{y_1 - y_2}{x_1 - x_2}$$

For a positional vector with an initial point at $(0, 0)$, the formula reduces to:

$$\text{slope} = \frac{y_1}{x_1}$$

And because the components of a position vector are the same as the coordinates of that vector's terminal point, the slope of $\bar{v}$ which has components $\langle\; v_1 \quad v_2 \;\rangle$ can be found with:

$$\bar{v}_{\text{slope}} = \frac{v_2}{v_1}$$

Ok, but… slope is only useful for vectors in two dimensions.

Here is another example where using position vectors simplifies calculations in three dimensions.

The terminal point (x_1, y_1, z_1) and initial point (x_2, y_2, z_2) of a vector $\bar{v}$ could be used to calculate the vector's magnitude using the distance formula derived previously.

$$\| \bar{v} \| = \sqrt{(x_1 - x_2)^2 + (y_1 - y_2)^2 + (z_1 - z_2)^2}$$

However, for a positional vector with an initial point at (0, 0, 0), the formula reduces to:

$$\| \bar{v} \| = \sqrt{x_1{}^2 + y_2{}^2 + z_3{}^2}$$

And because the components of a position vector are the same as the coordinates of that vector's terminal point, the magnitude of $\bar{v}$ with components of $\langle\; v_1 \quad v_2 \quad v_3 \;\rangle$ can be found with:

$$\| \bar{v} \| = \sqrt{v_1{}^2 + v_2{}^2 + v_3{}^2}$$

And these are just some simple examples. Position vectors are easy to work with in many situations. Position vectors will be used throughout the rest of the book.

To be clear, position vectors do not describe the purpose of the vector. That is, they are not solely for storing the position of objects. They may still be used to store the scale of objects, movement, velocity, forces, and more.

Yes, a position vector simply is a vector positioned at the origin. Remember also that vectors are equal if they have the same direction and magnitude. So, a position vector of $\langle\ v_x\ \ v_y\ \ v_z\ \rangle$ is still equal to the vector $\begin{bmatrix} v_x & v_y & v_z \end{bmatrix}$.

Activity: Critters

Vectors are used extensively in game engines, including Unity. For this activity, you will explore an existing game project to identify the various ways in which vectors are already being used and then add an enemy health bar that utilizes the *LookAt* and *Rotate* methods of the Transform class to ensure the healthbar is always facing the player.

1. Become familiar with the *Critters* game.

   Open *Scene01* of the Critters project from the Chapter 5 project files. The scene has a Directional Light, a CameraRig prefab, a Terrain, and Water. The Critters and Turrets are empty GameObjects in the hierarchy which will contain all the critters and turrets spawned during gameplay. A Canvas containing a UI Text component will be used to display the frame rate during gameplay.

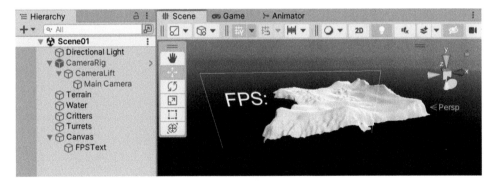

FIGURE 6.18 Scene01 of Critters Project displayed in Hierarchy and Scene windows.

When you play the game, you will see critters crawling all over the terrain.

FIGURE 6.19   Critters being fired at by turrets during gameplay.

The game begins with 20 critters and new critters spawn every half second. Critters are destroyed from the Scene when they crawl off the terrain.

> During gameplay, you can expand *Critters* in the Hierarchy to see all the critters that are currently crawling about in the game.

The FPSText UI element is set to update the current frame rate every second. You should see a gradually decrease in the frame rate as more critters spawn into the game.

> The frame rate will depend on your system specifications and on what other programs are running on your system.

The frame rate should continue to slow until critters are being destroyed at the same rate in which they are being spawned.

Use the keyboard and the mouse (or trackpad) to control the player's view. Pressing down the AWSD keys moves the camera to change your vantage point of the terrain. Scrolling zooms the player's view toward and away from the terrain.

While the CameraRig, CameraLift, and Main Camera are not visible in the game, it may be helpful to visualize them to better understand how the player is able to manipulate the camera.

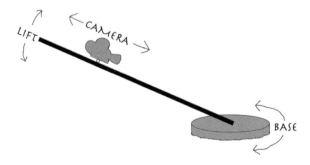

FIGURE 6.20   Illustration of camera rig with position and movements of base, lift, and camera.

With this rig, the camera is always looking at the base. Regardless of how the player manipulates their view, they will always be looking toward the center of the terrain where the base of the rig has been placed.

Pressing A and D, or the left and right arrow keys, rotates the base (the *CameraRig*) around the *z* axis, making the camera orbit around the terrain. Pressing W and S, or the up and down arrow keys, rotates the lift (i.e., the *CameraLift*) vertically. Scrolling with the mouse wheel or equivalent trackpad motion moves the camera closer or further away from the terrain, allowing the player to zoom in or out.

The *CameraRigController* script attached to the CameraRig provides the ability to modify the properties that define the camera's behavior.

While not adjustable in the editor, the speed of camera movement is doubled while the Shift key is held down.

Camera Rig Controller (Script)	
Script	CameraRigController
Horizontal Rotation Speed	45
Inverted Horizontal Rotation	☐
Vertical Rotation Speed	20
Inverted Vertical Rotation	☐
Zoom Speed	300
Zoom Max	300
Inverted Zoom	☑

FIGURE 6.21   CameraRigController viewed in Inspector.

The core gameplay involves strategically placing turrets to eliminate critters. Click anywhere on the terrain while playing to spawn a turret. Each turret will locate the nearest critter visible to it, rotate to face the critter, and fire a laser until the critter is destroyed.

> With each critter having an initial health value of 5 and each turret having the ability to cause 2.5 damage per second (dps), a critter being fired upon by one turret will be destroyed in 2 seconds.

2. Understand positioning with multiple coordinate systems.

Unity uses vectors to specify the positions of GameObjects, with values for the location of the GameObject on the *x*, *y*, and *z* axis. However, these location values are not always based on the *world* coordinate system—the coordinate system of the scene.

For this discussion, it would be helpful to see the entire terrain, including the lower portions that are currently underwater. Select the Water and then uncheck the box in the Inspector Window to deactivate it for the remainder of this lesson.

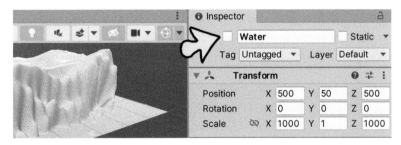

FIGURE 6.22   View of Scene with Water deactivated in the Inspector.

Consider the Empty GameObject named *Critters*. While the GameObject has no physical representation, it still has a transform, including a position vector.

Double-click on Critters in the Hierarchy to zoom to its location, select the move tool to reveal its precise location in the Scene Window, and scroll to zoom out until it is clear where Critters is located in the Scene.

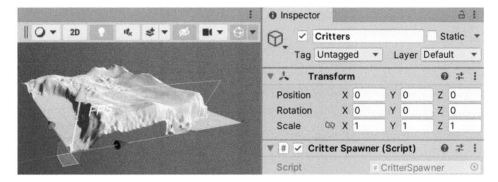

FIGURE 6.23   Critters selected with position of (0, 0, 0).

The Inspector reveals that the position of Critters is at the origin (0, 0, 0). Because Critters is a direct *child* of Scene01, as indicated by its indentation in the Hierarchy Window, it is positioned using the world coordinate system.

Now consider the initial position of the Main Camera. Select the camera with the move tool and modify the scene view so it is clear where the camera is positioned in the world.

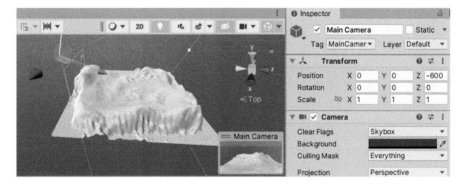

FIGURE 6.24   Main Camera selected with position of (0, 0, -600).

Notice the position values for the Main Camera shown in the Inspector are 0, 0, -600. If these were world system coordinates, the camera would be 600 units behind the Critters on the z axis. Instead, it appears to have the same z value as Critters moved away from the origin only on the x and y axes.

To understand the location values shown for the Main Camera, you must consider the hierarchy in which the Main Camera is placed. Specifically, the Main Camera is a child of the CameraLift, which is a child of the CameraRig, which is a child of Scene01.

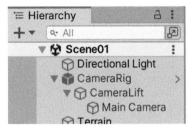

FIGURE 6.25   CameraRig expanded.

Let's begin with the CameraRig since we know its position is based on the world coordinate system. If you double-click on the CameraRig in the hierarchy, it zooms to the location of the Main Camera. Temporarily disable the CameraLift to avoid this behavior and then double-click on the CameraRig again to zoom to its actual position.

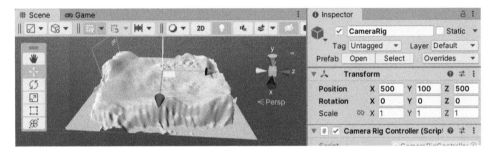

FIGURE 6.26   CameraRig selected with position above the center of terrain at (500, 100, 500).

The CameraRig appears in the Scene Window to have been placed directly above the center of the terrain. The Inspector shows the position of the CameraRig is at 500, 100, 500.

This appears to be the correct world coordinates given the terrain's position (i.e., its bottom corner at the origin) and the width and length of the terrain are both 1,000 units.

Mesh Resolution (On Terrain Data)	
Terrain Width	1000
Terrain Length	1000
Terrain Height	600

FIGURE 6.27   Terrain width and height.

The terrain dimensions can be found in the Inspector when the terrain is selected by clicking on the *Terrain Settings* gear icon of the Terrain component.

FIGURE 6.28   Terrain Settings.

Now, enable the CameraLift. Again, if you double-click the CameraLift in the hierarchy, Unity will zoom to the position of the Main Camera. Temporarily disable the Main Camera and then double-click the CameraLift to zoom to its actual position.

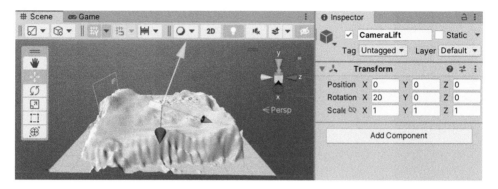

FIGURE 6.29 CameraLift selected with rotation around *x* axis of 20°.

While the rotation is different, the position of the CameraLift appears in the Scene to be in the same location as the CameraRig. However, the Inspector shows the position for the CameraLift to be at the origin (0, 0, 0). Clearly, this origin is not the same as the origin of the world coordinate system determined earlier to be at the bottom left corner of the terrain.

This is where multiple coordinate systems come into play.

I am ready for this!

Every GameObject has its own coordinate system with an origin at its pivot point, often the center of the GameObject. A GameObject placed as a child of another *parent* GameObject is positioned using the parent's coordinate system.

The unit size of a GameObject's coordinate system is based on the *scale* of the GameObject. A GameObject with scale 1, 1, 1 is at 100% of its original size, resulting in the same unit size as the coordinate system of the parent GameObject. A GameObject with scale 0.5, 0.5, 0.5 is at 50% of its original size, resulting in a unit size that is half of the unit size of the parent's coordinate system.

Selecting the CameraLift with the Move tool, you can see the arrow representing the *x*, *y*, and *z* axes of the CameraLift's coordinate plane. The coordinate system is tilted due to the CameraLift having an initial rotation on the *x* axis of 20.

One advantage to such a positioning system is that a GameObject can be moved forward on a single *local* axis, causing a more complex movement in its world position.

This is how the camera is able to easily zoom in and out by moving forward and backward on the *z* axis of the CameraLift's coordinate plane.

Finally, re-enable the Main Camera and adjust the Scene to get a good view of its world position.

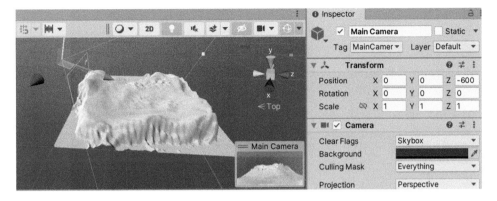

FIGURE 6.30   Main Camera pulled back on CameraLift to look downward at the terrain.

Now the Main Camera's position of (0, 0, -600) should make sense. These values define the local position of the Main Camera on the CameraLift's coordinate system. That is, the Main Camera is pulled back along the *z* axis 600 units from the CameraLift's origin.

 Note that the Main Camera has a rotation of 0, 0, 0. The Main Camera's rotation in the scene is due to the rotation of the CameraLift.

 Because the camera's view is in the forward direction on the z axis, the camera is facing directly at the origin of the CameraLift's coordinate system.

From this point forward, you should understand that every GameObject has both local and world values for position, rotation, and scale. While the local values for these properties are visible in the Transform component in the editor, the world values are not. However, the world

 Be sure to re-enable the Water so that turrets are unable to see the critters that are under the water's surface.

values are often needed and are therefore easily accessible through code.

3. Paying special attention to vectors, explore how the CameraRig is operated.

With an understanding of the mechanics of the CameraRig established, you should be prepared to analyze the code that allows the player to control it.

Open the CameraRigController script which contains the CameraRigController class and look at the class properties first.

```
 5   ☐public class CameraRigController : MonoBehaviour
 6    {
 7        private GameObject CameraLift;
 8
 9        public float horizontalRotationSpeed = 45f;    // degrees per second
10        public bool invertedHorizontalRotation = false;
11
12        public float verticalRotationSpeed = 20f;    // degrees per second
13        public bool invertedVerticalRotation = false;
14        private float minVerticalRotation = 10;
15        private float maxVerticalRotation = 50;
16
17        public float zoomSpeed = 300f; // distance per second
18        public float zoomMax = 300f;
19        private float minZoom;
20        private float maxZoom;
21        public bool invertedZoom = true;
22
23        private float speed;
24        private float speedMultiplier;
```

FIGURE 6.31   Lines 5 through 24 of the CameraRigController script.

The script needs access to all GameObjects in which the player will be able to move or rotate—the CameraRig, the CameraLift, and the Main Camera.

The Main Camera will be accessed through the Camera class. Specifically, Camera.main references the GameObject tagged as "MainCamera".

❶ Inspector			🔒 ⋮
☑ **Main Camera**		☐ Static ▼	
Tag MainCamera ▼	Layer Default ▼		

FIGURE 6.32   Main Camera tagged as MainCamera.

The script is attached to the CameraRig so it will automatically have access to it.

The *cameraLift* property declared on line 7 is initialized within the Start method on line 31 to serve as a reference to the CameraLift

The properties defined on lines 9 and 10 are used to define the speed and direction the CameraRig rotates when receiving player input. When the *invertedHorizontalRotation* is checked, the camera moves in the direction opposite of the directional key being pressed.

The properties defined on lines 12 to 15 are used to define the speed and direction of the CameraLift, as well as its rotation restrictions.

The properties defined on lines 17 to 21 are used to define the speed, direction, and restrictions for the movement of the Main Camera along the CameraLift.

The *speed* and *speedMultiplier* properties declared on lines 23 and 24 are used for movements. The values for these properties are calculated in the Update method.

The Start method on lines 26 to 32 initializes some of the properties that were not initialized upon declaration.

```
26    void Start()
27    {
28        minZoom = Camera.main.transform.localPosition.z;
29        maxZoom = Camera.main.transform.localPosition.z + zoomMax;
30
31        CameraLift = transform.Find("CameraLift").gameObject;
32    }
```

FIGURE 6.33   Lines 26 through 32 of the CameraRigController class.

Specifically, the *minZoom* property is initialized to the *z* value of the Main Camera's initial position. The player cannot zoom out beyond the initial position of the camera.

The camera will begin fully zoomed out.

The *maxZoom* property is then calculated by adding the value of the *zoomMax* property to the *z* value of the Main Camera's position.

It may be confusing to have both *maxZoom* and *zoomMax* properties. Remember that the *zoomMax* property is public and can be set in the editor while the *maxZoom* property is calculated.

The Update method contains the code that executes every frame to move the camera based on player input.

First, the *speedMultiplier* is set based on whether or not the player is holding down one of the Shift keys.

```
34    void Update()
35    {
36        // BOOST SPEED
37
38        speedMultiplier = 1;
39        if (Input.GetKey(KeyCode.LeftShift) || Input.GetKey(KeyCode.RightShift))
40        {
41            speedMultiplier = 2;
42        }
```

FIGURE 6.34   Lines 34 through 42 of the CameraRigController class.

When the shift key is up, the *speedMultiplier* is set to 1 so that the speed for a specific motion is unchanged. When the shift key is down, the *speedMultiplier* is set to 2 so that the speed for a specific motion is doubled.

Then, depending on player input, the Main Camera moves to zoom, the CameraLift rotates vertically, or the CameraRig rotates horizontally. The first block of code from lines 45 to 66 is for the zoom mechanic.

```
45      // ZOOM
46
47      speed = 0;
48
49      if (Input.GetAxis("Mouse ScrollWheel") > 0f)
50      {
51          speed += zoomSpeed * speedMultiplier;
52      }
53      else if (Input.GetAxis("Mouse ScrollWheel") < 0f)
54      {
55          speed -= zoomSpeed * speedMultiplier;
56      }
57
58      if (invertedZoom) speed *= -1;
59
60      float zNew = Camera.main.transform.localPosition.z + speed * Time.deltaTime;
61      if (zNew >= minZoom && zNew <= maxZoom)
62      {
63          Vector3 pos = Camera.main.transform.localPosition;
64          pos.z = zNew;
65          Camera.main.transform.localPosition = pos;
66      }
```

FIGURE 6.35   Lines 45 through 66 of the CameraRigController class.

The *speed* is initialized to 0 so that if no scrolling is detected, the Main Camera will not move. In lines 49 to 56, the value of *speed* is then increased or decreased if the player is scrolling. On line 58, the value of speed is negated if the *invertedZoom* property is true.

With the speed determined, the remaining code on lines 60 to 66 applies the movement. Line 60 initializes the local variable *zNew* to be the Main Camera's new *z* value when not restricted by the minimum and maximum zoom restrictions. Recall that speed should be multiplied by Time.deltaTime to factor in frame rate to the distance the Main Camera moves along the *z* axis.

As defined in the conditional statement on line 61, the code to move the Main Camera executes only if the zNew is within the acceptable range.

Why don't we just set the *z* value of the Main Camera's position with one line of code:

```
Camera.main.transform.localPosition.z = zNew;
```

The *x*, *y*, and *z* values are defined as read-only. This means you can **get** the *z* value of the camera's position, as was done in line 60, but you cannot directly **set** the *z* value. To modify a Vector3 that is not locally defined, you must assign it to a new Vector3.

The variable *pos* is created in line 63 to store a new Vector3 object with the same *x*, *y*, and *z* values of the camera's position. Then, the *z* value is updated on line 64.

Finally, on line 65 the camera's position is set to the new position which has the updated *z* value.

An alternate and arguably more elegant code for moving the camera uses vector mathematics. Lines 60 to 66 could be replaced with the following:

```
Vector3 newPos = Camera.main.transform.localPosition + Vector3.forward * speed * Time.deltaTime;
if (newPos.z >= minZoom && newPos.z <= maxZoom)
{
    Camera.main.transform.localPosition = newPos;
}
```

FIGURE 6.36　Alternate code for moving camera using vector mathematics.

The first line of this code uses the *Vector3.forward* property—a vector with *x*, *y*, and *z* values of 0, 0, and 1, respectively.

Because $\langle\, 0 \quad 0 \quad 1\, \rangle$ has a magnitude of 1, Vector3.forward is a normalized vector.

This information is provided when typing the property in Visual Studio.

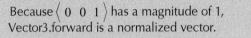

Multiplying *Vector3.forward* by the scalar value of *speed* changes the value of the vector only on the *z* axis. Adding the resulting "movement" vector (which still has an *x* and *y* value of zero) to the position vector of the camera moves the camera only on the *z* axis.

The next segment of code in the Update method for rotating the CameraRig is very similar to the zoom code.

```
69      // HORIZONTAL ROTATION
70
71      speed = 0;
72
73      if (Input.GetKey(KeyCode.LeftArrow) || Input.GetKey(KeyCode.A))
74      {
75          speed += horizontalRotationSpeed * speedMultiplier;
76      }
77
78      if (Input.GetKey(KeyCode.RightArrow) || Input.GetKey(KeyCode.D))
79      {
80          speed -= horizontalRotationSpeed * speedMultiplier;
81      }
82
83      if (invertedHorizontalRotation) speed *= -1;
84
85      transform.Rotate(Vector3.up, speed * Time.deltaTime);
```

FIGURE 6.37　Lines 69 through 85 of the CameraRigController class.

Lines 69 to 83 determine the speed of rotation based on keyboard input. With no restriction on how much the CameraRig may be rotated, only line 85 is needed to execute the rotation.

On line 85, *transform* is a reference to the Transform of the GameObject that the script is attached to—the CameraRig.

> The Rotate method of the Transform class rotates a GameObject around a specified axis by a specified amount.

In this case, the CameraRig is rotated around the *y* axis based on the calculated speed and frame rate.

> *Vector3.up* is equivalent to *Vector3(0, 1, 0)*.

The last segment of code in the Update method for vertically rotating the CameraLift is very similar to the code for rotating the CameraRig.

```
88          // VERTICAL ROTATION
89
90          speed = 0;
91
92          if (Input.GetKey(KeyCode.UpArrow) || Input.GetKey(KeyCode.W))
93          {
94              speed += verticalRotationSpeed * speedMultiplier;
95          }
96
97          if (Input.GetKey(KeyCode.DownArrow) || Input.GetKey(KeyCode.S))
98          {
99              speed -= verticalRotationSpeed * speedMultiplier;
100         }
101
102         if (invertedVerticalRotation) speed *= -1;
103
104         Quaternion originalRotation = cameraLift.transform.rotation;
105         cameraLift.transform.Rotate(Vector3.right, speed * Time.deltaTime);
106         float newX = cameraLift.transform.rotation.eulerAngles.x;
107         if (newX < minVerticalRotation || newX > maxVerticalRotation)
108         {
109             cameraLift.transform.rotation = originalRotation;
110         }
111     }
112 }
```

FIGURE 6.38   Lines 88 through 110 of the CameraRigController class.

Lines 90 to 102 again determine the speed of rotation based on keyboard input. Lines 104 to 110 are used to apply the rotation. This is a bit more complex due to the restrictions for rotation.

First, while the position and scale of a Transform are stored in Unity as a Vector3 object, the rotation of the Transform is stored as a *Quaternion*. A discussion of Quaternions is beyond the scope of this book, but fortunately Unity provides a way to access the Vector3 representation of Quaternions.

- In line 104, the *originalRotation* property is used to store the rotation of the CameraLift.
- In line 105, the CameraLift is rotated without attention to the rotation restrictions. *Vector3. right* is equivalent to Vector3(1, 0, 0).

- In line 106, the *newX* property is used to store the rotation value of the CameraLift around the *x* axis.

> While *rotation* is stored as a Quaternion, *rotation.eulerAngles* provides the Vector3 representation of the Quaternion which matches what is visible in the editor with *x*, *y*, and *z* values defining rotation on each axis in degrees.

- The conditional statement on lines 107 to 110 resets the rotation of the CameraLift back to its original position if the resulting rotation value is outside the acceptable range.

> So, the CameraRig is operated by applying vector addition to move and rotate the components for the CameraRig depending on the inputs received from the player.

4. Paying special attention to vectors, explore how critters are spawned and behave.

The *critterSpawner* and *critterBehavior* scripts both use vectors to position and move critters in the scene. Begin by analyzing the *critterSpawner* script that is attached to the *Critters* GameObject.

> *Critters* is the parent GameObject for all *Critter* GameObjects spawned during gameplay.

The *initialNumCritters* and *spawnFrequency* properties may be modified to control the number of critters in the scene.

The critterPrefabs property should specify the size of a list, and each list element should be set to a prefab from the Prefabs folder.

The terrain property should be set to the Terrain in the scene. This is used to get the bounds for where new critters may spawn.

When a critter is spawned, the prefab used is randomly selected from the critterPrefabs List.

> If spiders creep you out, change the size of the critterPrefabs List to 1 and drag the Termite from the Prefabs folder to be the only element.

FIGURE 6.39 CritterSpawner in Inspector.

The public properties visible in the editor and additional private properties are defined in lines 7 to 18 of the critterSpawner script.

```
5        public class CritterSpawner : MonoBehaviour
6        {
7            public int initialNumCritters = 10;
8            public float spawnFrequency = 1.5f;
9            public List<GameObject> critterPrefabs;
10           public Terrain terrain;
11
12           private float secondsSinceLastSpawn = 0;
13           private float minX, maxX, minZ, maxZ;
14           private float highestPoint;
15           private Vector3 startPosition;
16           private Quaternion startRotation;
17
18           private List<GameObject> critters = new List<GameObject>();
```

FIGURE 6.40   Lines 5 through 18 of the CritterSpawner class.

Of particular interest is the *critters* property on line 18 which is a List used to keep track of all critters that are spawned. While the property is private, code outside of the critterSpawner class will have access to the contents of the List using the public *GetCritters* method defined at the bottom of the script.

```
94       public List<GameObject> GetCritters()
95       {
96           return critters;
97       }
```

FIGURE 6.41   Lines 94 through 97 of the CritterSpawner class.

As usual, the Start method initializes many of the properties that were neither set in the editor nor initialized when declared. Additionally, the Start method includes a loop to spawn critters at random locations in the scene.

```
for (int i=0; i<initialNumCritters; i++)
{
    startPosition = new (Random.Range(minX, maxX), highestPoint, Random.Range(minZ, maxZ));
    startRotation = Quaternion.Euler(0, Random.Range(0, 360), 0);
    SpawnCritter(startPosition, startRotation);
}
```

FIGURE 6.42   Lines 29 through 34 of the CritterSpawner script.

The value of *initialNumCritters* determines how many times the code is repeated.

The *startPosition* property is a vector with a random *x* and *z* value to facilitate the random placement of a critter on the terrain. The *y* value is set to a value above the highest point in the terrain.

When spawned, the critter will need to be lowered so it will not float in the air above the terrain.

The *startRotation* is defined using the Euler method of the Quaternion class that takes in the *x*, *y*, and *z* rotation values in degrees and returns the equivalent Quaternion.

The startRotation will be used to rotate the critter around the *y* axis, defining the direction the critter will move when spawned.

The *startPosition* and *startRotation* are then passed to the custom *spawnCritter* method to spawn a critter at the specified position and rotation.

```
private void SpawnCritter(Vector3 pos, Quaternion rot)
{
    int index = Random.Range(0, critterPrefabs.Count);
    GameObject newCritter = Instantiate(critterPrefabs[index], pos, rot, this.gameObject.transform);
    newCritter.GetComponent<CritterBehavior>().SetCritterSpawner(this);
    critters.Add(newCritter);
}
```

FIGURE 6.43   SpawnCritter method on lines 80 through 86 of the CritterSpawner script.

The first line of the *spawnCritter* method randomly selects one of the index values of the critterPrefabs list. The next line uses Unity's *Instantiate* method to spawn a critter prefab at the position and rotation specified. The last argument specifies the transform the newly spawned GameObject will be a child of. In this case, *this.gameObject.transform* refers to the transform of the GameObject to which *this* script is attached.

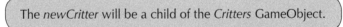

The *newCritter* will be a child of the *Critters* GameObject.

The next line of code in the *spawnCritter* method calls the custom *setCritterSpawner* method of the *CritterBehavior* class, sending *this CritterSpawner* as an argument. The *CritterBehavior* class needs access to the *CritterSpawner* class so that when a critter dies (in *CritterBehavior*), the List of critters (in the *CritterSpawner*) can be updated. Specifically, the *CritterBehavior* class needs to be able to call the *destroyCritter* method of the *CritterSpawner* class to remove the critter from the critters List and to destroy the critter from the scene.

```
88    public void DestroyCritter(GameObject c)
89    {
90        critters.Remove(c);
91        Destroy(c);
92    }
```

FIGURE 6.44   DestroyCritter method on lines 88 through 92 of the CritterSpawner script.

The last line of the *spawnCritter* method uses the *Add* method of the *List* class to add the newly instantiated GameObject to the *critters* List by passing *newCritter* as an argument. Doing this provides access to the instantiated critter after the method has been executed and the local variable *newCritter* ceases to exist.

Remember, newCritter has a limited scope—it exists only within the block of code in which it was declared.

The Update method tracks the time between each spawn and spawns a new critter based on the *spawnFrequency*.

The approach is very similar to how critters were spawned in the Start method with some added complexity in the random positioning to ensure the critter is spawned on a side of the terrain with a heading in the direction of the terrain.

Most of the vector mathematics related to critters occurs in the *CritterBehavior* script.

```
5     public class CritterBehavior : MonoBehaviour
6     {
7         public float speed = 1f;
8         public float health = 5f;
9
10        private float slopeRotation;
11        private CritterSpawner critterSpawner;
```

FIGURE 6.45 Lines 5 through 11 of the CritterBehavior class.

The public properties *speed* and *health* define the attributes of a critter.

The *slopeRotation* property is calculated based on the slope of the terrain directly below the critter's spawn location.

The slopeRotation of each critter is needed to rotate them according to the slope of the terrain at their location.

Compare the critter climbing up with and without a rotation to adjust for the slope of the terrain.

FIGURE 6.46 Critter rotated.

FIGURE 6.47 Critter not rotated.

Before rotating, a critter spawned in a random position above the terrain should be moved downward to sit on the terrain. This is done in the Start method using a *Raycast*.

Consistent with the mathematical definition, a *ray* in Unity is a line extending infinitely in one direction from a point.

The *Raycast* method of the *Physics* class casts (fires) the specified ray and returns a Boolean value of true if the ray hits a collider, or false if it does not. If the Raycast does result in a hit, information received from the *RayCast* method is stored in a *RaycastHit* object. The *RaycastHit* includes properties describing the collider that is hit and the relationship between the ray and that collider.

Figure 6.48 shows select properties of the *RaycastHit* class that are relevant to the concepts discussed in this book. A full list can be found on the RaycastHit page of the Unity API.

collider	The Collider that was hit.
distance	The distance from the ray's origin to the impact point.
normal	The normal of the surface the ray hit.
point	The impact point in world space where the ray hit the collider.
rigidbody	The Rigidbody of the collider that was hit. If the collider is not attached to a rigidbody then it is null.
transform	The Transform of the rigidbody or collider that was hit.

FIGURE 6.48   Select properties of the RaycastHit class defined in the Unity API.

Of particular interest for this project is:
- the *point* in world space where the ray hit the collider and
- the *normal*—the line through this point perpendicular to the surface.

Looking at the *Start* method, a *Raycast* is used to move the critter to a point on the terrain directly under the critter's position.

```
13    void Start()
14    {
15        RaycastHit hit;
16        Ray ray = new Ray(transform.position, Vector3.down);
17        if (Physics.Raycast(ray, out hit))
18        {
19            transform.position = hit.point;
20        }
21        else
22        {
23            Debug.Log("No surface found for " + transform.name);
24            Die();
25        }
26    }
```

FIGURE 6.49   Start method on lines 13 through 26 of the CritterBehavior script.

The *hit* property defined on line 15 is used to store information about a successful Raycast. The *Ray* object instantiated on line 16 begins at the critter's position and has a downward direction. The *Raycast* on line 17 fires the ray and stores the RaycastHit information in the *hit* property.

If the *Raycast* is successful, the position of the critter is updated on line 19 to the point in which the ray hits the terrain. If unsuccessful, a relevant message is printed on line 23 and the critter's *die* method is called.

In a similar fashion, the *Update* method also uses a *Raycast* to keep the critter at the correct elevation as it moves across the terrain and to continually rotate it based on the slope of the terrain under the critter.

```
28   void Update()
29   {
30       if (critterSpawner == null) return;
31
32       Ray ray = new Ray(this.transform.position + Vector3.up * 10.0f, Vector3.down);
33       RaycastHit hit = new RaycastHit();
34       if (Physics.Raycast(ray, out hit))
35       {
36           // move
37           transform.position += transform.forward * Time.deltaTime * speed;
38           // rotate
39           transform.rotation = Quaternion.FromToRotation(transform.up, hit.normal) * transform.rotation;
40       }
41       else
42       {
43           Die();
44       }
45   }
```

FIGURE 6.50   Update method on lines 28 through 45 of the CritterBehavior script.

The ray created on line 32 has a downward direction as before, but vector addition and scalar multiplication are used to specify an origin for the ray to be 10 units above the creature. This is done to avoid the critter being moved under the terrain where firing a ray downward from the critter would no longer result in a hit.

So, the ray is fired downward from above the critter's position to ensure that the Raycast successfully hits the terrain.

An alternate approach would be to cast a second upward-facing ray if the initial downward-facing *Raycast* fails to hit the terrain.

Line 37 uses vector addition and multiplication to move the critter. On line 39, the rotation of the critter is updated using the normal vector to the point on the terrain where the Raycast hit.

5. Set up a healthbar for the critter prefabs to display each critter's current health.

Double-click on the Termite prefab from the Prefabs folder in the project window to open it.

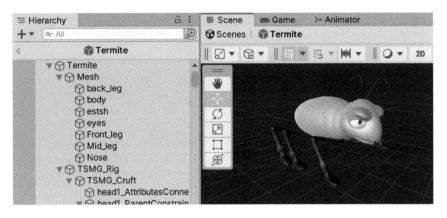

FIGURE 6.51 Termite Prefab open in Hierarchy and Scenes Window.

Add a *Plane* as a child of Critter to use for the healthbar.

FIGURE 6.52 Right-click in the Hierarchy on the Termite and select 3D Object → Plane.

Rename the plane to "Healthbar".

Modify the transform of the Healthbar to orient it above the Critter and facing in the same direction as the critter. You may use the same position, rotation, and scale values shown here.

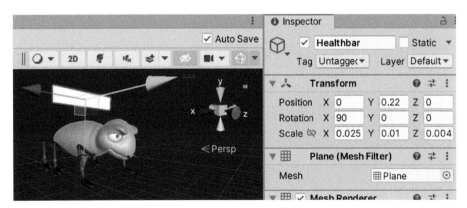

FIGURE 6.53 Plane renamed and transformed to be a healthbar above the Termite.

Like all GameObjects in Unity, a Plane is simply a GameObject with a set of predefined components. Components may be added or removed. In this case, the Plane has a Mesh Collider which is not useful.

Remove the Mesh Collider by clicking on the icon with three dots next to the component name and selecting "Remove Component".

FIGURE 6.54   Remove Component.

Next, create a new material for the Healthbar.

- In the Project Window, right-click within the Materials folder and select *Create → Material*.

- Rename the material "HealthbarMat".

FIGURE 6.55   HealthbarMat.

Drag the new material from the Project Window onto the Healthbar. With the Healthbar selected, scroll down in the Inspector Window to locate the newly added HealthbarMat. Set the color for the Albedo property and set the *Metallic* and *Smoothness* properties to 0.

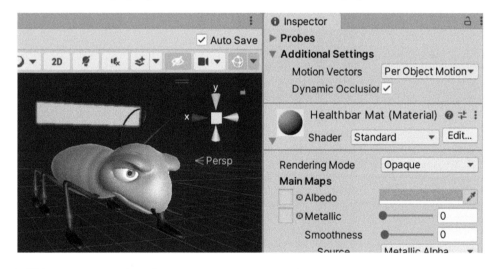

FIGURE 6.56   Material with desired color added as a component of the Healthbar.

Add a Plane as a child of Healthbar and name it "Health". The Healthbar and Health GameObjects will together provide the fixed-sized frame in which the changing amount of health will be shown.

FIGURE 6.57   Health.

Set the *y* value for the position of the Health to slightly above zero so that it appears in front of the Healthbar. Decrease the scale of the Health on the *x* and *z* axes so that the Healthbar provides a border for the Health. Adjust the Scene view so that you can see how the Healthbar looks when looking at the Critter straight on.

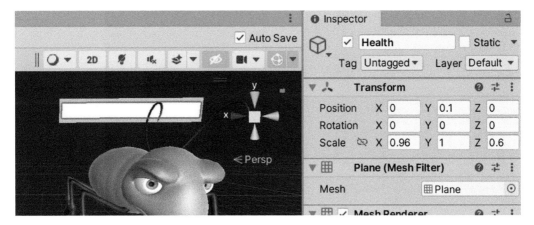

FIGURE 6.58　Health transformed to be framed by Healthbar.

Remove the *Mesh Renderer* and *Mesh Collider* components from Health leaving only the *Transform* and the *Plane (Mesh Filter)* components.

The Health will not be visible. It will serve only as a container for the *HealthFill*.

Create a Plane as a child of *Health* and name it "HealthFill".

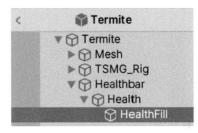

FIGURE 6.59　HealthFill.

Remove the Mesh Collider component from the HealthFill and make sure that its position is at the origin, the rotation is zeroed out, and the scale is 1 on each axis so that it takes up 100% of the container.

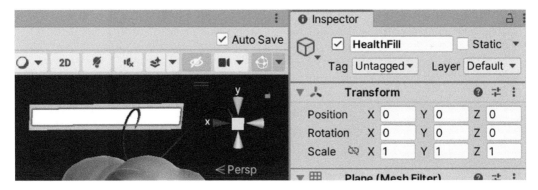

FIGURE 6.60　HealthFill covering entire Health container.

Create a new material named "HealthFillMat" and apply it to the HealthFill.

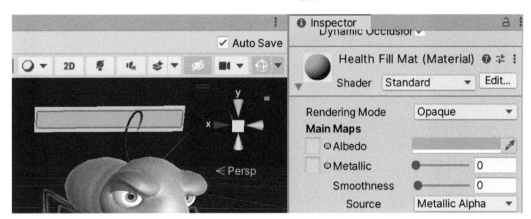

FIGURE 6.61   Green HealthFillMat Material attached to HealthFill GameObject.

With the Healthbar set up for the Termite, we are ready to apply the same Healthbar to the other critters. Copy the Healthbar from the Hierarchy and paste it in the Red Spider prefab. The spiders are taller than the termite so you may need to adjust the Healthbars position accordingly.

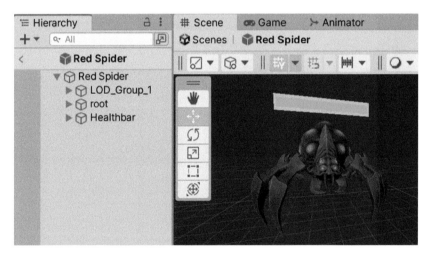

FIGURE 6.62   Healthbar added to Red Spider prefab.

Paste the Healthbar in the Blue Spider and Yellow Spider prefabs as well. A Prefab of the Healthbar could have been made so that subsequent changes to it would affect all Healthbars on all critters. Not using a Prefab allows for variation between the Healthbars of different critters.

When you play the game now, you should see a healthbar appear on top of all Critters that are moving toward the camera.

The healthbars of the critters moving away from the camera are not visible because planes in Unity are transparent when viewed from the backside.

FIGURE 6.63   Healthbars above camera-facing critters.

To complete the healthbar feature, the HealthFill needs to get smaller as the critter's health value decreases. Also, the Healthbar needs to constantly rotate to face the camera. These tasks can be done in the *CritterBehavior* class.

6. Adjust the size of the HealthFill when a critter is damaged.

With the *CritterBehavior* script open, add properties to use as reference to the *Healthbar* and *HealthFill* GameObjects.

```
 5  public class CritterBehavior : MonoBehaviour
 6  {
 7      public GameObject healthbar;
 8      public GameObject healthFill;
 9
10      public float speed = 1f;
11      public float health = 5f;
```

FIGURE 6.64   healthbar and healthFill properties added to CritterBehavior class.

Save the script, return to Unity, and open the Termite prefab.

Critter Behavior (Script)		
Script	# CritterBehavior	⊙
Healthbar	⊕ Healthbar	⊙
Health Fill	⊕ HealthFill	⊙
Speed	20	
Health	4	

With the Termite selected, scroll down in the Inspector to locate the CritterBehavior script. Then drag the Healthbar and HealthFill GameObjects from the Hierarchy Window to set the newly created properties. Do this for the blue, red, and yellow spider prefabs as well.

FIGURE 6.65   healthbar and healthFill set.

I notice the speed and health are different for each critter type.

Because the HealthFill needs to be displayed as a percent of the maximum health possible, create a *maxHealth* property to store this maximum possible value for health. In the Start method, initialize *maxHealth* to the initial value of the *health* property.

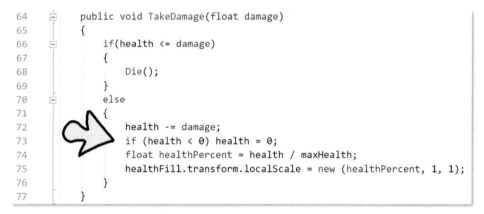

```
10          public float speed = 1f;
11          public float health = 5f;
12          private float maxHealth;
13
14          private float slopeRotation;
15          private CritterSpawner critterSpawner;
16
17   ⊟      void Start()
18          {
19              maxHealth = health;
```

So, all critters will begin with full health.

FIGURE 6.66   maxHealth property added and initialized in Start method.

Finally, modify the *takeDamage* method to update the size of the HealthFill every time the value of *health* is reduced.

```
64   ⊟      public void TakeDamage(float damage)
65          {
66   ⊟          if(health <= damage)
67              {
68                  Die();
69              }
70   ⊟          else
71              {
72                  health -= damage;
73                  if (health < 0) health = 0;
74                  float healthPercent = health / maxHealth;
75                  healthFill.transform.localScale = new (healthPercent, 1, 1);
76              }
77          }
```

FIGURE 6.67   TakeDamage method modified to update the healthbar.

Recall that the HealthFill has an initial scale of 1 on each axis so that it is the same size as its parent GameObject. To change the width of the HealthFill, its scale on the *x* axis should change to the percent of the *maxHealth* that remains.

Play the game now and you should see the health of each critter facing the camera decline as they are being fired upon.

7. Continually rotate the healthbar to face the camera.

In Unity, the forward direction of a transform is in the direction of the *z* axis, represented by the blue arrow. Typically, objects are created so their forward-facing direction is consistent with this. A plane, however, is not.

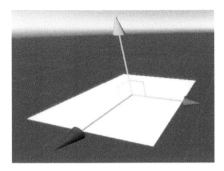

The forward direction of a plane is not the same as the normal to the plane as you might expect it to be.

In Unity, the visible portion of a plane with zero rotation faces upward along the *y* axis, as indicated by the green arrow.

FIGURE 6.68   Plane in an empty scene

This characteristic of planes explains why the Healthbar was rotated around the *x* axis (i.e., the red arrow) by 90 degrees to face the same direction as the critter.

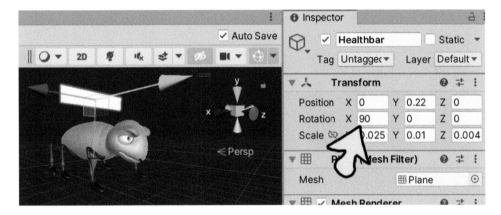

FIGURE 6.69   Healthbar plane rotated 90 degrees around the *x* axis.

In the *CritterBehavior* script, add a command at the end of the *Update* method to rotate the healthbar so that it is looking at the camera.

```
52              healthbar.transform.LookAt(Camera.main.transform);
53         }
```

FIGURE 6.70   Code added at end of the Update method to face healthbar toward the camera.

Here, the *LookAt* method of the Transform class is used to rotate the transform of the Healthbar so that it is facing the main camera.

More specifically, facing the origin of the main camera's transform.

When you play the game now, you see none of the healthbars! If you pause the game and look at one of the critters in the Scene view, you will discover that the forward direction of the plane (as shown by the blue axis) is facing toward the camera.

> Right. The face of the plane does is not its forward direction!

FIGURE 6.71   Healthbar not facing camera.

To get the face of the plane to face toward the camera, the plane needs to be rotated around the *x* axis (as shown by the red arrow) by 90 degrees so that the plane's *y* axis (as shown by the green arrow) is facing the camera.

Stop the game and add another line of code at the end of the Update method to do this.

```
53                  healthbar.transform.Rotate(Vector3.right, 90f);
54          }
```

FIGURE 6.72   Code added at end of the Update method to rotate the healthbar.

Playing the game now, the healthbar should always be facing the camera regardless of the direction critters are moving or where the player moves the camera.

FIGURE 6.73   Healthbars facing camera.

Challenges

Math & Coding challenges

For the math and coding challenges, you should become familiar with the *TurretBehavior* class, which is attached as a component of the Turret prefab.

1. Use square magnitudes to determine the closest critter.

   Like computer programming in general, game development requires attention to efficiencies that lower the processing requirements of the software. For games, this can help improve framerate and minimize lag.

   In the *Critters* game, the distance between a turret and each critter is calculated for every frame in which the turret does not already have a target. Our game would be more efficient if we were able to less frequently determine which critter is closest.

Locate the code that finds a new target for a turret starting on line 30 of *TurretBehavior* script.

```
26          if(target == null)
27          {
28              HideLaser();
29
30              // find new target
31              List<GameObject> critters = critterSpawner.GetCritters();
32
33              float closestCritterDistance = Mathf.Infinity;
34              foreach (GameObject critter in critters)
35              {
```

FIGURE 6.74   Lines 26 through 34 of the TurretBehavior script.

Let's break down the code before we improve on it.

- This code is within the Update method but only executes when the Turret has no target due to the conditional statement on line 26.
- On line 28, the laser is hidden using a *HideLaser* method defined elsewhere in the class.
- On line 31, the local variable *critters* is declared and initialized to access a List of all critters that have been spawned. This list is returned by the public *GetCritters* method defined in the *CritterSpawner* class.
- The local variable *closestCritterDistance* is initialized to the largest float value possible using the *Infinity* property of the *Mathf* class.
- Finally, a foreach loop is used to loop through each *critter* GameObject stored in the *critters* List. The first time through the loop, *critter* references the first GameObject of the *critters* list; in the second iteration, *critter* references the second GameObject of the list; and so on.

The purpose of the loop is to look at each critter, one at a time, to see if it is a closer target than any other critter that was previously looked at. The first visible critter will always be closer when compared to the initial "infinity" value of *closestCritterDistance*. As soon as a closer critter is found, the *target* can be set and the *closestCritterDistance* property updated to the distance from the gun to that target.

Look at the code within the foreach loop that repeats for each critter.

```
Vector3 directionToCritter = critter.transform.position - gun.transform.position;
float distanceToCritter = Vector3.Distance(critter.transform.position, transform.position);

RaycastHit hit;
if (Physics.Raycast(gun.transform.position, directionToCritter, out hit, distanceToCritter + 1))
{
    if (hit.transform.gameObject == critter)
    {
        // critter is visible (line of site established)
        if (distanceToCritter < closestCritterDistance)
        {
            target = critter;
            closestCritterDistance = distanceToCritter;
        }
    }
}
```

FIGURE 6.75   Code within the foreach loop—lines 36 through 51 of the TurretBehavior script.

The first two local variables declared in the loop store the direction from the gun to the critter and the distance between them.

The *directionToCritter* is calculated using Vector subtraction!

The *distanceToCritter* is initialized to the value returned by the Distance method of the Vector3 class.

The first conditional statement checks to see whether or not a ray fired from the gun toward the critter hits something. This should always be true. Needed information is stored in the *hit* property when the Raycast is completed.

The second condition checks to see if the object that was hit by the ray is in fact the critter the ray was pointing at. This is not always true because another GameObject may be blocking the line of sight between the gun and the critter.

Another critter, another turret, the terrain, or any other object in the game may be between the critter and the gun.

If the critter is visible to the gun, a final check is done to determine if the distance to the critter is less than *closestCritterDistance*. If so, the *target* and the *closestCritterDistance* are updated.

So, how can this be more efficient?

We could compare square magnitudes instead of distances.

Recall from Chapter 4 that the distance between two objects in 2D space can be calculated using the distance formula $d = \sqrt{\Delta x^2 + \Delta y^2}$ and similarly, the distance between two objects in 3D space can be calculated using the distance formula $d = \sqrt{\Delta x^2 + \Delta y^2 + \Delta z^2}$. Regardless of whether you are working in 2D or 3D, calculating distance requires calculating the square root—a relatively slow process that can slow performance, especially when used repeatedly.

Fortunately, the actual distance is not needed to compare distances!

Let $\mathbf{m}_1$ be the magnitude (i.e., the distance) between one critter and the gun; and $\mathbf{m}_2$ is the magnitude between another critter and the gun.

If $\mathbf{m}_1 > \mathbf{m}_2$ then $(\mathbf{m}_1)^2 > (\mathbf{m}_2)^2$ and if $\mathbf{m}_1 < \mathbf{m}_2$ then $(\mathbf{m}_1)^2 < (\mathbf{m}_2)^2$

Proven by just squaring both sides of the inequality.

The relationship between magnitudes is the same as the relationship between square magnitudes. Therefore, instead of calculating the magnitude with

$$m = \sqrt{\Delta x^2 + \Delta y^2 + \Delta z^2}$$

only the *square magnitude* needs to be calculated using

$$m^2 = \Delta x^2 + \Delta y^2 + \Delta z^2.$$

> Then, the smallest square magnitude is the closest!

Modify the code to compare square magnitudes instead of distances to determine the closest critter. You may use the formula by plugging in the correct values and operators, or you may use the *SqrMagnitude* property of the Vector3 class.

> You should update variable names to avoid confusion. Specifically, *distanceToCritter* should be something like *squareMag* and *closestCritterDistance* should be something like *smallestSquareMag*.

2. Improve on maximum sight distance for the turrets.

You may have noticed that a *sightDistance* property was included in the TurretBehavior class. The property is defined on line 7 of the TurretBehavior script and is visible in the Inspector when the Turret prefab is open.

▼ # ✓ **Turret Behavior (Script)** ❷ ⇅ ⁝	
Script	# TurretBehavior ⊙
Movement Speed	2
Sight Distance	400
Dps	2.5

FIGURE 6.76   TurretBehavior in Inspector.

The *sightDistance* does limit the turrets from finding targets beyond 400 units away. You can see this by placing several turrets in one corner of the map and watching after they destroy the nearby critters that they never fire across the map to far away critters. Recalling the terrain is 1,000×1,000 units, turrets should not be able to see or target critters beyond the sight distance specified.

The relevant code for implementing the sight distance feature begins in the else block that runs each frame in which a turret already has a target.

```
57      if (distanceToCritter > sightDistance)
58      {
59          target = null;
60      }
61      else
62      {
63          // rotate gun towards target
```

FIGURE 6.77   Lines 57 through 63 of the TurretBehavior script.

> If the first reach goal was completed, line 57 should be modified to compare square magnitudes.
> if (squareMag > sightDistance * sightDistance)

Simply, if the distance to the critter is greater than the sight distance, the target is set back to null and the turret will begin to search for a new target in the next frame. This code is needed for when a critter moves out of range after already having been targeted.

However, currently the sightDistance is not being used when finding a new target. This means that a turret could target a critter that is beyond its sight distance, and the next frame this code would set the target back to null, and the next frame it would invalidly target the same critter again, and so on.

It would be more efficient to never target a critter that is beyond the sight distance of the turret.

Locate the code beginning on line 30 that finds a new target. Identify what, if anything, is limiting the length of the ray that is being cast toward the direction of a critter when a new target is being searched for. It may help to read about *Physics.Raycast* method in the Unity API. Modify the code so that the ray is only cast out as far as the specified sight distance.

 Design & Coding challenges

1. Modify the *sightDistance* property of the Turret prefab in the Inspector to make it more difficult to destroy critters.

2. Modify the health to be left-aligned within the healthbar instead of center-aligned.

3. Limit the number of turrets that can be added in the same manner that the number of bombs were limited in the Bombs Away game. Show the number of turrets available for use as a UI element.

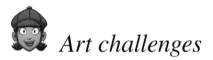 *Art challenges*

1. Modify the laser and/or the health so that they are not the same color.

2. Apply a variety of seamless textures to the terrain to create visual interest and make various areas more distinctive.

Achievements

The mathematics of game development is bound to game programming. Game engines often provide classes (such as Vector3), properties (such as Vector3.forward) and methods (such as Vector3.Normalize, Vector3.Distance, and Vectro3.sqrMagnitude) to lessen the amount of coding required to quickly achieve desired results. However, an understanding of mathematics is still needed to know when and how to use these tools.

In this chapter you:

- Learned how vectors may be used to:
    - Represent positions and change in position.
    - Add a movement vector to an object's position to find its resulting position.
    - Subtract the position vectors of two objects to find the vector from one of the objects to the other.
    - Transpose a vector to make it compatible with other vectors.
    - Normalize vectors to describe direction consistently without variation in magnitude.
    - Use scalar multiplication to scale the directional vector of an object so that the object is moved based on its speed.
    - Negate a directional vector to find the vector in the opposite direction.
- Explored the use of vectors within an existing game project.
- Took on the role of developer to implement a healthbar.

Exercises

What is the magnitude of the following vectors?

1. Vector2.up

2. Vector3.forward

3. Vector3.one

Vector $\bar{p} = \langle\ 5\ \ 6\ \ 7\ \rangle$ represents the position of the player, and Vector $\bar{e} = \langle\ 12\ \ 8\ \ 4\ \rangle$ represents the position of an enemy.

4. What vector would describe both the direction the player would need to face to move toward the enemy **and** the distance the player is from the enemy?

5. What is the unit vector that would describe only the direction the player would need to face to move toward the enemy?

6. What vector would describe both the direction the enemy would need to face to move toward the player **and** the distance the enemy is from the player?

7. What is the unit vector that would describe only the direction the enemy would need to face to move toward the player?

A 2D game allows the player to use AWSD keys to move their character horizontally and vertically. The player may also hold down two keys simultaneously to move diagonally. For example, the player may hold W to move up, D to move right, or W and D together to move diagonally up and to the right.

The movement of the player over one second is calculated by multiplying the speed by the direction vector $\bar{w} = \langle\ 0\ \ 1\ \ 0\ \rangle$ when the W key is pressed, and by $\bar{d} = \langle\ 1\ \ 0\ \ 0\ \rangle$ when the D key is pressed. When the W and D keys are both being pressed, the movement is calculated by multiplying the speed by $\left(\bar{w} + \bar{d}\right)$.

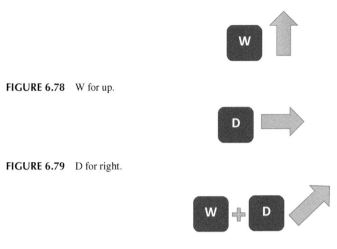

FIGURE 6.78   W for up.

FIGURE 6.79   D for right.

FIGURE 6.80   W and D for up and right.

8. If the player's speed is 5 meters per second, how far will the player move in one second when using:

   W key only: _____D key only: _____Both the W and D key: _____

9. How will the movement speed along the diagonals differ from the horizontal and vertical movement speed?

10. Adding the $\bar{w}$ and $\bar{d}$ vectors together results in a diagonal movement vector of $\langle\ 1\ \ 1\ \ 0\ \rangle$. What directional vector could be used instead to ensure the speed of the player is consistent in every direction?

7

Sinusoidal Functions | Sine and Cosine

Introduction

The periodic functions of Sine and Cosine will be discussed in this chapter along with the sinusoidal functions that result from applying transformations to the Sine and Cosine functions. These functions are useful in game development, including when you want an object to oscillate between two points while also easing the speed of the objects near the endpoints.

The Math

Special Right Triangles

A right triangle with a hypotenuse of 5 units and legs of 3 units and 4 units is a special right triangle in which all sides are integers.

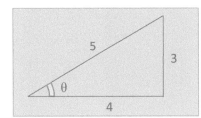

This "3-4-5 right triangle" can be proven to have a 90-degree angle using the Pythagorean Theorem.

$$\text{leg}^2 + \text{leg}^2 = \text{hypotensue}^2$$
$$3^2 + 4^2 = 5^2$$
$$9 + 16 = 25$$

FIGURE 7.1   3-4-5 Right triangle with θ as the smallest angle.

A triangle with sides of 30°, 60°, and 90° forms another special right triangle. Regardless of the size of the triangle, the lengths of the sides are always in the ratio of $1 : \sqrt{3} : 2$ where the shortest side is always half the length of the hypotenuse.

Lastly, a triangle with sides of 45°, 45°, and 90° forms another special right triangle. Regardless of the size of the triangle, the lengths of the sides are always in the ratio of $1 : 1 : \sqrt{2}$ where the legs are equal in length and the hypotenuse is $\sqrt{2}$ times longer than each leg.

Being familiar with the 3-4-5, the 30-60-90, and the 45-45-90 right triangles will be useful throughout this lesson.

Rethinking Sine and Cosine

In Chapter 4, the Sine function was defined for a given angle of a right triangle to be the ratio of the length of the side opposite the given angle over the length of the hypotenuse.

DOI: 10.1201/9781032701431-8

$$\sin\theta = \frac{\text{opposite}}{\text{hypotenuse}}$$

This technical definition is extremely useful. The equation gives a relationship between three values—one of the acute angles of a right triangle, the length of the side opposite the angle, and the hypotenuse. With any two known values, this formula can be used to solve for the unknown.

Let's drill down on the meaning of Sine by looking at how trigonometric functions apply to 2D vectors.

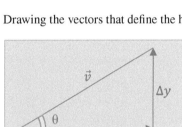

Consider a vector $\bar{v}$ in a direction defined by an angle θ.

I will imagine the vector represents the vector from an enemy to a player.

FIGURE 7.2 $\bar{v}$ in a direction of θ.

Drawing the vectors that define the horizontal and vertical components of $\bar{v}$ will form a right triangle.

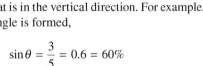

The vector opposite θ represents the vertical component of $\bar{v}$.

The magnitude of a vector is always positive—so for the vertical portion of $\bar{v}$, the magnitude is the $|\Delta y|$.

FIGURE 7.3   Right triangle with $\bar{v}$.

Adapting the sine function,

$$\sin\theta = \frac{\text{opposite}}{\text{hypotenuse}} = \frac{|\Delta y|}{\|\bar{v}\|}$$

This ratio describes the portion of $\bar{v}$ that is in the vertical direction. For example, if $\|\bar{v}\| = 5$ and the direction of $\bar{v}$ is such that a 3-4-5 right triangle is formed,

$$\sin\theta = \frac{3}{5} = 0.6 = 60\%$$

That is, three-fifths, or 60%, of $\bar{v}$ is in the vertical direction.

Indeed, 60% of 5 is 3.

For a vector with a direction defined by an angle θ, $\sin\theta$ gives the fraction of the vector that is in the vertical direction.

Thinking of sine in this way is new to me!

What about cosine?

Remember, the mathematical definition is

$$\cos\theta = \frac{\text{adjacent}}{\text{hypotenuse}}$$

So, how is cosine defined in relation to vectors?

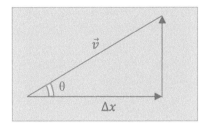

Consider again vector $\vec{v}$ in a direction defined by an angle θ.

The vector adjacent to θ represents the horizontal component. The magnitude of this vector, the Δx, is positive because it represents the length of the side of the triangle.

FIGURE 7.4 Δx of $\vec{v}$ along the leg of the right triangle.

Adapting the cosine function,

$$\cos\theta = \frac{\text{adjacent}}{\text{hypotenuse}} = \frac{|\Delta x|}{\|\vec{v}\|}$$

This ratio describes the portion of the vector that is in the horizontal direction. For example, if $\|\vec{v}\| = 5$ and the direction of $\vec{v}$ is such that a 3-4-5 right triangle is formed,

$$\sin\theta = \frac{4}{5} = 0.8 = 80\%$$

That is, four-fifths, or 80%, of the vector is in the horizontal direction. Indeed, 80% of 5 is 4.

For a vector with a direction defined by an angle θ,

$\cos\theta$ gives the fraction of the vector that is in the horizontal direction.

Horizontal and Vertical Projections

Let's drill down further on the use of sine and cosine on vectors.

Consider two vectors $\vec{a}$ and $\vec{b}$.

It is often useful to know how much a vector $\vec{a}$ moves in the direction of a vector $\vec{b}$? This is equivalent to asking what the projection of $\vec{a}$ onto $\vec{b}$ is.

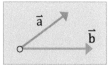

FIGURE 7.5 $\vec{a}$ and $\vec{b}$.

The sine and cosine functions are projections for the special case of projecting a vector onto a completely horizontal or vertical vector.

Consider the vectors $\vec{a}$ and $\vec{b}$ where $\vec{b}$ has a completely horizontal direction.

You can imagine a flashlight pointing in the direction perpendicular to $\vec{b}$ such that a shadow from $\vec{a}$ is projected onto $\vec{b}$. The length of the shadow in the same direction as $\vec{b}$ is a vector ($\vec{p}$ in the illustration) and this vector is the projection of $\vec{a}$ onto $\vec{b}$.

Hopefully, this looks familiar. We use cosine to determine how much $\vec{a}$ moves in the horizontal direction, or how much of $\vec{a}$ is projected onto a horizontal vector.

$$\cos\theta = \frac{\|\vec{p}\|}{\|\vec{a}\|}$$

where θ is the measure of the angle between $\vec{a}$ and $\vec{b}$.

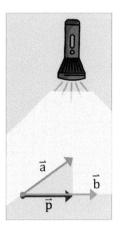

FIGURE 7.6   Flashlight projecting $\vec{a}$ onto $\vec{b}$.

Multiply both sides of this formula by the magnitude of $\vec{a}$ to solve for the magnitude of $\vec{p}$.

$$\|\vec{p}\| = \|\vec{a}\| \cdot \cos\theta$$

With the magnitude and direction of $\vec{a}$ known, the projection onto a completely horizontal vector can be calculated with this formula.

Think about the right side of this equation. The $\cos\theta$ represents the fraction of $\vec{a}$ that is in the horizontal direction. This fraction would be the same regardless of the magnitude of $\vec{a}$. For example, if $\cos\theta = \frac{1}{2}$. Half of $\vec{a}$ is in the horizontal direction, regardless of the magnitude of $\vec{a}$.

Similarly, if $\vec{b}$ has a completely vertical direction, you could imagine the flashlight turned to create a projection in the vertical direction.

We could use sine to determine how much of $\vec{a}$ is in the vertical direction, or what the projection of $\vec{a}$ onto a completely vertical vector is.

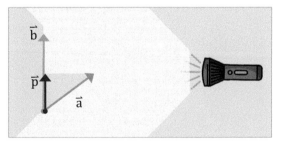

FIGURE 7.7   Projection of $\vec{a}$ onto a vertical vector.

Defining sine and cosine functions in terms of projections,

For a vector with a direction defined by an angle θ,

$\sin\theta$ gives the projection of the vector in the vertical direction.
$\cos\theta$ gives the projection of the vector in the horizontal direction.

Projections will be discussed in depth in Chapter 10, including how to find the projection of a vector onto another vector that is not completely horizontal or vertical.

Values of Sine and Cosine

Values resulting from the sine and cosine functions depend on the angle that is given to the function. Using θ as the angle that defines the direction of vector $\bar{v}$, let's look at some of the resulting values.

When θ is zero, a projection downward onto the horizontal would result in a vector of the same size as $\bar{v}$. 100% of $\bar{v}$ is in the horizontal direction.

Indeed,

$$\cos\theta = \frac{\text{adjacent}}{\text{hypotenuse}} = \frac{\|\bar{v}\|}{\|\bar{v}\|} = 1$$

When θ is zero, a projection sideways onto the vertical would result in a vector with no magnitude. 0% of $\bar{v}$ is in the vertical direction.

Indeed,

$$\sin\theta = \frac{\text{opposite}}{\text{hypotenuse}} = \frac{0}{\|\bar{v}\|} = 0$$

$\theta=0°$ (0 rad)

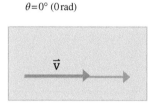

FIGURE 7.8 Horizontal vector $\bar{v}$ projected onto another horizontal vector.

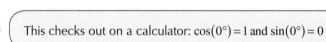

This checks out on a calculator: $\cos(0°)=1$ and $\sin(0°)=0$

Let's find the sine and cosine of a 30° ($\pi/6$ rad) angle.

Because the ratio of the shortest leg of a 30-60-90 triangle is half the hypotenuse, and the shortest leg is opposite the 30° angle,

$$\sin\theta = \frac{\text{opposite}}{\text{hypotenuse}} = \frac{1}{2} = 0.5$$

Because the ratio of the longest leg of a 30-60-90 triangle to the hypotenuse is $\sqrt{3}:2$, and the longest leg is adjacent to the 30° angle,

$$\cos\theta = \frac{\text{adjacent}}{\text{hypotenuse}} = \frac{\sqrt{3}}{2} \approx 0.866$$

$\theta=30°$ ($\pi/6$ rad)

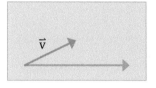

FIGURE 7.9 $\bar{v}$ with 30° heading projected onto a horizontal vector.

This also checks out on a calculator: $\cos(30°) \approx 0.866$ and $\sin(30°) = 0.5$

Let's also find the sine and cosine of a 45° (π / 4 rad) angle.

Because the ratio of each side of a 45-45-90 triangle is $1 : \sqrt{2}$,

$$\sin\theta = \frac{1}{\sqrt{2}} \approx 0.707$$

$$\cos\theta = \frac{1}{\sqrt{2}} \approx 0.707$$

$\theta = 45°$ (π / 4 rad)

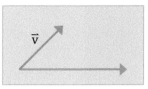

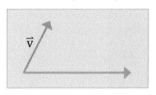

FIGURE 7.10 $\vec{v}$ with 45° heading projected onto a horizontal vector.

Let's work out one more. Find the sine and cosine of a 60° (π / 3 rad) angle.

Because the ratio of the shortest leg of a 30-60-90 triangle is half the hypotenuse, and the shortest leg is adjacent to the 60° angle,

$$\cos\theta = \frac{\text{adjacent}}{\text{hypotenuse}} = \frac{1}{2} = 0.5$$

$\theta = 60°$ (π / 3 rad)

FIGURE 7.11 $\vec{v}$ with 60° heading projected onto a horizontal vector.

Because the ratio of the longest leg of a 30-60-90 triangle to the hypotenuse is $\sqrt{3} : 2$, and the longest leg is opposite the 60° angle,

$$\sin\theta = \frac{\text{opposite}}{\text{hypotenuse}} = \frac{\sqrt{3}}{2} \approx 0.866$$

Use the same logic to find the sin and cosine of 90° that was used to find the sin and cosine of 0°.

Or just use a calculator.

You should find $\cos(90°) = 0$ and $\sin(90°) = 1$.

What is the relationship between all of these values? Let's start plotting.

Thus far, we have determined:

θ	$\sin\theta$	$\cos\theta$
0	0	1
π / 6	0.5	0.866
π / 4	0.707	0.707
π / 3	0.866	0.5
π / 2	1	0

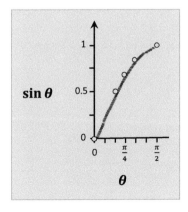

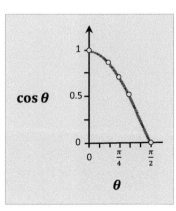

FIGURE 7.12 $\sin\theta$ plotted.   **FIGURE 7.13** $\cos\theta$ plotted.

If you plot more values for angles between 0 and $\pi/2$ radians, you get the curves shown in Figures 7.12 and 7.13. However, looking at angles in just the first quadrant gives only a limited view of the range of values that could result from applying the sine and cosine functions.

What values of sine and cosine result from angles beyond 90°? Let's consider positional vectors defined by these larger angles, starting with those angles in the second quadrant.

Imagine a light shining downward onto a vector that has a direction defined by an angle θ between 90° and 180°

A downward projection creates a right triangle that does not include θ. Instead, it includes the supplementary angle of $180 - \theta$. So, the projection of $\bar{v}$ onto the horizontal can be found from the $\cos(180° - \theta)$.

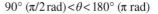
$$90° \, (\pi/2\,\text{rad}) < \theta < 180° \, (\pi\,\text{rad})$$

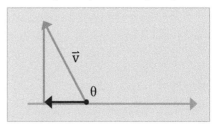

FIGURE 7.14 $\bar{v}$ with the second quadrant heading projected onto horizontal.

While this will give you the correct magnitude of the projection onto the horizontal, the projection vector will be in the opposite direction.

Consider the specific case in which θ is 120° ($2\pi/3$ rad). The supplemental angle is $180° - 120°$, or 60°. This is a 30-60-90 right triangle. As demonstrated in a previous example,

$$\cos(60°) = \frac{\text{adjacent}}{\text{hypotenuse}} = \frac{1}{2} = 0.5$$

However, this result is based on an input angle of 60° defining a vector in the first quadrant. Our vector defined by an angle of 120° is in the second quadrant.

With $\bar{v}$ placed as a positional vector on the coordinate plane and $\bar{r}$ defining the reflection of that vector over the y-axis, it is clear they both form right triangles that have congruent sides.

Specifically, the projection of $\bar{v}$ onto the x-axis has the same magnitude as the projection of $\bar{r}$ onto the x-axis, but the projections are in opposite directions.

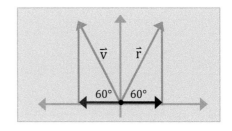

FIGURE 7.15 $\bar{v}$ and $\bar{r}$ reflected around y-axis *projected onto horizontal.*

With cosine giving the horizontal projection of a vector and sine giving the vertical projection, determining whether the sine and cosine of an angle are positive or negative should be intuitive.

A positional vector in quadrant I moves both horizontally and vertically in the positive direction. Therefore, the cosine and the sine of the angle are positive.

A positional vector in the second quadrant moves horizontally in the negative direction and vertically in the positive direction. Therefore, the cosine of the angle is negative and the sine is positive.

A positional vector in the third quadrant moves both horizontally and vertically in the negative direction. Therefore, the cosine and sine of the angle are negative.

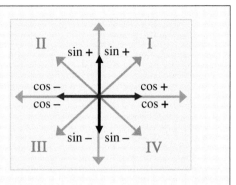

FIGURE 7.16   Position vectors in each quadrant with projections to show signs of sine and cosine.

A positional vector in the fourth quadrant moves horizontally in the positive direction and vertically in the negative direction. Therefore, the cosine of the angle is positive and the sine is negative.

Projections will be discussed further in later chapters along with reflections.

The remainder of this chapter will focus on the sine and cosine curves.

If you continue calculating values for sine and cosine for angles in all four quadrants—for angles of $0°$ ($0\,\text{rad}$) to $360°$ ($2\pi\,\text{rad}$)—you find a relationship between the direction of horizontal and vertical projections.

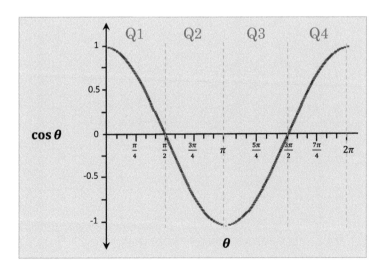

When graphed, the horizontal projections given by the cosine function form a curve.

As expected, the values for $\cos\theta$ are negative for angles in the second and third quadrants.

FIGURE 7.17 $\cos\theta$ for values of θ between 0 and 2π radians.

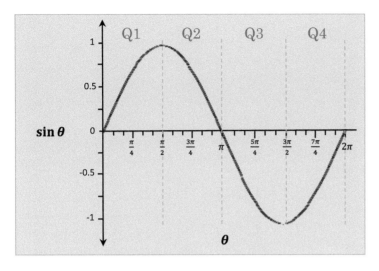

FIGURE 7.18 sin θ for values of θ between 0 and 2π radians.

When graphed, the vertical projections given by the sine function form a similar curve.

As expected, the values for sin θ are negative for angles in the third and fourth quadrants.

Both the sine and cosine functions are a ratio of sides of a right triangle, with the longest side—the hypotenuse—as the denominator. As the numerator will always be less than or equal to the denominator, we know the resulting values will be less than or equal to 1.

 Of course. The portion of a vector that is in the horizontal or vertical direction would never exceed 100% of that vector's magnitude.

What about sine and cosine values for angles not between 0 and 2π radians? Recall from Chapter 5 that adding or subtracting 360 degrees (2π radians) changes the number of rotations but results in the same angle between the initial and final directions. For example, the sine and cosine of a 400° angle is the same as the sine and cosine of a 40° angle. And the sine and cosine of a −60° angle is the same as the sine and cosine of a 300° angle.

 Hmm… if angles just repeat every full 360° rotation, then it makes sense that the values that make up the sine and cosine curves also repeat on the same interval.

Plotting out more values of cosine and sine, you find the curves repeat on an interval of 2π radians.

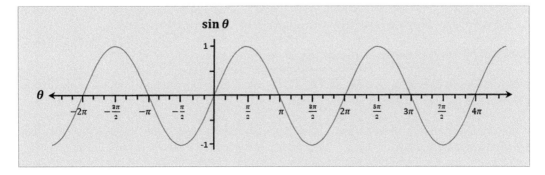

FIGURE 7.19 Graph of sin θ for values of θ between −2π and 4π radians.

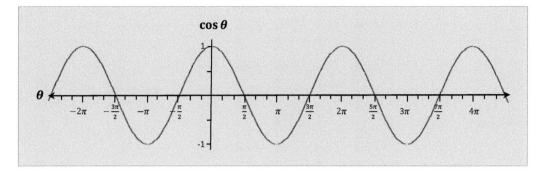

FIGURE 7.20   Graph of $\cos\theta$ for values of θ between -2π and 4π radians.

Now those are the trusty sin and cos waves that I am used to.

Sinusoidal Functions

Sinusoidal functions have the same general shape as a sine or cosine function but may be shifted in position and stretched or condensed horizontally and vertically. Before making any such transformations, consider the position, size, and shape of the sine and cosine functions further.

Sine and cosine are both *periodic functions* because they repeat values at regular intervals. The regular interval, or *period*, of the sine and cosine waves is 2π.

For example, $\sin(1-2\pi) = \sin(1) = \sin(1+2\pi) = \sin(1+4\pi)$, and so on.

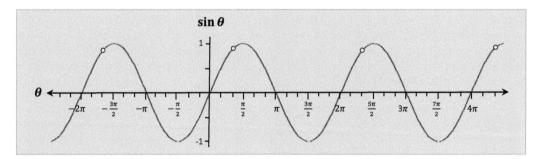

FIGURE 7.21   Sine wave showing sin (1) is equal to sin of 1 increased or decreased by multiples of 2π.

While the input to a sine and cosine function (the x value) can be any real number, the value returned by the function (the y value) oscillates between a minimum of -1 and a maximum of 1.

Because the curves are centered vertically around the x-axis, the *median* of the functions is 0.

Finally, both functions have an *amplitude* of 1. The amplitude is the distance from the median to the maximum, or half the distance from the minimum to maximum.

While sinusoidal functions have the same general shape as the sine and cosine functions, they may have a different position and a different size. The function in Figure 7.22 could be a transformation of either the sine or cosine function shifted horizontally and vertically to a new position, stretched horizontally to have a period of 12 units, and stretched vertically to have an amplitude of 2 units.

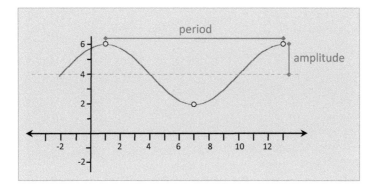

FIGURE 7.22 Sinusoidal function with max at 6, min at 2, median at 4, period of 12, and amplitude of 2.

The general form of sinusoidal functions can be used to map a sinusoidal curve to its function or vice versa.

$$y = A\sin\big(B(x+C)\big) + D$$

and

$$y = A\cos\big(B(x+C)\big) + D$$

 So, the sine and cosine functions result when A and B are one and C and D are zero.

 Yes. And any other values cause a transformation.

From this general form, we can determine the size and position of the curve. Specifically,

- The amplitude is $|A|$.
  - If A is negative, the curve will be reflected around the x axis.
- The period is $\dfrac{2\pi}{|B|}$.
  - If $|B| = 1$, the period is 2π.
  - If $|B| > 1$, the period is less than 2π and the function undergoes a horizontal compression.
  - If $|B| < 1$, the period is greater than 2π and the function undergoes a horizontal stretch.
- The horizontal shift, or *phase shift*, is the opposite of C.
  - If C is positive, the phase shift is to the left.
  - If C is negative, the phase shift is to the right.
- The vertical shift is D.

Sometimes you might want to find the function to fit a desired curve. For example, the function shown in Figure 7.22 could be determined using the general form with either sine or cosine.

In either case, the amplitude is 2 units, so $A=2$; and the vertical shift upward is 4 units, so $D=4$; and the period is 12 units, which will help us calculate the value of B.

$$\text{Period} = 12 = \frac{2\pi}{|B|}$$

$$12 \cdot |B| = 2\pi$$

$$|B| = \frac{2\pi}{12}$$

$$B = \frac{\pi}{6}$$

The value of C depends on whether you are making a phase shift on the sin curve or the cosine curve.

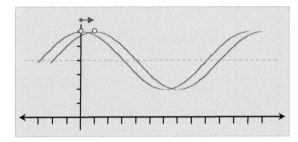

The cosine curve intersects the y axis at its maximum value. That point needs to shift one unit to the right, so $C=-1$.

$$y = 2\cos\left(\frac{\pi}{6}(x + -1)\right) + 4$$

FIGURE 7.23   Cosine curve shifted one unit to the right.

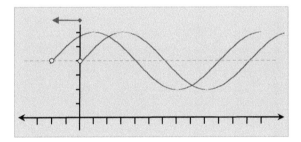

The sine curve intersects the y axis at the median. That point needs to shift two units to the left, so $C=2$.

$$y = 2\sin\left(\frac{\pi}{6}(x + 2)\right) + 4$$

FIGURE 7.24   Sine curve shifted two units to the left.

Using a graphing calculator, such as the desmos.com/calculator that was used to graph the two functions in Figure 7.25, confirm the sinusoidal functions are equivalent.

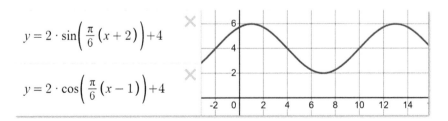

FIGURE 7.25   Equivalent functions graphed with a graphing calculator.

Sometimes you might want to find the curve given by a sinusoidal function. You can do this by writing the function in the general form and extracting the needed information.

For example, you may want to graph the curve defined by:

$$y = -\frac{1}{2}\sin\left(\frac{\pi}{4}x\right)$$

In general form, this is:

$$y = -\frac{1}{2}\sin\left(\frac{\pi}{4}(x+0)\right)+0$$

For the period:

$$P = \frac{2\pi}{|B|} = \frac{2\pi}{\left|\frac{\pi}{4}\right|} = 2\pi \cdot \frac{4}{\pi} = 2(4) = 8$$

For the amplitude:

$$A = \left|-\frac{1}{2}\right| = \frac{1}{2}$$

Because we are using the general formula that includes sine, and there is no shift horizontally or vertically, the curve will go through the origin at its median.

$$y = -\frac{1}{2}\cdot\sin\left(\frac{\pi}{4}x\right)$$

FIGURE 7.26   Sinusoidal function graphed with a graphing calculator.

As expected, the curve intersects the origin, has a period of 8 units, and an amplitude of half a unit. However, if you are a keen observer, you may have noticed that the curve is inverted.

I see. Unlike the sine function, the curve moves from the origin downward into the fourth quadrant instead of upward into the first quadrant.

One explanation for this could be that there was a phase shift of 4 units. However, it is clear from the formula that no phase shift is occurring. For this function, the reflection of the curve around the median is due to the amplitude being negative.

Activity: Headbob

Projections will be discussed in later chapters along with reflections. For the activity of this chapter, we will use sinusoidal waves to create oscillating motion with easing. For example, imagine a platform that moves back and forth, slowing down before coming to a stop and changing direction, and then speeding up again as it takes off.

This acceleration and deceleration can be accomplished, along with the desired oscillation, using the sine or cosine waves. The input of the function might be time while the return value is position along a given axis.

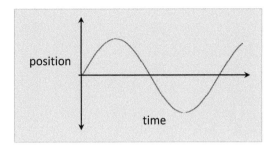

As time passes, the platform position will oscillate between the minimum and maximum points. Additionally, the platform's change in position over time (i.e., its speed) will be slow near these points and fastest when equidistant between these points.

FIGURE 7.27   Sinusoidal function defining the relationship between time and position.

For this activity, we will be adding a headbob motion to a player movement script.

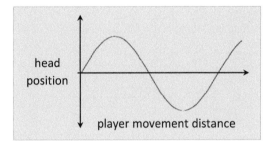

The camera that serves as the head of the first-person player will oscillate on the *y*-axis between its high and low points. Doing this over a given amount of time would not account for the player's speed. Instead, the head will oscillate over the player's movement distance.

FIGURE 7.28   Sinusoidal function defining the relationship between head position and player movement distance.

To get started, open the headbob project for this chapter and look at the FirstPersonPlayer GameObject.

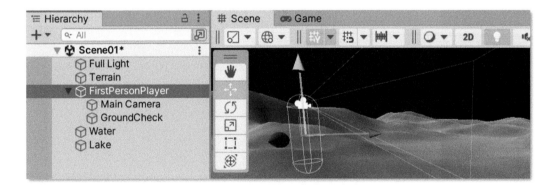

FIGURE 7.29   FirstPersonPlayer GameObject visible in the Scene and expanded in the Hierarchy.

The Main Camera which serves as the eyes of the player is a child of the *FirstPersonPlayer*. This setup ensures the camera moves with the player. For this activity, think of the Main Camera as the player's head. It is this Main Camera that we will apply a headbob too.

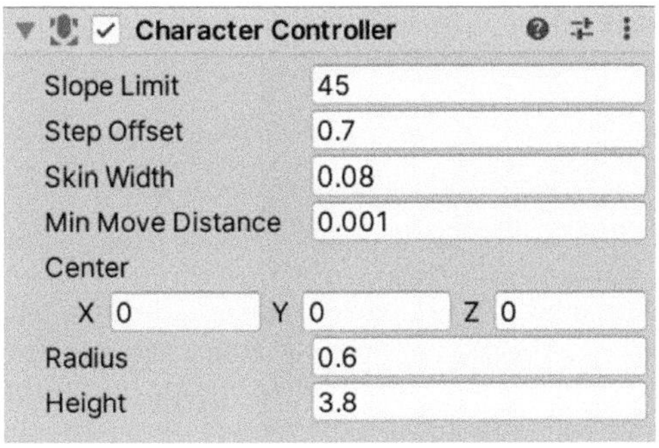

FIGURE 7.30   CharacterController in Inspector.

A *CharacterController* component is attached to the FirstPersonPlayer. While not visible in the inspector, this component includes a *CapsuleCollider* that is visible when the FirstPersonPlayer is selected (see Figure 7.29). This collider serves as the body of the player, and the *radius* and *height* properties of the CharacterController define its size.

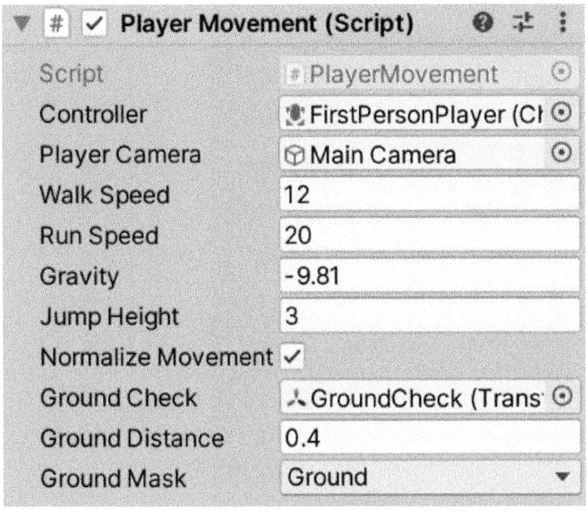

FIGURE 7.31   PlayerMovement in Inspector.

The *PlayerMovement* script is also attached to the FirstPersonPlayer. The controller property is a reference to the CharacterController, allowing the script to use members of the CharacterController such as the Move method.

Notice the *walkSpeed* and *runSpeed* properties. The speed of the headbob will need to match the speed of the player.

Unlike a Rigidbody, a CharacterController is not affected by forces such as gravity. This is why a gravity property has been added to the PlayerMovement class.

Play the game and use the AWSD keys to walk around. Hold the shift key down while moving to run. Notice that it feels as though you are sliding around. This is not how human movement feels. When humans walk or run, their head goes up and down. We need to adjust the PlayerMovement script to add this behavior.

Open the PlayerMovement script to get started. Add the following properties and Start method just above the existing Update method.

```
22
23        public float bobbingAmount = 0.1f;
24
25        float initCamY;
26        float moveAmount = 0;
27        float camY;
28        bool bobbingUp = true;
29
30        void Start()
31        {
32            initCamY = playerCamera.transform.localPosition.y;
33        }
34
```

FIGURE 7.32   Properties and Start method added to the PlayerMovement script.

The *bobbingAmount* is the only public property being added. Later, you will be able to adjust the value in the inspector if the default value of 0.1 does not give the desired amount of head movement. The other properties added are private and will not be adjustable through the inspector.

The *initCamY* property is initialized to the *y* value of the camera's position. The camera will simply move up and down on its *y*-axis while the player is walking or running to create a headbob.

The *moveAmount* property starts at 0 and will continually update to store the amount the player has moved. Remember, we will be using the amount of player movement as our input to a periodic function to get the desired head position along a sinusoidal curve.

The *camY* property will continually change based on the output of the periodic function used.

Lastly, the *bobbingUp* property will be used to keep track of the direction the head is currently moving. This property is not actually needed to accomplish the headbob but will be useful later when we want a particular event to occur when the camera reaches its lowest point.

I wonder what that event will be?

Next, locate the line of code that moves the player.

```
56              controller.Move(move * speed * Time.deltaTime);
```

FIGURE 7.33   Existing line of code that moves the player forward.

Immediately after the player is moved, add code to update the *y* position of the camera.

```
58          // Bobbing
59          float camX = playerCamera.transform.localPosition.x;
60          float camZ = playerCamera.transform.localPosition.z;
61          float previousCamY = camY;
62          if (move == Vector3.zero)
63          {
64              moveAmount = 0;
65              camY = Mathf.Lerp(playerCamera.transform.localPosition.y,
66                                initCamY, Time.deltaTime * speed);
67          }
68          else
69          {
70              moveAmount += speed * Time.deltaTime;
71              camY = initCamY + Mathf.Sin(moveAmount) * bobbingAmount;
72          }
73          playerCamera.transform.localPosition = new (camX, camY, camZ);
```

FIGURE 7.34   Bobbing code added to the PlayerMovement script.

The *camX* and *camZ* variables store the current position of the camera on the *x* and *z* axis after the player has moved. These local variables serve as quick references to the values (see line 73 of Figure 7.34).

The position of *camY* previously defined as a class property needs to be calculated. Before changing the value of *camY* however, its value is stored in the local variable *previousCamY*. This variable is not needed to achieve the bobbing behavior but will be useful when we want a particular event to occur when the camera reaches its lowest point.

What event? The suspense is killing me.

The value for *camY* depends on whether the player is moving or not.

If the players' *move* vector is zero, the moveAmount is set back to zero and the *y* value of the camera is set back to its initial value using the Lerp function. While the value of *camY* could be immediately set to *initCamY*, using the Lerp function will move it towards the *initCamY* over several frames to avoid an abrupt change in head position.

If the player is moving, the *moveAmount* is increased and *camY* is calculated using a sinusoidal function.

Written in the general form of $y = A \sin\big(B(x + C)\big) + D$, the function is defined on line 71 of Figure 7.34 is:

$$y = bobbingAmount \cdot \sin\big(1(moveAmount + 0)\big) + initCamY$$

The amplitude is $\big|A\big|$. In our formula, the *bobbingAmount* is the amplitude.

The period is $\dfrac{2\pi}{\big|B\big|}$. In our formula, *B* is 1 so the period is 2π.

The phase shift is *C*. Because *C*=0, there is no phase shift.

The vertical shift is *D*. In our formula, the *initCamY* is the amount the curve is shifted upward.

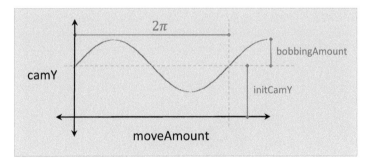

FIGURE 7.35   Curve of the sinusoidal function used for camera movement.

So, for any given player movement amount (moveAmount), the formula gives us the position of the head on the *y*-axis (camY).

And when the player is not moving (moveAmount=0), the camera is positioned at its initial placement on the body (camY=initCamY).

If you were to play the game now, you might feel the camera moving up and down as you move. However, this is currently very subtle because the amplitude is very small. Make the headbob more noticeable by changing the *bobbingAmount* in the inspector window to 1. This might be too high but will be great while working on the headbob feature. Play the game and you should definitely feel the head moving up and down as you move around.

Likely, you will want to adjust the bobbingAmount so that the headbob is subtle, increasing immersion without distracting the player from the core gameplay.

An alternate solution to the headbob using sinusoidal functions would be to use time as the input and adjust the period using the speed. This would involve replacing the *moveAmount* with a *time* property.

```
time += Time.deltaTime;
camY = initCamY + Mathf.Sin(time * speed) * bobbingAmount;
```

FIGURE 7.36 Preview of code that uses time as the input instead of moveAmount.

This formula in general form would be:

$$y = bobbingAmount \cdot \sin\big(speed(time + 0)\big) + initCamY$$

The period is $\dfrac{2\pi}{|B|}$. With *speed* as the *B*, the period would be $\dfrac{2\pi}{speed}$.

In our project, this solution would be problematic because the speed of the player changes depending on whether they are walking or running. This would cause the period to change every time the player presses or releases the shift key.

While I did implement this solution with success, I prefer using an unchanging sinusoidal function—one in which the period never changes.

Congratulations on using a sinusoidal wave to create a headbob! Next, let's add an event that occurs when the head is at its lowest point.

Finally!

What event should occur when the player steps down? A footstep sound effect of course!

I didn't see that coming. [*rolls eyes with sarcasm*]

To get started, add an *AudioSource* component to the *FirstPersonPlayer* and drag the *Footsteps_Grass* audio file from the *Audio* folder to set the *AudioClip* property.

Also, uncheck the *Play On Awake* checkbox so that the audio clip does not play until we explicitly tell it to via code.

▼ ◀ ✓ **Audio Source**	❷ ⇄ ⋮
AudioClip	♪ Footsteps_Grass ⊙
Output	None (Audio Mixer Grou ⊙
Mute	☐
Bypass Effects	☐
Bypass Listener Effec	☐
Bypass Reverb Zones	☐
Play On Awake	☐
Loop	☐
Priority	129

FIGURE 7.37   AudioSource on FirstPersonPlayer.

Next, add a private property named footsteps and initialize it in the Start method to the AudioSource component that you just attached to the player.

```
28        bool bobbingUp = true;
29        AudioSource footsteps;
30
31        void Start()
32        {
33            initCamY = playerCamera.transform.localPosition.y;
34            footsteps = GetComponent<AudioSource>();
35        }
```

FIGURE 7.38   Updates to the PlayerMovement script to provide access to the AudioSource component.

Lastly, you need to add code to play the audio source when the camera is at its lowest point. At first thought, the solution sounds easy.

```
// Footsteps SFX
float minCamPos = initCamY - bobbingAmount;
if (camY == minCamPos)
{
    footsteps.Play(0);
}
```

FIGURE 7.39   Code to play AudioClip when the camera is at the lowest position.

However, this will likely never execute because the camera will likely never be exactly at the lowest possible point. You could instead play the audio when the camera is close to its lowest possible point.

```
// Footsteps SFX
float minCamPos = initCamY - bobbingAmount;
if (Mathf.Abs(camY - minCamPos) < 0.001f)
{
    footsteps.Play(0);
}
```

FIGURE 7.40   Code to play AudioClip when the camera is near its lowest position.

However, what threshold should be used. Too small and the audio will not play. Too large and it might play multiple times. Additionally, the change in camY will vary depending on the frame rate.

So, to ensure the audio plays once and only once, add the following code for *Footsteps SFX* just under the block of code where the *Bobbing* code was added, just before the *Jumping* code.

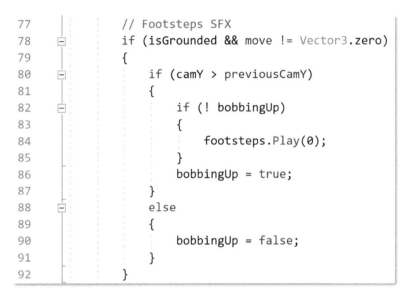

```
77          // Footsteps SFX
78          if (isGrounded && move != Vector3.zero)
79          {
80              if (camY > previousCamY)
81              {
82                  if (! bobbingUp)
83                  {
84                      footsteps.Play(0);
85                  }
86                  bobbingUp = true;
87              }
88              else
89              {
90                  bobbingUp = false;
91              }
92          }
```

FIGURE 7.41   Updates to the PlayerMovement script to play footsteps audio when upward bob begins.

This code only executes when the player is on the ground and moving. If the value of camY is greater than its previous value, we know the head is currently moving upward. However, we do not want to play the sound every frame that it moves up. It should only play when the head **begins** moving up. The value of 0 sent to the Play method makes the audio play from the beginning, 0 seconds from the start.

When you save and play the game again, you should hear footsteps playing. Change the bobbingAmount in the Inspector window to various values while playing and notice that the amount of time between footsteps is consistent regardless of how far up and down the head moves. This is because changing the amplitude has no effect on the period.

 Of course, if you run you will hear the footsteps more frequently. But this is not because the period changed but instead because the moveAmount is changing at a faster rate.

Challenges

 *Art & Coding challenges*

1. The player can jump by pressing the space bar. However, the landing is silent. Play the footstep sound or another audio file when the player lands from a jump or fall.

2. Implement a variety of footstep sounds so that it adjusts to the surface the player is on. The sound of walking on grass would be different than the sound of walking on sand or ice.

Math & Coding challenges

1. Add an obstacle that oscillates between two points in the world.

2. Add a light source over an object you want the player to notice. Continually change the intensity of the light using a sinusoidal function so that it has a throbbing feel.

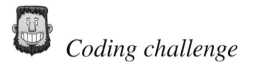

Coding challenge

1. The player is unable to jump while running. Fix that bug!

Achievements

Sinusoidal functions are useful in game development anytime you need a variable to oscillate between two values. While this could be done using other techniques, including linear functions, the easing inherent in sinusoidal functions is often desired.

In this chapter you:

- Learned how to:
    - Find the vector projection of a vector onto an axis.
    - Graph the curve of sinusoidal functions.
    - Write the sine and cosine function that defines a given sinusoidal curve.
- Implemented a headbob feature using a sinusoidal function.
- Detected the moment a sinusoidal function changed directions to play a sound effect.

Exercises

Given $\bar{v}$ has direction defined by θ,

1. How do you find the percentage of $\bar{v}$ that is in the vertical direction?

2. How do you find the percentage of $\bar{v}$ that is in the horizontal direction?

Given α is an angle between 90 and 180 degrees, what is the range of possible values for:

3. $\sin \alpha$

4. $\cos \alpha$

5. How are the sin and cos curves similar?

6. How are the sin and cos curves different?

7. Find an equation that fits the sinusoidal curve:

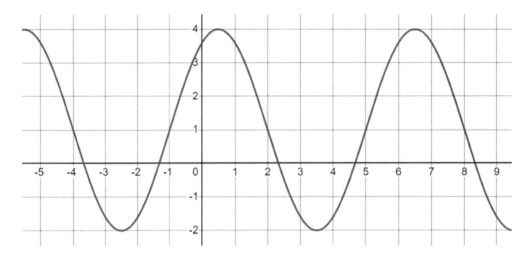

FIGURE 7.42   Sinusoidal curve.

8. Find a formula to define the position on the *x*-axis of a moving platform that oscillates horizontally over time following a sinusoidal curve. The platform should move 3 units to the left and right of its initial position and should complete a full oscillation every 2 seconds.

8

Directionality | Dot Product

Introduction

"Multiplication" of vectors involves multiplication of elements, but is quite unique. In fact, there are two completely different methods for multiplying vectors. The details of one such method will be covered in this chapter, and the details of the other methods will be covered in Chapter 9.

We begin with the *dot product*.

The dot product results in a scalar and is therefore also called the *scalar product*.

While the dot product may be used to multiply vectors, it is also used when multiplying matrices. This is where we begin the lesson.

The Math

Multiplying Matrices

The dimensions of the matrices determine whether they can be multiplied or not. Matrices can be multiplied if the number of columns in the first matrix matches the number of rows in the second matrix. Furthermore, the matrix that results from the multiplication will have the same number of rows as the first matrix and the same number of columns as the second matrix.

Consider the following two matrices A and B.

$$A = \begin{bmatrix} 1 & 2 & 3 \end{bmatrix} \quad B = \begin{bmatrix} 6 & 3 \\ 5 & 1 \\ 7 & 4 \end{bmatrix}$$

Matrix A is a 1×3 ("one by three") matrix because it has 1 row and 3 columns. Matrix B is a 3×2 matrix because it has 3 rows and two columns. The order matters when multiplying matrices. $A \cdot B$ is not the same as $B \cdot A$. The multiplication of $A \cdot B$ is possible because A has three columns and B has three rows. The resulting matrix will be 1×2 because A has one row and B has two columns.

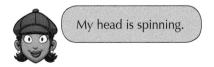

My head is spinning.

DOI: 10.1201/9781032701431-9

Fortunately, writing out the dimensions of the vectors will allow you to quickly see if they may be multiplied and, if so, what the dimensions of the resulting matrix will be. If the inner values match, you can multiply and the resulting matrix will have the dimensions of the outer values.

size of resulting matrix

$$(1 \times 3)(3 \times 2)$$

must match

Now we quickly determined that:

$$[1 \quad 2 \quad 3] \cdot \begin{bmatrix} 6 & 3 \\ 5 & 1 \\ 7 & 4 \end{bmatrix} = [\square \quad \square]$$

Writing a concise rule for multiplying matrices is difficult. Let's tackle the problem by using the *dot product* to calculate each value of our resulting matrix.

To find the value that belongs in row 1 and column 1, multiply the values in row 1 of the first matrix with the corresponding values in column 1 of the second matrix, and then add the products together.

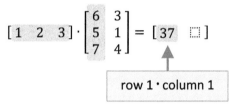

row 1 · column 1

In our example,

$(1 \cdot 6) + (2 \cdot 5) + (3 \cdot 7)$

$6 + 10 + 21$

37

Similarly,

To find the value that belongs in row 1 and column 2, multiply the values in row 1 of the first matrix with the corresponding values in column 2 of the second matrix, and then add the products together.

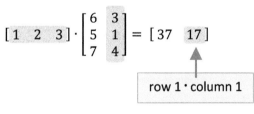

row 1 · column 1

In our example,

$(1 \cdot 3) + (2 \cdot 1) + (3 \cdot 4)$

$3 + 2 + 12$

17

At last, we have completed the matrix multiplication: $AB = \begin{bmatrix} 37 & 17 \end{bmatrix}$

Any two compatible matrices may be multiplied by using the dot product to find each value of a resulting matrix.

Multiplying Vectors (Dot Product)

Multiplying vectors requires only a single use of the dot product, and the result is always a scalar.

Consider multiply vector $\vec{a}$ by vector $\vec{b}$ where $\vec{a} = \begin{bmatrix} 3 & 4 & 0 \end{bmatrix}$ and $\vec{b} = \begin{bmatrix} 5 & 6 & 2 \end{bmatrix}$.

A dot is placed between the vectors to express the dot product. This is read as "a dot b".

$$\vec{a} \cdot \vec{b}$$

$$\begin{bmatrix} 3 & 4 & 0 \end{bmatrix} \cdot \begin{bmatrix} 5 & 6 & 2 \end{bmatrix}$$

A 1×3 vector cannot be multiplied by another 1×3 vector. Transpose the second matrix so they are compatible. A 1×3 vector can be multiplied by a 3×1 vector to get a 1×1 vector—a scalar value.

$$\begin{bmatrix} 3 & 4 & 0 \end{bmatrix} \cdot \begin{bmatrix} 5 \\ 6 \\ 2 \end{bmatrix} = \square$$

Using the dot product:

$$\vec{a} \cdot \vec{b} \;=\; (3 \cdot 5) + (4 \cdot 6) + (0 \cdot 2) \;=\; 15 + 24 + 0 \;=\; 39$$

> So, the dot product of two vectors is found by adding up the products of corresponding components.

A formula can be used to express this method of finding the dot product.

Given $\vec{v} = \langle\, v_1 \;\; v_2 \;\; v_3 \,\rangle$ and $\vec{w} = \langle\, w_1 \;\; w_2 \;\; w_3 \,\rangle$

$$\vec{v} \cdot \vec{w} = v_1 w_1 + v_2 w_2 + v_3 w_3$$

Properties of the dot product include:

- Communitive: $\vec{a} \cdot \vec{b} = \vec{b} \cdot \vec{a}$
- Distributive: $\vec{a} \cdot \left(\vec{b} + \vec{c} \right) = \vec{a} \cdot \vec{b} + \vec{a} \cdot \vec{c}$
- Associative: $C \left(\vec{a} \cdot \vec{b} \right) = (C \cdot \vec{a}) \cdot \vec{b} = \vec{a} \cdot (C \cdot \vec{b})$

An interesting property emerges when you take the dot product of a vector with itself. Consider:

$$\vec{v} = \begin{bmatrix} v_1 & v_2 & v_3 \end{bmatrix}$$

Then,

$$\vec{v} \cdot \vec{v} = \begin{bmatrix} v_1 & v_2 & v_3 \end{bmatrix} \cdot \begin{bmatrix} v_1 & v_2 & v_3 \end{bmatrix}$$

$$= v_1{}^2 + v_2{}^2 + v_3{}^2$$

This might look familiar. Recall from Chapter 5 that the magnitude of vector $\bar{v}$ is given by

$$\|\bar{v}\| = \sqrt{v_1{}^2 + v_2{}^2 + v_3{}^2}$$

If you square both sides, you will get the *square magnitude*.

$$\|\bar{v}\|^2 = v_1{}^2 + v_2{}^2 + v_3{}^2$$

That leads to the property:

The dot product of a vector with itself is the square magnitude of that vector.

$$\bar{v} \cdot \bar{v} = \|\bar{v}\|^2$$

A much longer proof involving the *Law of Cosines* would lead you to another interesting property.

$$\bar{v} \cdot \bar{w} = \|\bar{v}\| \cdot \|\bar{w}\| \cos\theta$$

where θ is the angle between position vectors $\bar{v}$ and $\bar{w}$ and $0 \le \theta \le \pi$.

This provides an alternate method of finding dot product when the angle between vectors is known.

While a dot placed between two vectors denotes a dot product, a dot placed between two scalars denotes simple scalar multiplication.

And magnitudes such as $\bar{v}$ and $\bar{w}$ are scalars.

So, if the components of two vectors are known, find the dot product with:

$$\bar{v} \cdot \bar{w} = v_1 w_1 + v_2 w_2 + v_3 w_3$$

And if the magnitudes and the angle between them are known, use:

$$\bar{v} \cdot \bar{w} = \|\bar{v}\|\|\bar{w}\| \cos\theta$$

Solving this new formula for θ results in a formula for finding the angle between any two vectors.

$$\theta = \cos^{-1}\left(\frac{\bar{v} \cdot \bar{w}}{\|\bar{v}\| \cdot \|\bar{w}\|}\right)$$

where θ is the angle between vectors $\bar{v}$ and $\bar{w}$, and $0 \le \theta \le \pi$

Consider why the angle is restricted to the range of 0 to π radians.

This formula provides the measure of the *smallest* angle between two vectors. If an angle goes beyond π rad, it is no longer the smallest angle between the vectors.

Let's work through an example. Consider again vectors $\vec{a} = \begin{bmatrix} 3 & 4 & 0 \end{bmatrix}$ and vector $\vec{b} = \begin{bmatrix} 5 & 6 & 2 \end{bmatrix}$.

To find the angle θ between the vectors, use some variation of the formula:

$$\vec{v} \cdot \vec{w} = \| \vec{v} \| \cdot \| \vec{w} \| \cos\theta \qquad \cos\theta = \frac{\vec{v} \cdot \vec{w}}{\| \vec{v} \| \cdot \| \vec{w} \|} \qquad \theta = \cos^{-1}\left(\frac{\vec{v} \cdot \vec{w}}{\| \vec{v} \| \cdot \| \vec{w} \|} \right)$$

Starting with the middle formula, we could first solve for $\cos\theta$.

$$\cos\theta = \frac{\vec{a} \cdot \vec{b}}{\| \vec{a} \| \cdot \| \vec{b} \|} = \frac{(3)(5) + (4)(6) + (0)(2)}{\left(3^2 + 4^2 + 0^2\right) \cdot \left(5^2 + 6^2 + 2^2\right)} = \frac{15 + 24 + 2}{25 \cdot 65} = \frac{41}{1625}$$

Then you take the inverse cosine of both sides of the equation to solve for θ.

$$\theta = \cos^{-1}\left(\frac{41}{1625} \right) \approx 88.55°$$

The angle between vectors can be used to determine if the vectors are parallel or perpendicular.

If $\theta = 0$ or $\theta = \pi$, the vectors are parallel.

If $\theta = \dfrac{\pi}{2}$, the vectors are perpendicular.

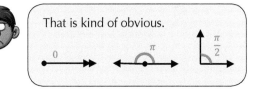

That is kind of obvious.

In 3D space, the terms *orthogonal* and *normal* are often used to describe perpendicular vectors.

A vector is not limited to being perpendicular to vectors.

For example, in Chapter 6, the normal vector was discussed in relation to its intersection of a plane or curved surface.

While finding the angle between two vectors is sometimes useful, it is not necessary if you just need to know if the vectors are orthogonal. Consider our second formula for finding the dot product.

$$\vec{v} \cdot \vec{w} = \|\vec{v}\| \cdot \|\vec{w}\| \cos\theta$$

As we just established, $\theta = \dfrac{\pi}{2}$ when $\vec{v}$ and $\vec{w}$ are perpendicular.

$$\vec{v} \cdot \vec{w} = \|\vec{v}\| \cdot \|\vec{w}\| \cos\dfrac{\pi}{2}$$

Because $\cos\dfrac{\pi}{2} = 0$, this can be simplified to:

$$\vec{v} \cdot \vec{w} = \|\vec{v}\| \cdot \|\vec{w}\| \cdot 0$$

Regardless of the magnitudes of $\vec{v}$ and $\vec{w}$, this simplifies further to:

$$\vec{v} \cdot \vec{w} = 0$$

And there you have it.

The dot product of perpendicular vectors is zero.

Now let's consider what could be said about the dot product when the angle between vectors is acute or obtuse.

For acute angles, $0 < \theta < \dfrac{\pi}{2}$. In this range, $\cos\theta$ is always positive. By definition, the magnitudes of the vectors are also positive. Because the dot product of vectors that form an acute angle is the product of three positive values (i.e., $\|\vec{v}\| \cdot \|\vec{w}\| \cdot \cos\theta$), the dot product itself must be positive.

Likewise, for obtuse angles, $\dfrac{\pi}{2} < \theta < \pi$. In this range, $\cos\theta$ is always negative. Because the dot product of vectors that form an acute angle is the product of two positive values and one negative value, the dot product itself must be negative.

Vectors form an acute angle if their dot product is positive.

Vectors are orthogonal if their dot product is zero.

Vectors form an obtuse angle if their dot product is negative.

The relationship between the dot product and the directionality of vectors can be taken a step further when working with unit vectors.

Because the magnitudes of unit vectors are one, the formula for dot product can be simplified from:

$$\vec{v} \cdot \vec{w} = \|\vec{v}\| \cdot \|\vec{w}\| \cos\theta$$

to:

$$\hat{v} \cdot \hat{w} = \cos\theta$$

In the range of possible angles formed by two vectors (i.e., $0 < \theta < \pi$), $\cos\theta$ is in the range of -1 to 1; and because the dot product of unit vectors is equal to $\cos\theta$,

> Unit vectors face the same direction if their dot product is 1.
>
> Unit vectors are orthogonal if their dot product is 0.
>
> Unit vectors face opposite directions if their dot product is -1.

$$\hat{v} \cdot \hat{w} = \cos\theta$$

applies to any angle θ between any two unit vectors $\hat{v}$ and $\hat{w}$.

For example,

$$\text{if } \theta = \frac{\pi}{4}\text{rad}, \hat{v} \cdot \hat{w} \approx 0.7071$$

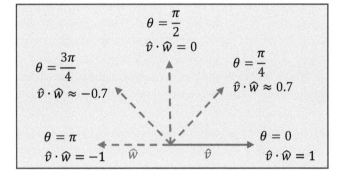

FIGURE 8.1 Dot product for vectors forming various angles.

Multiple vectors perpendicular to each other are *mutually orthogonal*. In 3D space, there are an infinite number of orthogonal vectors to any given vector.

You can visualize this by imagining one vector spinning around another. Each rotation requires a different vector.

Alternatively, you could imagine the length of one vector changing in size. While all the vectors would be unique, they would all have the same direction.

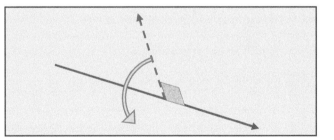

FIGURE 8.2 Vector rotating around an orthogonal vector.

Consider the directional vectors that align with the x, y, and z axis.

- The unit vector $\langle\; 1 \quad 0 \quad 0 \;\rangle$ represents the vector in the positive direction of the x-axis.
- The unit vector $\langle\; 0 \quad 1 \quad 0 \;\rangle$ represents the vector in the positive direction of the y-axis.
- The unit vector $\langle\; 0 \quad 0 \quad 1 \;\rangle$ represents the vector in the positive direction of the z-axis.

By definition of the Cartesian coordinate system, these vectors are orthogonal. Still, the relationship can be proven by confirming the dot product of each pair of vectors is 0.

For example, $\langle\; 1 \quad 0 \quad 0 \;\rangle \cdot \langle\; 0 \quad 1 \quad 0 \;\rangle = (1 \cdot 0) + (0 \cdot 1) + (0 \cdot 0) = 0$

Showing this relationship for each pair of vectors in the set proves the vectors are mutually orthogonal.

I could visualize orthogonal vectors with the same starting point being moved to have different starting points such that the lines never intersect. Would they still be orthogonal?

I like your brain. Let's try it out. Consider the same example using vectors with no defined position instead of position vectors. The math is the same.

$$\begin{bmatrix} 1 & 0 & 0 \end{bmatrix} \cdot \begin{bmatrix} 0 & 1 & 0 \end{bmatrix} = (1 \cdot 0) + (0 \cdot 1) + (0 \cdot 0) = 0$$

While position vectors have a starting point at the origin, vectors in general do not have a position. They are defined only by **direction** and **magnitude**. So, yes, vectors that have a dot product of 0 are orthogonal regardless of where you might imagine their position to be.

In summary, you have two options for checking if vectors are orthogonal.

Option 1: Use the dot product to find the angle between the vectors. The vectors are perpendicular if the angle is $\frac{\pi}{2}$.

Option 2: Find the dot product. The vectors are perpendicular if the dot product is 0.

So, we don't need to find the angle between vectors to know if they are orthogonal. Is there also an easier way to know if vectors are parallel? Absolutely!

To determine if vectors are parallel,

Option 1: Use the dot product to find the angle between the vectors. The vectors are parallel if the angle is 0 or π.

Option 2: Parallel vectors have the same or opposite direction. Vectors are parallel if they are *scalar multiples*.

Vectors are scalar multiples if one vector can be multiplied by a scalar to get the other vector.

Vectors $\bar{v}$ and $\bar{w}$ are scalar multiples if a scalar C exists in which

$$\bar{v} = C \cdot \bar{w}$$

For example, $\left\langle \begin{array}{ccc} 14 & -2 & 0 \end{array} \right\rangle$ is a scalar multiple of $\left\langle \begin{array}{ccc} -7 & 1 & 0 \end{array} \right\rangle$ because:

$$-2 \cdot \left\langle \begin{array}{ccc} -7 & 1 & 0 \end{array} \right\rangle = \left\langle \begin{array}{ccc} 14 & -2 & 0 \end{array} \right\rangle$$

A quick way to check if vectors $\bar{v} = \langle\ v_1\ \ v_2\ \ v_3\ \rangle$ and $\bar{w} = \langle\ w_1\ \ w_2\ \ w_3\ \rangle$ are scalar multiples is to divide v_1 by w_1 to get a scalar that could be multiplied by v_1 to get w_1. If the scalar can also be multiplied by v_2 to get w_2 and by v_3 to get w_3, the vectors are scalar multiples.

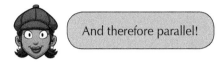

And therefore parallel!

Activity: Speed Racer

The dot product is applicable to game programmers in many situations. This activity will provide you with two such cases, both involving the behavior of UI elements.

1. Become familiar with the *Speed Racer* game.

   Open *Scene01* of the Speed Racer project from the Chapter 8 project files.

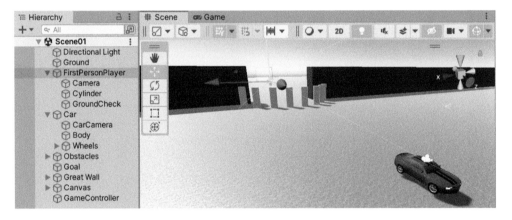

FIGURE 8.3   Scene01 of Speed Racer viewed in the Hierarchy and Scene windows.

The *FirstPersonPlayer* is controlled by the player and includes a *Camera* initially used when the scene loads. The Car also has a Camera which is used when the player enters and begins to control the car. Play the game to see how the camera and controls switch when the car is entered. Use the AWSD or arrow keys to move and the space bar to jump.

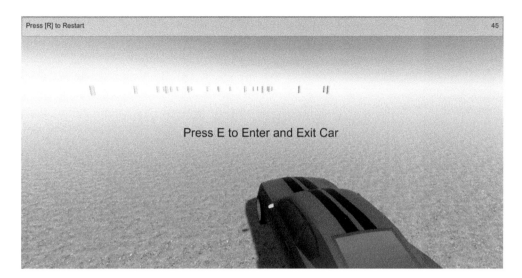

FIGURE 8.4   Message appearing when the player approaches the car during gameplay.

As you play, notice:
- You win the game when you reach the goal—the green cylinder.
- You lose the game if you do not reach the goal within 60 seconds.
- A UI message displays the region you are entering when passing the Great Wall.

> The message appears regardless of which direction you pass. Currently, "Hazard Valley" is displayed when you enter <u>and</u> exit the area.

> That is confusing. In most games, the name of an area only appears when the player enters that area.

- A UI message appears when you approach the car with instructions on how to enter and exit it.

> Yea, that doesn't work so great either. The instructions should not be visible when the player is looking away from the car.

2. Improve the UI for entering a new region.

Currently, *Gap* is being used as a trigger to detect when the player passes through the wall. With Gap selected in the hierarchy, you should be able to see the light green edges of the box collider. Additionally, if the move tool is selected, you can see its forward direction, which is always in the positive direction of the z-axis.

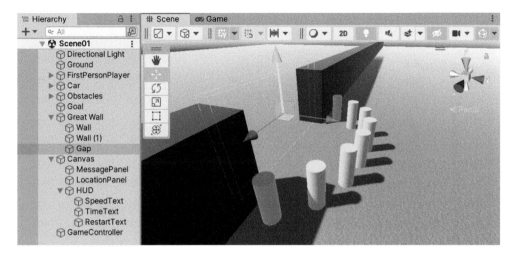

FIGURE 8.5   Gap selected with the blue arrow indicating its forward direction.

A *one-way trigger* would be more appropriate here. While Unity does not provide any such component, it can easily be coded by comparing the directionality of the relevant vectors.

 The trick is knowing which vectors to compare!

Displaying a newly entered area is implemented in the EnterAreaBehaviour script.

With the Gap selected, the initial values of the attached script's public properties are visible in the Inspector.

▼ #	**Enter Area Behaviour (Script)** ❷ ⌲ ⋮
Script	# EnterAreaBehaviour ⊙
Area Name	Hazard Valley
Location Panel	☺ LocationPanel ⊙
Duration	2
Player Character	☺ FirstPersonPlayer ⊙

FIGURE 8.6   EnterAreaBehaviour in Inspector.

Open the script in Visual Studio to take a closer look.

```
 6    public class EnterAreaBehaviour : MonoBehaviour
 7    {
 8        public string areaName;
 9        public GameObject locationPanel;
10        public float duration = 2.0f;
11        public GameObject playerCharacter;
12
13        void OnTriggerEnter(Collider other)
14        {
15            if (other.gameObject == playerCharacter)
16            {
17                Debug.Log(other.gameObject.name + " entered " + areaName);
18
19                locationPanel.GetComponent<Text>().text = areaName;
20                locationPanel.SetActive(true);
21                Invoke("HideLocationPanel", duration);
22            }
23        }
24
25        void HideLocationPanel()
26        {
27            locationPanel.GetComponent<Text>().text = "";
28            locationPanel.SetActive(false);
29        }
30    }
```

FIGURE 8.7   Lines 6 through 30 of EnterAreaBehaviour script.

The *OnTriggerEnter* method executes when another collider comes into contact with the Gap. The conditional statement on line 15 ensures that only a collision with the *playerCharacter* will cause the *areaName* to appear.

Notice the *HideLocationPanel* method defined on line 25 is called on line 21 in an atypical manner. Instead of simply calling the method as usual, the name of the method is passed as a string to the Invoke method along with a duration.

The Invoke method causes a delay before the named method is called. With the duration initialized to 2 in the Inspector, the message will remain on the screen for two seconds before the method to hide it is called.

The issue already mentioned is that the script behaves the same regardless of which direction the player moves through the collider. Recall that the Gap is facing forward toward the area with the car named "Hidden Valley". You might try checking if the player is facing in that same direction when the collision occurs.

```
13      void OnTriggerEnter(Collider other)
14      {
15          if (other.gameObject == playerCharacter)
16          {
17              Vector3 gapForward = this.gameObject.transform.forward;
18              Vector3 playerForward = playerCharacter.transform.forward;
19
20              float dot = gapForward.x * playerForward.x
21                        + gapForward.y * playerForward.y
22                        + gapForward.z * playerForward.z;
23
24              if(dot > 0)
25              {
26                  Debug.Log(other.gameObject.name + " entered " + areaName);
27
28                  locationPanel.GetComponent<Text>().text = areaName;
29                  locationPanel.SetActive(true);
30                  Invoke("HideLocationPanel", duration);
31              }
32          }
33      }
```

FIGURE 8.8   Updated code for the OnTriggerEnter method of the EnterAreaBehaviour class.

With these updates to the OnTriggerEnter method, the forward direction of the Gap is being compared to the forward direction of the playerCharacter. The dot product is calculated by adding the products of the corresponding components of the vectors. If the dot product is positive, the angle between the vectors is acute indicating the Player is facing *generally* in the same direction as the wall, and the code for showing the area name is executed.

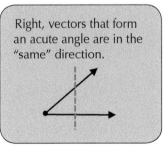
Right, vectors that form an acute angle are in the "same" direction.

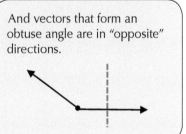
And vectors that form an obtuse angle are in "opposite" directions.

This may initially feel like it is working when you run the game. However, there is a problem when moving through the gap backward. In this case, the area name is shown when leaving the area and not shown when entering the area.

Well, yea, why would you assume that the player will be facing in the same direction they are moving?

A better solution to creating the one-way trigger is to compare the forward direction of the Gap to the direction the player is actually moving instead of the direction they are facing. Fortunately, the vector representing the playerCharacter's current velocity can be accessed through the public *GetVelocity* method of the *PlayerMovement* class.

Update the relevant code (i.e., lines 17–22) of the OnTriggerEnter method accordingly.

```
Vector3 gapForward = this.gameObject.transform.forward;
Vector3 playerVelocity = playerCharacter.GetComponent<PlayerMovement>().GetVelocity();

float dot = gapForward.x * playerVelocity.x
          + gapForward.y * playerVelocity.y
          + gapForward.z * playerVelocity.z;
```

FIGURE 8.9   Improved code for the OnTriggerEnter method.

Running the program now should have the desired result of showing "Hidden Valley" only when moving into that area, regardless of the player's orientation.

3. Improve the UI for instructions to use interactable objects.

Let's move on to the instructional message that appears when the player approaches the car. The message appears when the playerCharacter hits the BoxCollider that has been added to the Car, which is slightly visible when the Car is selected.

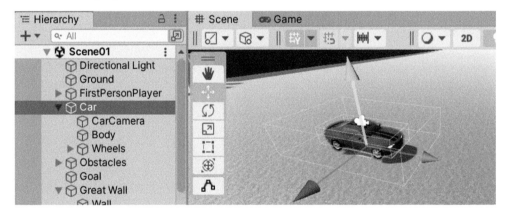

FIGURE 8.10   BoxCollider of Car viewed in Scene Window.

This logic for the collision can be seen in the *OnTriggerEnter* and *OnTriggerExit* methods of the *CarEntryZoneBehaviour* class.

```
12          void OnTriggerEnter(Collider other)
13          {
14              if (other.gameObject == playerCharacter)
15              {
16                  Debug.Log("Player entered car entry zone");
17                  ShowInstructions();
18              }
19          }
20
21          void OnTriggerExit(Collider other)
22          {
23              if (other.gameObject == playerCharacter)
24              {
25                  Debug.Log("Player exited car entry zone");
26                  HideInstructions();
27              }
28          }
```

FIGURE 8.11   Lines 12 through 28 of the CarEntryZoneBehaviour script.

The problem is that the message is displayed when the playerCharacter is in the BoxCollider regardless of whether or not they are looking at the car. We need to update the script to ensure the message only appears when the car is in the player's view.

Sounds like a job for the dot product. Again, the trick is knowing which vectors to compare!

It is no longer sufficient to rely solely on the OnTriggerEnter and OnTriggerExit methods to determine when to show and hide the instructions for entering the car. This is because the player could look toward and away from the car from within the Car's BoxCollider without moving. Now, you will need to use the *OnTriggerStay* method which will execute every frame in which the player is within the collider.

First, update the existing methods so they update the *inEntryZone* property. The player should be in the entry zone when they are inside the collider, whether they are looking at the car or not. Additionally, while the instructions should be hidden when the player leaves the entry zone they will not necessarily be shown when the player enters the entry zone.

```
12    void OnTriggerEnter(Collider other)
13    {
14        if (other.gameObject == playerCharacter)
15        {
16            Debug.Log("Player entered car entry zone");
17            inEntryZone = true;
18        }
19    }
20
21    void OnTriggerExit(Collider other)
22    {
23        if (other.gameObject == playerCharacter)
24        {
25            Debug.Log("Player exited car entry zone");
26            inEntryZone = false;
27            HideInstructions();
28        }
29    }
```

FIGURE 8.12   Updated code in CarEntryZoneBehaviour class.

Now add an *OnTriggerStay* method as follows.

```
31    private void OnTriggerStay(Collider other)
32    {
33        if (other.gameObject == playerCharacter)
34        {
35            Vector3 playerPos = playerCharacter.transform.position;
36            Vector3 carPos = this.gameObject.transform.position;
37            Vector3 playerToCar = carPos - playerPos;
38
39            Vector3 playerForward = playerCharacter.transform.forward;
40
41            float dot = playerToCar.x * playerForward.x
42                      + playerToCar.y * playerForward.y
43                      + playerToCar.z * playerForward.z;
44
45            if (dot > 0)
46            {
47                ShowInstructions();
48            }
49            else
50            {
51                HideInstructions();
52            }
53        }
54    }
```

FIGURE 8.13   OnTriggerStay method added to the CarEntryZoneBehaviour class.

In each frame, this method calculates the vector from the player to the car on line 37 by subtracting the Car's position from the player's position. This *playerToCar* vector represents the direction the player would need to face to be looking directly at the car. The *playerForward* vector, on the other hand, is the direction the player is actually looking.

Next, the dot product of that *playerToCar* vector and the *playerForward* vector is calculated to compare their directions. If the dot product is positive, the angle formed by the vectors is acute and the instructions are shown. Otherwise, if the angle formed by the vectors is right (i.e. the dot product is zero) or obtuse (i.e. the dot product is negative), the instructions are hidden.

This script works pretty well at making the instructions appear only when near the car and looking in the direction of the car. However, you may have noticed strange behavior when facing the car while in the entry zone and looking up at the sky. Clearly, this is a time when the player is not looking toward the car but still seeing the instructions.

That behavior makes sense based on how the player controls are defined in the *PlayerMovement* script. Moving the mouse to the left and right rotates the playerCharacter around the *y* axis causing a change in its forward direction. However, moving the mouse up and down does not rotate the playerCharacter at all, but instead rotates the attached camera around the *x* axis.

The solution to this bug is to use the forward direction of the camera instead of the player. Indeed, the forward vector of the camera is the true vector representing the direction the player is looking. These changes should all be done within the conditional statement of the *OnTriggerStay* method.

```
Transform cam = playerCharacter.transform.Find("Camera").transform;
Vector3 playerLookAtCar = this.gameObject.transform.position - cam.position;

Vector3 playerForward = playerCharacter.transform.forward;
Vector3 playerLook = new (playerForward.x, cam.forward.y, playerForward.z);

float dot = playerLookAtCar.x * playerLook.x
          + playerLookAtCar.y * playerLook.y
          + playerLookAtCar.z * playerLook.z;
```

FIGURE 8.14   Updated code in OnTriggerStay method of the CarEntryZoneBehaviour class.

This updated script first stores the *Transform* of the *Camera* which is attached to the *playerCharacter* as *cam*. Then the vector *playerLookAtCar* is calculated by subtracting the position of *cam* from the position of *Car*.

The vector from the player's camera to the car is a better choice than the vector from the player to the car. The vector from the Camera, which you can see in the inspector is positioned 1.15 units above its FirstPersonPlayer parent, aligns with the actual viewpoint of the player.

The *playerForward* property is only defined to provide a way to quickly access the playerCharacter's forward vector. Then, *playerLook* is created using the *x* and *z* components of that *playerForward* vector and the *y* component of the *playerCam* vector.

Finally, the dot product is calculated to determine the directionality between the vector that defines where the player is looking (i.e., *playerLook*) and the vector that defines where the player would need to look to face directly at the car (i.e., *playerLookAtCar*).

Challenges

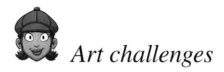

Art challenges

Swap the car with your own custom vehicle or 3D model from the Unity Asset store. Be sure the controls for driving the car still work correctly.

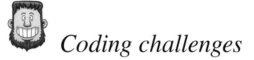

Coding challenges

1. Replace the formula used for calculating the dot product in both parts of the activity with the Vector3 method which returns the dot product between any two given vectors.

2. Replace the *areaName* property of the EnterAreaBehaviour script with the properties *areaNameInFront* and *areaNameBehind*. Then, change the behavior such that the correct area name is shown based on the direction the player moves through the Gap.

   With the trigger causing an area name to appear in both directions, a minor issue arises. If the player enters one area and then quickly re-enters back into the other area, the Invoke command to hide the message may cause the message to disappear too quickly. To address this bug, research how to stop all previous Invokes before creating a new Invoke.

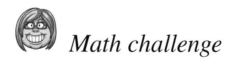

Math challenge

Modify the CarEntryZoneBehaviour class so that the instructional message appears only when looking more directly at the car (e.g., using a 90-degree field of view instead of 180 degrees). To achieve this, you will need to normalize the vectors before taking the dot product to ensure the result is between −1 and 1.

Just use the normalized property of the Vector3 class. For example,

```
playerLook.normalized
```

Achievements

In this chapter, you learned how to find and use the dot product. You performed this new operation to find the angles between vectors and to check if vectors are parallel or perpendicular to each other.

You then applied what you learned in a game to show messages to the player as they pass through a trigger in a specific direction, and again while they are within a trigger looking in the direction of an interactable object.

Additional uses of the dot product will be discussed in the next chapters.

In this chapter you:

- Calculated the dot product of two vectors.
- Used the dot product to check whether or not vectors are orthogonal.
- Used the dot product to find the angle between vectors.
- Used the angle to check if vectors are parallel.
- Used the dot product to determine which direction a player enters a trigger.
- Used the dot product to determine if the player is looking toward an object.

Exercises

1. Find the angle between $\langle\ 12\ \ -3\ \ 0\ \rangle$ and $\langle\ 4\ \ -5\ \ -2\ \rangle$

2. Are vectors $\langle\ 2\ \ 3\ \ -1\ \rangle$ and $\langle\ 2\ \ -1\ \ 1\ \rangle$ parallel?

3. Are vectors $\langle\ 2\ \ 3\ \ -1\ \rangle$ and $\langle\ 2\ \ -1\ \ 1\ \rangle$ orthogonal?

4. Are vectors $\langle\ -2\ \ -3\ \ 6\ \rangle$ and $\langle\ \frac{2}{3}\ \ 1\ \ -2\ \rangle$ parallel?

5. Are vectors $\langle\ -2\ \ -3\ \ 6\ \rangle$ and $\langle\ \frac{2}{3}\ \ 1\ \ -2\ \rangle$ orthogonal?

6. What is the largest possible set of mutually orthogonal vectors?

7. Classify the angle formed by each vector with the vector $\langle\ 3\ \ 4\ \ -5\ \rangle$ as acute, obtuse, or neither. If neither, specify if the vectors are orthogonal or parallel. If parallel, specify if the vectors are in the same or opposite directions.

   a. $\langle\ 1\ \ 1\ \ 1\ \rangle$

   b. $\langle\ 1\ \ 0\ \ 0\ \rangle$

   c. $\langle\ -1\ \ 2\ \ 1\ \rangle$

   d. $\langle\ 6\ \ 8\ \ -10\ \rangle$

   e. $\langle\ -3\ \ -4\ \ 5\ \rangle$

9

Orthogonal Directionality | Cross Product

Introduction

In the previous chapter, the dot product was used to multiply matrices and vectors. Now we look at another method of multiplying vectors—the *cross product*.

The cross product results in a vector and is therefore also called the *vector product*

The Math

ijk Notation

So far, we have discussed vectors using component form.

$\begin{bmatrix} 3 & 5 & -2 \end{bmatrix}$, for example, describes a vector based on the change on the x, y, and z axes from its initial point to its endpoint. $\langle\ 3\ \ 5\ \ -2\ \rangle$, also in component form, is a position vector with an initial point at (0, 0, 0) and an endpoint at (3, 5, −2). In both cases, you are describing a vector using x, y, and z components.

However, there is another notation for writing vectors that aligns with the definition of a vector as having a direction and magnitude.

Consider that $\langle\ 3\ \ 5\ \ -2\ \rangle$ could be written as:

$$\langle\ 3\ \ 0\ \ 0\ \rangle + \langle\ 0\ \ 5\ \ 0\ \rangle + \langle\ 0\ \ 0\ \ -2\ \rangle$$

That should be correct. Adding vectors simply involves adding up the corresponding elements of those vectors.

DOI: 10.1201/9781032701431-10

With some factoring, this could be written as:

$$3 \cdot \langle\ 1\quad 0\quad 0\ \rangle + 5 \cdot \langle\ 0\quad 1\quad 0\ \rangle - 2 \cdot \langle\ 0\quad 0\quad 1\ \rangle$$

Sure. Scalar multiplication simply involves multiplying each component of a vector with the scalar.

Now we have a vector defined by the sum of three other vectors, each described by their magnitude and direction.

- The vector $3 \cdot \langle\ 1\quad 0\quad 0\ \rangle$ has a magnitude of 3 in the direction of the x axis.
- The vector $5 \cdot \langle\ 0\quad 1\quad 0\ \rangle$ has a magnitude of 5 in the y-direction.
- The vector $-2 \cdot \langle\ 0\quad 0\quad 1\ \rangle$ has a magnitude of -2 in the z-direction.

Of course, $3 \cdot \langle\ 1\quad 0\quad 0\ \rangle + 5 \cdot \langle\ 0\quad 1\quad 0\ \rangle - 2 \cdot \langle\ 0\quad 0\quad 1\ \rangle$ is a bit much to write out to describe a single vector. To simplify this, $\hat{i}, \hat{j},$ and $\hat{k}$ are commonly used to represent the unit vectors in the direction of the x, y, and z axes, respectively.

$$\hat{i} = \langle\ 1\quad 0\quad 0\ \rangle \quad \hat{j} = \langle\ 0\quad 1\quad 0\ \rangle \quad \hat{k} = \langle\ 0\quad 0\quad 1\ \rangle$$

The component form of $\langle\ 3\quad 5\quad -2\ \rangle$ may be written in ijk form as $3\hat{i} + 5\hat{j} - 2\hat{k}$.

VECTOR NOTATION

Component form: $\langle\ v_1\quad v_2\quad v_3\ \rangle$

ijk form: $v_1 \hat{i} + v_2 \hat{j} + v_3 \hat{k}$

You may be wondering why two forms exist for expressing the same vector. Simply, it is sometimes easier to work with vectors when expressed in one form or the other depending on the unique circumstances. For example, the ijk form is useful to express a vector as an algebraic expression and to find the cross product of two vectors.

Could this be a lead-in to learning about cross products?

Multiplying Vectors (Cross Product)

The cross product is a method of multiplying two vectors which results in a vector that is *orthogonal* to both vectors being multiplied. That is, they form a right angle with both vectors.

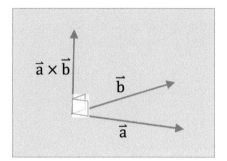

Here, $\vec{a} \times \vec{b}$, read as "A cross B", is a vector orthogonal to both $\vec{a}$ and $\vec{b}$.

Note, the angle formed by $\vec{a}$ and $\vec{b}$ does not need to be a right angle.

FIGURE 9.1 $\vec{a} \times \vec{b}$.

The direction of $\vec{a} \times \vec{b}$ can be determined using the right-hand rule.

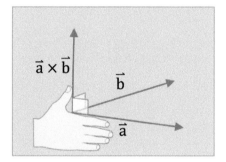

With your right hand on $\vec{a}$, fingers pointing in the direction of $\vec{a}$ and palm facing $\vec{b}$, the direction of $\vec{a} \times \vec{b}$ is indicated by the raised thumb.

FIGURE 9.2 Right-hand $\vec{a} \times \vec{b}$.

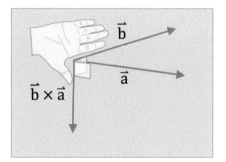

If you are flexible enough to position your right hand along $\vec{b}$ with the palm facing $\vec{a}$, you can see $\vec{b} \times \vec{a}$ is a vector in the opposite direction of $\vec{a} \times \vec{b}$.

So,

$$\vec{a} \times \vec{b} = -(\vec{b} \times \vec{a})$$

FIGURE 9.3 Right-hand $\vec{b} \times \vec{a}$.

To calculate a cross product, you will need to calculate the *determinant* of 2×2 and 3×3 matrices.

Start with embracing a clear distinction:

- The determinant of a 2×2 matrix is always a scalar.
- The determinant of a 3×3 matrix is always a vector.

The determinant of a 2×2 matrix is calculated by subtracting the product of the second element of row 1 and first element of row 2 from the product of the first element of row 1 and second element of row 2.

$$\det\begin{bmatrix} a & b \\ c & d \end{bmatrix} = ad - bc$$

For example, if $\mathbf{X} = \begin{bmatrix} 8 & 4 \\ -2 & 9 \end{bmatrix}$, the determinant of $\mathbf{X} = 8(9) - 4(-2) = 72 + 8 = \boxed{80}$

 I can visualize the order in which the multiplication and subtraction should occur.

The logo for **Visual Studio** might help you remember this!

Actually, the logo for **Visual Studio Code** would be better.

Calculating the determinant of a 3×3 matrix can be done in 4 simple steps.

Step 1 | Multiply the scalar a by the determinant of the 2×2 matrix that remains when the row and column of a is removed.

$$\begin{bmatrix} a & b & c \\ d & e & f \\ g & h & i \end{bmatrix} = a \cdot \det\begin{bmatrix} e & f \\ h & i \end{bmatrix} = a\,(ei - fh)$$

Step 2 | Multiply the opposite of the scalar b by the determinant of the 2×2 matrix that remains when the row and column of b are removed.

$$\begin{bmatrix} a & b & c \\ d & e & f \\ g & h & i \end{bmatrix} = -b \cdot \det\begin{bmatrix} d & f \\ g & i \end{bmatrix} = -b\,(di - fg)$$

The opposite of b is $-b$

Step 3 | Multiply the scalar c by the determinant of the 2×2 matrix that remains when the row and column of c are removed.

$$\begin{bmatrix} a & b & c \\ d & e & f \\ g & h & i \end{bmatrix} = c \cdot \det\begin{bmatrix} d & e \\ g & h \end{bmatrix} = c\,(dh - eg)$$

Step 4 | Add the results from the first three steps together.

$$\det\begin{bmatrix} a & b & c \\ d & e & f \\ g & h & i \end{bmatrix} = \boxed{a(ei - fh)} + \boxed{-b(di - fg)} + \boxed{c(dh - eg)}$$

The 4-step process is fairly easy to remember and works every time! You may still want a general formula for finding the determinant of a 3×3 matrix.

Here it is!

$$\det\begin{bmatrix} a & b & c \\ d & e & f \\ g & h & i \end{bmatrix} = a\cdot\det\begin{bmatrix} e & f \\ h & i \end{bmatrix} - b\cdot\det\begin{bmatrix} d & f \\ g & i \end{bmatrix} + c\cdot\det\begin{bmatrix} d & e \\ g & h \end{bmatrix}$$

 Well, yea, this formula just describes the 4-step process.

You could simplify the formula by solving each of the 2×2 determinants.

$$\det\begin{bmatrix} a & b & c \\ d & e & f \\ g & h & i \end{bmatrix} = a\left(ei - fh\right) - b\left(di - fg\right) + c\left(dh - eg\right)$$

 Hello, this formula is shown previously in the 4th and last step.

Then, if you simplify the second term by distributing the negative, you get the *standard form* for the formula for finding the determinant of a 3×3 matrix.

$$\det\begin{bmatrix} a & b & c \\ d & e & f \\ g & h & i \end{bmatrix} = a\left(ei - fh\right) + b\left(fg - di\right) + c\left(dh - eg\right)$$

With a firm understanding of how to calculate determinants, you are ready to find the cross product of two vectors. The cross product is the determinant of a 3×3 matrix formed by the unit vectors for each axis and the vectors being crossed.

$$\text{For } \vec{v} = \left\langle\, v_1 \quad v_2 \quad v_3 \,\right\rangle \text{ and } \vec{w} = \left\langle\, w_1 \quad w_2 \quad w_3 \,\right\rangle,$$

$$\vec{v} \times \vec{w} = \det\begin{bmatrix} \hat{i} & \hat{j} & \hat{k} \\ v_1 & v_2 & v_3 \\ w_1 & w_2 & w_3 \end{bmatrix}$$

Solving for the determinant and distributing the negative on the second term gives a formula for finding the cross product.

Using ijk notation:

$$\vec{v} \times \vec{w} = \hat{i}(v_2 w_3 - v_3 w_2) + \hat{j}(v_3 w_1 - v_1 w_3) + \hat{k}(v_1 w_2 - v_2 w_1)$$

In component from:

$$\vec{v} \times \vec{w} = \left\langle \quad v_2 w_3 - v_3 w_2 \quad v_3 w_1 - v_1 w_3 \quad v_1 w_2 - v_2 w_1 \quad \right\rangle$$

I can see why learning the 4-step process would be easier than memorizing the formula.

Still, the formula would be useful in writing a function that would calculate the cross product of any two vectors.

The vector $\vec{a} \times \vec{b}$ is not the only vector orthogonal to $\vec{a}$ and $\vec{b}$. Other orthogonal vectors include those which have the same direction but a different magnitude than $\vec{a} \times \vec{b}$ or those which are in the opposite direction of $\vec{a} \times \vec{b}$.

This brings us to the magnitude of $\vec{a} \times \vec{b}$.

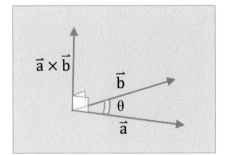

It turns out, $\left\| \vec{a} \times \vec{b} \right\|$ is related to the individual magnitudes of $\vec{a}$ and $\vec{b}$, and the angle between them.

Let's expand on our previous visual of $\vec{a} \times \vec{b}$ to include θ as the measure of the angle formed by $\vec{a}$ and $\vec{b}$.

FIGURE 9.4 θ between $\vec{a}$ and $\vec{b}$.

To find $\left\| \vec{a} \times \vec{b} \right\|$, we start with a formula derived in Chapter 8.

$$\left\| \vec{v} \right\|^2 = \vec{v} \cdot \vec{v}$$

Because $\vec{a} \times \vec{b}$ is a vector,

$$\left\| \vec{a} \times \vec{b} \right\|^2 = (\vec{a} \times \vec{b}) \cdot (\vec{a} \times \vec{b})$$

Letting $\vec{a} = \left\langle a_1 \quad a_2 \quad a_3 \right\rangle$ and $\vec{b} = \left\langle b_1 \quad b_2 \quad b_3 \right\rangle$, plug in the formula for cross product.

$$\left\| \vec{a} \times \vec{b} \right\|^2 = \left\langle a_2 b_3 - a_3 b_2 \quad a_3 b_1 - a_1 b_3 \quad a_1 b_2 - a_2 b_1 \right\rangle \cdot \left\langle a_2 b_3 - a_3 b_2 \quad a_3 b_1 - a_1 b_3 \quad a_1 b_2 - a_2 b_1 \right\rangle$$

Remember you simply multiply corresponding elements to find the dot product.

$$\left\| \vec{a} \times \vec{b} \right\|^2 = (a_2b_3 - a_3b_2)(a_2b_3 - a_3b_2) + (a_3b_1 - a_1b_3)(a_3b_1 - a_1b_3) + (a_1b_2 - a_2b_1)(a_1b_2 - a_2b_1)$$

From this, we can derive the formula $\left\| \vec{a} \times \vec{b} \right\| = \left\| \vec{a} \right\| \cdot \left\| \vec{b} \right\| \cdot \sin\theta$.

What? I am not seeing how that could be.

Well, this is a book about math, so I'll take some time to show you the proof!

With *a little* algebra...

$$\left\| \vec{a} \times \vec{b} \right\|^2 = (a_2b_3 - a_3b_2)(a_2b_3 - a_3b_2) + (a_3b_1 - a_1b_3)(a_3b_1 - a_1b_3) + (a_1b_2 - a_2b_1)(a_1b_2 - a_2b_1)$$

$$= (a_2b_3)(a_2b_3) + (a_2b_3)(-a_3b_2) + (-a_3b_2)(a_2b_3) + (-a_3b_2)(-a_3b_2)$$
$$+ (a_3b_1)(a_3b_1) + (a_3b_1)(-a_1b_3) + (-a_1b_3)(a_3b_1) + (-a_1b_3)(-a_1b_3)$$
$$+ (a_1b_2)(a_1b_2) + (a_1b_2)(-a_2b_1) + (-a_2b_1)(a_1b_2) + (-a_2b_1)(-a_2b_1)$$

$$= (a_2b_3)^2 - a_2b_2a_3b_3 - a_2b_2a_3b_3 + (-a_3b_2)^2$$
$$+ (a_3b_1)^2 - a_1b_1a_3b_3 - a_1b_1a_3b_3 + (-a_1b_3)^2$$
$$+ (a_1b_2)^2 - a_1b_1a_2b_2 - a_1b_1a_2b_2 + (-a_2b_1)^2$$

$$= a_2{}^2b_3{}^2 - a_2b_2a_3b_3 - a_2b_2a_3b_3 + a_3{}^2b_2{}^2$$
$$+ a_3{}^2b_1{}^2 - a_1b_1a_3b_3 - a_1b_1a_3b_3 + a_1{}^2b_3{}^2$$
$$+ a_1{}^2b_2{}^2 - a_1b_1a_2b_2 - a_1b_1a_2b_2 + a_2{}^2b_1{}^2$$

$$= a_2{}^2b_3{}^2 + a_3{}^2b_2{}^2 + a_3{}^2b_1{}^2 + a_1{}^2b_3{}^2 + a_1{}^2b_2{}^2 + a_2{}^2b_1{}^2$$
$$- 2a_2b_2a_3b_3 - 2a_1b_1a_3b_3 - 2a_1b_1a_2b_2$$

$$= a_2{}^2b_3{}^2 + a_3{}^2b_2{}^2 + a_3{}^2b_1{}^2 + a_1{}^2b_3{}^2 + a_1{}^2b_2{}^2 + a_2{}^2b_1{}^2 + a_1{}^2b_1{}^2 + a_2{}^2b_2{}^2 + a_3{}^2b_3{}^2$$
$$- 2a_2b_2a_3b_3 - 2a_1b_1a_3b_3 - 2a_1b_1a_2b_2 - a_1{}^2b_1{}^2 - a_2{}^2b_2{}^2 - a_3{}^2b_3{}^2$$

$$= a_2{}^2 b_3{}^2 + a_3{}^2 b_2{}^2 + a_3{}^2 b_1{}^2 + a_1{}^2 b_3{}^2 + a_1{}^2 b_2{}^2 + a_2{}^2 b_1{}^2 + a_1{}^2 b_1{}^2 + a_2{}^2 b_2{}^2 + a_3{}^2 b_3{}^2$$

$$- \left(2a_2 b_2 a_3 b_3 + 2a_1 b_1 a_3 b_3 + 2a_1 b_1 a_2 b_2 + a_1{}^2 b_1{}^2 + a_2{}^2 b_2{}^2 + a_3{}^2 b_3{}^2 \right)$$

$$= a_1{}^2 b_1{}^2 + a_1{}^2 b_2{}^2 + a_1{}^2 b_3{}^2 + a_2{}^2 b_1{}^2 + a_2{}^2 b_2{}^2 + a_2{}^2 b_3{}^2 + a_3{}^2 b_1{}^2 + a_3{}^2 b_2{}^2 + a_3{}^2 b_3{}^2$$

$$- \left(2a_2 b_2 a_3 b_3 + 2a_1 b_1 a_3 b_3 + 2a_1 b_1 a_2 b_2 + a_1{}^2 b_1{}^2 + a_2{}^2 b_2{}^2 + a_3{}^2 b_3{}^2 \right)$$

$$= \left(a_1{}^2 + a_2{}^2 + a_3{}^2 \right)\left(b_1{}^2 + b_2{}^2 + b_3{}^2 \right) - \left(a_1 b_1 + a_2 b_2 + a_3 b_3 \right)\left(a_1 b_1 + a_2 b_2 + a_3 b_3 \right)$$

you get:

$$\left\| \vec{a} \times \vec{b} \right\|^2 = \left(a_1{}^2 + a_2{}^2 + a_3{}^2 \right)\left(b_1{}^2 + b_2{}^2 + b_3{}^2 \right) - \left(a_1 b_1 + a_2 b_2 + a_3 b_3 \right)^2$$

And this is where the fun begins!

$$\text{Notice}: a_1{}^2 + a_2{}^2 + a_3{}^2 = \| \vec{a} \|^2$$

$$b_1{}^2 + b_2{}^2 + b_3{}^2 = \| \vec{b} \|^2$$

$$\left(a_1 b_1 + a_2 b_2 + a_3 b_3 \right)\left(a_1 b_1 + a_2 b_2 + a_3 b_3 \right) = \vec{a} \cdot \vec{b}$$

Substitute in to get:

$$\left\| \vec{a} \times \vec{b} \right\|^2 = \| \vec{a} \|^2 \cdot \| \vec{b} \|^2 - \left(\vec{a} \cdot \vec{b} \right)^2$$

Plugging in our formula for dot product,

$$\left\| \vec{a} \times \vec{b} \right\|^2 = \| \vec{a} \|^2 \cdot \| \vec{b} \|^2 - \left(\| \vec{a} \| \cdot \| \vec{b} \| \cdot \cos\theta \right)^2$$

which simplifies to:

$$\left\| \vec{a} \times \vec{b} \right\|^2 = \| \vec{a} \|^2 \cdot \| \vec{b} \|^2 - \| \vec{a} \|^2 \cdot \| \vec{b} \|^2 \cdot \cos^2\theta$$

Factoring out the $\| \vec{a} \|^2 \cdot \| \vec{b} \|^2$ we get:

$$\left\| \vec{a} \times \vec{b} \right\|^2 = \| \vec{a} \|^2 \cdot \| \vec{b} \|^2 \left(1 - \cos^2\theta \right)$$

Because $1 - \cos^2\theta = \sin^2\theta$, this simplifies to:

$$\left\| \vec{a} \times \vec{b} \right\|^2 = \| \vec{a} \|^2 \cdot \| \vec{b} \|^2 \cdot \sin^2\theta$$

Finally, you can square root both sides to solve for the magnitude of the cross product.

$$\left\| \vec{a} \times \vec{b} \right\| = \| \vec{a} \| \cdot \| \vec{b} \| \cdot \sin\theta$$

Wait. I remember from my algebra class that there are two solutions when solving for a square. For example, if $x^2 = 9$, then $x = \pm 3$. That is, $3^2 = 9$ and $(-3)^2 = 9$.

Good catch. I think I can help with this.

Magnitudes are always positive, so $\|\vec{a}\|$ and $\|\vec{b}\|$ must be positive. Also, we know θ is between 0 and π because it is an angle formed by two vectors, and sin is positive for values from 0 to π. So, we also know $\sin\theta$ is positive.

So, finally, we have a formula to find the magnitude of the cross product!

$$\|\vec{a}\times\vec{b}\| = \|\vec{a}\|\cdot\|\vec{b}\|\cdot\sin\theta$$

where θ is the angle between $\vec{a}$ and $\vec{b}$.

This is similar to the dot product formula: $\vec{a}\cdot\vec{b} = \|\vec{a}\|\cdot\|\vec{b}\|\cdot\cos\theta$

Furthermore, we can quickly derive another formula for finding the cross product.

Remember, a vector is comprised of a direction and a magnitude.

$$\vec{v} = \|\vec{v}\|\cdot\hat{u} \text{ where } \hat{u} \text{ is the unit vector in the direction of } \vec{v}$$

Because $\vec{a}\times\vec{b}$ is a vector,

$$\vec{a}\times\vec{b} = \|\vec{a}\times\vec{b}\|\cdot\hat{u}$$

And plugging in our formula for $\|\vec{a}\times\vec{b}\|$,

$$\vec{a}\times\vec{b} = \|\vec{a}\|\cdot\|\vec{b}\|\cdot\sin\theta\cdot\hat{u}$$

where $\hat{u}$ is the unit vector in the direction of $\vec{a}\times\vec{b}$.

Having two formulas for cross product has the same benefit as having two formulas for dot product. One of the formulas is useful when the angle between the vectors is known, and the other formula is better when the angle is unknown.

Time for an example. Let's find a vector that is orthogonal to both of the following vectors.

$$\vec{a} = \left\langle 3 \quad 4 \quad 0 \right\rangle \quad \vec{b} = \left\langle 5 \quad 6 \quad 2 \right\rangle$$

$\bar{a} \times \bar{b}$ is such a vector! Use the formula for cross product that does not require the angle between the vectors. That is the formula that involves determinants.

To find $\bar{a} \times \bar{b}$, first arrange the vectors into a 3×3 matrix. Use the directional vectors $\hat{i}, \hat{j},$ and $\hat{k}$ in the first row. Then place the values of $\bar{a}$ in the middle row and the values of $\bar{b}$ in the last row.

$$\begin{bmatrix} \hat{i} & \hat{j} & \hat{k} \\ 3 & 4 & 0 \\ 5 & 6 & 2 \end{bmatrix}$$

Then use our handy 4-step process to find the determinant of the 3×3 matrix.

$$\begin{bmatrix} \hat{i} & \hat{j} & \hat{k} \\ 3 & 4 & 0 \\ 5 & 6 & 2 \end{bmatrix}$$

$$\hat{i}\begin{bmatrix} 4 & 0 \\ 6 & 2 \end{bmatrix}$$

$$\hat{i}(4*2-0*6)$$

$$\hat{i}(8-0)$$

$$8\hat{i}$$

$$\begin{bmatrix} \hat{i} & \hat{j} & \hat{k} \\ 3 & 4 & 0 \\ 5 & 6 & 2 \end{bmatrix}$$

$$-\hat{j}\begin{bmatrix} 3 & 0 \\ 5 & 2 \end{bmatrix}$$

$$-\hat{j}(3*2-0*5)$$

$$-\hat{j}(6-0)$$

$$-6\hat{j}$$

$$\begin{bmatrix} \hat{i} & \hat{j} & \hat{k} \\ 3 & 4 & 0 \\ 5 & 6 & 2 \end{bmatrix}$$

$$\hat{k}\begin{bmatrix} 3 & 4 \\ 5 & 6 \end{bmatrix}$$

$$\hat{k}(3*6-4*5)$$

$$\hat{k}(18-20)$$

$$-2\hat{k}$$

$$\bar{a} \times \bar{b} = \det\begin{bmatrix} \hat{i} & \hat{j} & \hat{k} \\ 3 & 4 & 0 \\ 5 & 6 & 2 \end{bmatrix} = 8\hat{i} - 6\hat{j} - 2\hat{k}$$

Written in component form, $\bar{a} \times \bar{b} = \langle\, 8 \quad -6 \quad -2 \,\rangle$

Remember from the previous chapter that the dot product of two perpendicular vectors is zero. A quick check *partially* confirms our result by ensuring it has a valid direction.

$$\bar{a} \cdot \left(\bar{a} \times \bar{b}\right)$$

$$\langle\, 3 \quad 4 \quad 0 \,\rangle \cdot \langle\, 8 \quad -6 \quad -2 \,\rangle$$

$$(3 \cdot 8) + (4 \cdot -6) + (0 \cdot -2)$$

$$24 + -24 + 0$$

$$0$$

$$\bar{b} \cdot \left(\bar{a} \times \bar{b}\right)$$

$$\langle\, 5 \quad 6 \quad 2 \,\rangle \cdot \langle\, 8 \quad -6 \quad -2 \,\rangle$$

$$(5 \cdot 8) + (6 \cdot -6) + (2 \cdot -2)$$

$$40 + -36 + -4$$

$$0$$

Let's also find $\left\| \bar{a} \times \bar{b} \right\|$.

If you know the magnitude of the vectors being crossed and the angle between those vectors, use:

$$\left\| \bar{a} \times \bar{b} \right\| = \left\| \bar{a} \right\| \cdot \left\| \bar{b} \right\| \cdot \sin\theta$$

Otherwise, if you know the components of the vectors, find the cross product and then use the distance formula to find its magnitude.

The latter is the better option in this example because we do not know the angle between the vectors. It is also nice that we have already found $\bar{a} \times \bar{b}$.

$$\left\| \bar{a} \times \bar{b} \right\| = \left\| \left\langle \begin{array}{ccc} 8 & -6 & -2 \end{array} \right\rangle \right\| = \sqrt{(8)^2 + (-6)^2 + (-2)^2} = \sqrt{64 + 36 + 4} = \sqrt{104}$$

Just as there are corollaries related to vectors which have a dot product of 0, so too are there corollaries related to vectors which have a cross product of 0.

Let's consider the case of $\bar{a} \times \bar{b} = 0$.

Substitute the recently derived formula for cross product gives:

$$\left\| \bar{a} \right\| \cdot \left\| \bar{b} \right\| \cdot \sin\theta \cdot \hat{u} = 0$$

For this to be true, one of the factors must be zero. Assuming the vectors both have some length, their magnitudes are non-zero, they have a direction, and their cross product has a direction orthogonal to both. This suggests that the only factor that could be 0 is $\sin\theta$.

$$\text{If } \bar{a} \times \bar{b} = 0, \text{ then } \sin\theta = 0.$$

For what angles does $\sin\theta = 0$? Recall that for the angle θ between two vectors, $0 \geq \theta \geq \pi$. In this range,

$$\sin\theta = 0 \text{ only when } \theta = 0 \text{ or } \pi$$

Therefore, when $\bar{a} \times \bar{b} = 0$, the angle between the vectors is either 0 (they have the same direction) or π (they are in opposite directions). In either case, the vectors are parallel.

To summarize, for any two vectors $\bar{v}$ and $\bar{w}$:

if $\bar{v} \cdot \bar{w} = 0$, then $\bar{v} \perp \bar{w}$	If $\bar{v} \times \bar{w} = 0$, then $\bar{v} \parallel \bar{w}$
Vectors with a dot product of 0 are orthogonal.	*Vectors with a cross product of 0 are parallel.*

Using Cross Product to Find Area

You might be surprised to see a sub-section focused on area in a chapter about the cross product of vectors. The discussion about the magnitude of a cross product is about to get more interesting.

You probably remember how to find the area of a rectangle—multiply the height and base.

$$A_R = h \cdot b$$

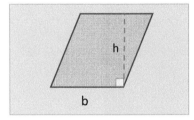

A rectangle that has a base of 5 units and a height of 3 units has an area of 15 square units.

Algebra, trigonometry, vector mathematics, and now geometry!

FIGURE 9.5   3 by 5 rectangle.

Can the formula for the area of a rectangle be generalized to all parallelograms?

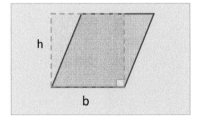

Consider the parallelogram shown. The height of a parallelogram is the line segment which forms a right angle with the base.

FIGURE 9.6   Parallelogram.

Consider the rectangle with the same base and height as the parallelogram.

If the triangles have the same size and shape (i.e., they are congruent), you could imagine moving the blue triangle on top of the yellow triangle to demonstrate the areas are the same.

We just need to prove that the triangles are congruent.

FIGURE 9.7   Parallelogram and square with same base and height.

The orange triangle has a right angle because all angles of a rectangle are 90°.

The *Linear Pair Postulate* confirms the blue triangle also has a right angle.

If two angles form a linear pair, then they are supplementary.

The right angles of the triangle are congruent. They both are 90°.

Corresponding Angles Postulate confirms another set of congruent angles.

When parallel lines are cut by a transversal, corresponding angles have the same measure.

The hypotenuses are congruent because opposite sides of a parallelogram have the same length.

Finally, we have sufficient information to determine the triangles are congruent.

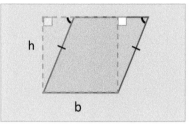

FIGURE 9.8 Congruent triangles formed by square and parallelogram.

The *Angle-Angle-Side (AAS) Postulate* confirms that these two triangles are congruent.

If two angles and a non-included side of one triangle are congruent to the corresponding two angles and non-included side of another triangle, then the triangles are congruent.

Having established the two triangles are congruent, we know their areas are equal.

Furthermore, because the area of each parallelogram consists of a shared trapezoid and one triangle, the areas of the two parallelograms are equal.

This demonstrates that the area of any parallelogram is the product of its height and base.

$$A_P = h \cdot b$$

Ok, the geometry review is nice, but how does this relate to vectors and cross product?

I am about to make that connection!

Consider a parallelogram formed by two vectors $\vec{a}$ and $\vec{b}$.

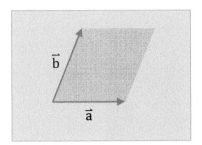

FIGURE 9.9 $\vec{a}$ and $\vec{b}$ as adjacent sides of a parallelogram.

Remember $\vec{a} \times \vec{b}$ is a vector orthogonal to $\vec{a}$ and $\vec{b}$. If $\vec{a}$ and $\vec{b}$ are on the plane facing you (i.e., the plane of the page or screen that you are reading from), then $\vec{a} \times \vec{b}$ would be pointing directly at you.

Also, the length of $\vec{a} \times \vec{b}$ is given by:

$$\left\| \vec{a} \times \vec{b} \right\| = \left\| \vec{a} \right\| \cdot \left\| \vec{b} \right\| \cdot \sin\theta$$

To find the area of the parallelogram, we need to know the height and base.

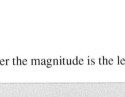

> It looks like the base is $\vec{a}$.

> No, no, no. Have you learned nothing? The base is the length of a side—a scalar.
>
> $\vec{a}$ is a vector, not a scalar.

Remember the magnitude is the length of a vector. Therefore, the base of the parallelogram is $\left\| \vec{a} \right\|$.

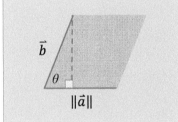

FIGURE 9.10 Right Triangle formed with hypotenuse $\left\| \vec{b} \right\|$.

To find the height, consider the right triangle formed by the line segment for the height. The hypotenuse is $\left\| \vec{b} \right\|$.

If θ is the angle formed by $\vec{a}$ and $\vec{b}$, then: $\sin\theta = \dfrac{\text{height}}{\left\| \vec{b} \right\|}$

Solving, we get: $\text{height} = \left\| \vec{b} \right\| \sin\theta$

With the base and height determined, they may be multiplied to find the area of the parallelogram.

$$\text{Area} = \left\| \vec{a} \right\| \cdot \left\| \vec{b} \right\| \cdot \sin\theta$$

What a discovery! The formula for area is the same as the formula for the magnitude of a cross product.

$$A_P = \left\| \vec{a} \times \vec{b} \right\|$$

Where A_P is the area of the parallelogram formed by vectors $\vec{a}$ and $\vec{b}$.

As the angle between $\vec{a}$ and $\vec{b}$ approaches $0°$ or $180°$, the parallelogram flattens out to having no area and so the magnitude of the cross product approaches 0. Furthermore, the magnitude of the cross product is maximized for two vectors of set magnitudes when the angle between the vectors is $90°$.

What about the area of a triangle formed by two vectors?

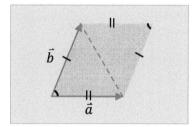

The triangle formed by the vectors has half the area of the parallelogram formed by the vectors.

Of course, this could be proven by showing that the triangles formed by the line connecting the end-points of the vectors are congruent.

FIGURE 9.11 Congruent triangles of a parallelogram.

The angle formed by the vectors is congruent to the opposite angle of the parallelogram because opposite angles of a parallelogram are equal. Additionally, opposite sides of a parallelogram are equal.

The *Side-Angle-Side (SAS) Postulate* confirms that these two triangles are congruent.

Two triangles are congruent if two sides and the included angle of one triangle are congruent to two sides and the included angle of another triangle.

Without a doubt, the area of the triangle is simply half the area of the parallelogram.

$$A_T = \frac{\left\| \vec{a} \times \vec{b} \right\|}{2}$$

Where A_T is the area of the triangle formed by vectors $\vec{a}$ and $\vec{b}$.

The Normal

Recall, the normal vector is a vector that is perpendicular to a surface at a given point. The normal vector, often called the "normal", can be calculated for a point on a plane or a curved surface.

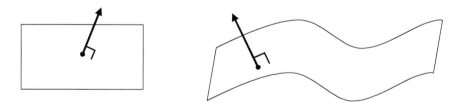

FIGURE 9.12 A normal drawn on a plane and a curved surface.

Do not confuse terms.

A <u>vector norm</u> is another term for magnitude. It is simply the length of the vector.

A <u>normal</u> is a vector that is orthogonal to a surface.

A <u>normalized</u> vector has a magnitude of one—it is a unit vector. <u>Normalizing</u> a vector is scaling it to have a magnitude of one while maintaining the same direction.

There is also the unit normal, which of course is just a normalized normal.

Let's first discuss the normal to a plane. The normal of a plane can be found given any two vectors on the plane which are not parallel. Simply find the cross product of the two vectors.

A plane can be defined by 3 non-collinear points. Consider a plane containing non-collinear points Q, R, and S. In this example, $\overrightarrow{QR}$ and $\overrightarrow{QS}$ are non-parallel vectors on the plane. Therefore, $\overrightarrow{QR} \times \overrightarrow{QS}$ is a normal to the plane in one direction and $\overrightarrow{QS} \times \overrightarrow{QR}$ is a normal to the plane in the opposite direction.

A plane may also be defined by a single point and its normal. The properties and methods of a *Plane* in Unity include.

- The *Set3Points* method "Sets a plane using three points that lie within it. The points go around clockwise as you look down on the top surface of the plane."
- The *SetNormalAndPosition* method "Sets a plane using a point that lies within it along with a normal to orient it."
- The *normal* property stores the Vector that is normal to the plane.

For a full list of methods and properties defined in the Plane class, check the Unity documentation. https://docs.unity3d.com/ScriptReference/Plane.html

Achievements

In this chapter, you learned about the cross product. While no activities or challenges are included in this chapter, the cross product will be needed in the next chapter to understand the mathematics behind vector reflections.

Exercises

1. $\bar{u} = \left\langle\ -3\ \ 1\ \ -2\ \right\rangle$

   $\bar{v} = \left\langle\ 1\ \ 1\ \ 1\ \right\rangle$

   Find three vectors that are orthogonal to both $\bar{u}$ and $\bar{v}$.

2. A plane is defined by the following points:

   A = (3, –1, 5)   B = (0, 0, 0)   C = (–5, 9, 3)

   Define the same plane with a single point on the plane and the normal to the plane.

3. Two vectors, each with a magnitude of 7 units, form a 45° angle. What is the magnitude of their cross product?

4. What is the area of the triangle with vertices at the following points?

   A = (–20, 16, 0)   B = (7, –7, 4)   C = (12, 14, –2)

10

Reflections | Vector Projection and Reflection

Introduction

Often in game programming, you need to know how much one vector is in the direction of another vector. Mathematically, that requires finding the *projection* of a vector onto another vector. One example of the need for vector projections is to find the *reflection* of a vector off another vector. As you might imagine, this is commonly being done by the physics engine every time there is a collision to determine what new direction an object should move after the collision. This chapter will cover both vector projections and vector reflections.

The Math

We have established that dot products can be used to compare the directionality of two vectors and to find angles between vectors. These are examples of when the dot product operation is useful, but they do not really define what a dot product is.

Sadly, you are still not quite ready for that. To understand what the dot product actually represents, you must first understand *scalar* and *vector projection*.

Consider two vectors $\vec{a}$ and $\vec{b}$.

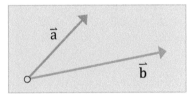

FIGURE 10.1   vectors $\vec{a}$ and $\vec{b}$.

How much does $\vec{a}$ move in the direction of $\vec{b}$? The answer involves the projection of $\vec{a}$ onto $\vec{b}$.

The projection of $\vec{a}$ onto $\vec{b}$ is denoted as:

$$Proj_{\vec{b}}\vec{a}$$

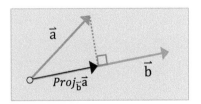

FIGURE 10.2 $\vec{a}$ projected onto $\vec{b}$.

DOI: 10.1201/9781032701431-11

While $Proj_b\bar{a}$ describes the vector resulting from vector projection, the magnitude of $Proj_b\bar{a}$ denoted by $Comp_b\bar{a}$ describes the *component* or *scalar* projection.

So, vector projection always results in a vector, and component projection always results in a scalar.

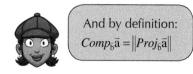
And by definition:
$Comp_b\bar{a} = \left\| Proj_b\bar{a} \right\|$

You might ask yourself, how much of the vector $\bar{a}$ is being applied in the vector $\bar{b}$ direction?

If the direction of $\bar{b}$ is known, this is really just a magnitude question. You should find $Comp_b\bar{a}$.

Look again at the right triangle formed from the vector projection.

$Comp_b\bar{a}$ is the length of one leg of a right triangle.

$\|\bar{a}\|$ is the length of the hypotenuse.

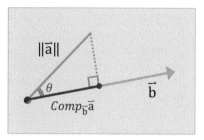

FIGURE 10.3   Component of $\bar{a}$ that is in the direction of $\bar{b}$.

Plugging this information into the trig formula of $\cos\theta = \dfrac{\text{adjacent}}{\text{hypotenuse}}$ gives:

$$\cos\theta = \frac{Comp_b\bar{a}}{\|\bar{a}\|}$$

And now you can solve to get a formula for component projection.

$$Comp_b\bar{a} = \|\bar{a}\|\cos\theta$$

where θ is the angle between $\bar{a}$ and $\bar{b}$

Take this a step further. Recall the formula established in Chapter 8 which uses the dot product to find the angle between two vectors.

$$\cos\theta = \frac{\bar{a}\cdot\bar{b}}{\|\bar{a}\|\cdot\|\bar{b}\|}$$

Substituting in the value for $\cos\theta$ gives another formula for finding the component projection.

$$Comp_b\bar{a} = \|\bar{a}\|\cdot\frac{\bar{a}\cdot\bar{b}}{\|\bar{a}\|\cdot\|\bar{b}\|}$$

Simplified, this is

$$Comp_{\vec{b}}\vec{a} = \frac{\vec{a} \cdot \vec{b}}{\| \vec{b} \|}$$

So, I can find the component projection when θ is known using: $Comp_{\vec{b}}\vec{a} = \| \vec{a} \| \cos$
And when θ is unknown, I can use: $Comp_{\vec{b}}\vec{a} = \frac{\vec{a} \cdot \vec{b}}{\| \vec{b} \|}$

Now we can use the component projection to derive a formula for vector projection.

Recall that a vector can be defined by its magnitude multiplied by its direction.

$$\text{vector} = \text{magnitude} \cdot \text{direction}$$

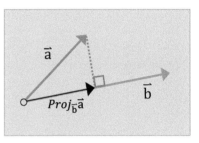

FIGURE 10.4 $\vec{a}$ projected onto $\vec{b}$.

Applying this to the projection of a onto b:

$$Proj_{\vec{b}}\vec{a} = \| Proj_{\vec{b}}\vec{a} \| \cdot \text{unit vector of } Proj_{\vec{b}}\vec{a}$$

The direction of $Proj_{\vec{b}}\vec{a}$ is the same direction of $\vec{b}$. Therefore, they share the same unit vector and:

$$Proj_{\vec{b}}\vec{a} = \| Proj_{\vec{b}}\vec{a} \| \cdot \text{unit vector of } \vec{b}$$

This simplifies to $Proj_{\vec{b}}\vec{a} = Comp_{\vec{b}}\vec{a} \cdot \frac{\vec{b}}{\| \vec{b} \|}$

The magnitude of $Proj_{\vec{b}}\vec{a}$ is $Comp_{\vec{b}}\vec{a}$

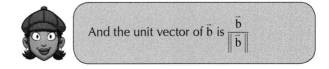

And the unit vector of $\vec{b}$ is $\frac{\vec{b}}{\| \vec{b} \|}$

Using our previously established formula for component projection, substitute $\dfrac{\bar{a} \cdot \bar{b}}{\left\| \bar{b} \right\|}$ for $Comp_{\bar{b}}\bar{a}$.

$$Proj_{\bar{b}}\bar{a} = \frac{\bar{a} \cdot \bar{b}}{\left\| \bar{b} \right\|} \cdot \frac{\bar{b}}{\left\| \bar{b} \right\|}$$

With a bit of simplifying, we now have a formula for finding vector projection.

$$Proj_{\bar{b}}\bar{a} = \frac{\bar{a} \cdot \bar{b}}{\left\| \bar{b} \right\|^2} \cdot \bar{b}$$

Another version of this formula could be written if $\bar{b}$ was a unit vector, $\hat{b}$.

$$Proj_{\hat{b}}\bar{a} = \frac{\bar{a} \cdot \hat{b}}{\left\| \hat{b} \right\|^2} \cdot \hat{b}$$

Knowing the magnitude of a unit vector is 1, this simplifies to:

$$Proj_{\hat{b}}\bar{a} = \bar{a} \cdot \hat{b} \cdot \hat{b}$$

So, finding a vector projection requires taking the dot product twice!

While there are unique cases in game programming where vector projection is useful, it will be used in this book as a step toward vector reflections.

Imagine an object moving along a vector $\bar{v}$ until it collides with a wall as shown. The incoming angle θ is formed by $\bar{v}$ and a vector $\bar{n}$ normal to the wall. For visualization purposes, this vector is drawn through the point in which $\bar{v}$ contacts the wall. The magnitude $\bar{n}$ is arbitrary.

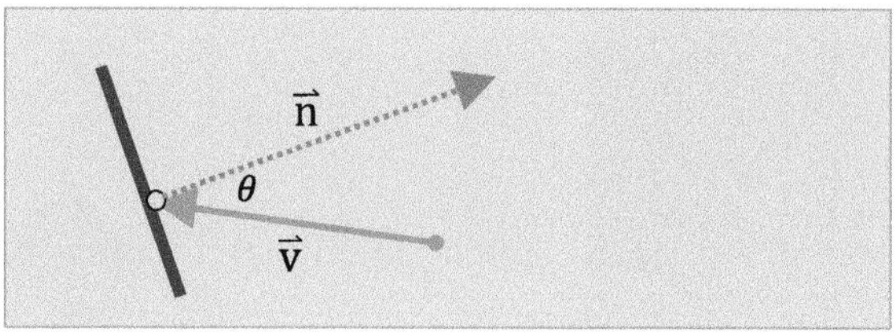

FIGURE 10.5   Normal of a wall at endpoint of $\bar{v}$.

A *reflection* describes the vector that would be reflected on the other side of the normal as if bouncing off a mirror.

Assuming there is no loss of energy from the impact, the object will bounce off the wall at the same speed and with the same outgoing angle as the incoming angle.

In this example, $\overrightarrow{v_r}$ is the *perfect reflection* of $\vec{v}$ around the normal of the wall.

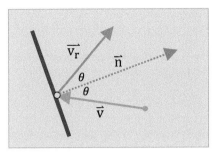

 With a perfect reflection, the magnitudes of the incoming and outgoing vectors are the same.

FIGURE 10.6   Perfect reflection of $\vec{v}$.

One game example of where perfect reflections might be used is within the physics engine itself. If a very elastic ball were to collide with a wall, it might bounce in a perfect reflection.

 Another fun example might be a puzzle game that involves a laser bouncing off mirrors that the player can strategically place and rotate.

Our goal is to find a formula for the reflected vector.

Recall that a vector is defined only by magnitude and direction and could have any position.

For this proof, it is helpful to position $\overrightarrow{v_r}$ so it has the same initial point as $\vec{v}$, and then position $\vec{v}$ again so its initial point is at the terminal point of $\overrightarrow{v_r}$.

As the normal now traverses a set of parallel vectors, the alternate interior angles are equal.

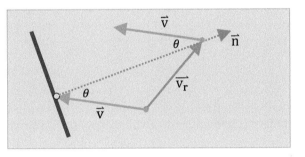

FIGURE 10.7 $\vec{v}$ at initial and terminal point of $\overrightarrow{v_r}$.

Now to put our vector projection to use.

Projecting $\vec{v}$ onto the normal vector gives the vector $Proj_{\vec{n}}\vec{v}$ as shown.

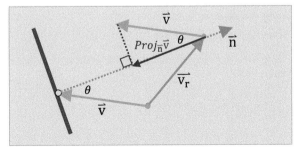

FIGURE 10.8   Projection of $\vec{v}$ on the normal.

Extending the perpendicular side from the end of the projection creates another triangle which also has a right angle, an angle with a measure of θ, and a hypotenuse of length $\| \bar{v} \|$.

These two triangles are congruent as per the *Angle-Angle-Side (AAS) Postulate*.

As congruent triangles, the lengths of the legs adjacent to θ are equal. They both have a length equal to the magnitude of $Proj_{\bar{n}}\bar{v}$. These sides are also co-linear.

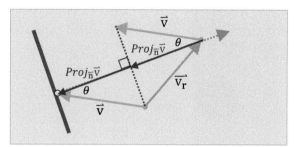

FIGURE 10.9   Projection on the normal repeated.

Multiplying $Proj_{\bar{n}}\bar{v}$ by two results in a vector from the terminal point of $\bar{v_r}$ to the terminal point of $\bar{v}$.

Further multiplying by -1 changes the vector to point in the opposite direction, with an initial point at the terminal point of $\bar{v}$ and a terminal point at the terminal point of $\bar{v_r}$.

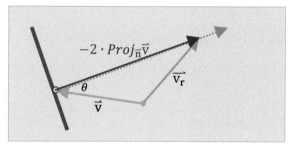

FIGURE 10.10   Opposite of doubled projection.

Recall the sum of two vectors can be visualized by placing the initial point of one of the vectors at the terminal point of the other. This provides a general formula for vector reflection.

$$\bar{v_r} = \bar{v} - 2 \cdot Proj_{\bar{n}}\bar{v}$$

Where $\bar{v_r}$ is the vector reflection of $\bar{v}$ around $\bar{n}$.

Activity: The Octagon

The activity for this chapter provides an opportunity to apply vector reflections to provide prediction motion paths.

1. Become familiar with *The Octagon* game.

   Open *Scene01* of The Octagon project from the Chapter 10 project files. Notice the naming scheme for the balls that are children of the *Balls* GameObject.

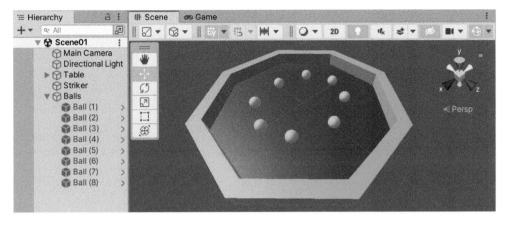

FIGURE 10.11 Scene01 of The Octagon open in Hierarchy and Scene windows.

To play the game, click the mouse to strike the red ball. You can also press the tab to change the target ball which can be easily identified by its red material.

The blue line represents the "striker" and is always drawn from the mouse position directly to the target ball. The yellow line shows the path the target ball will follow when hit.

Knock the balls around until you get the hang of the game. Notice, the length of the blue striker relates to the force in which the target ball is hit.

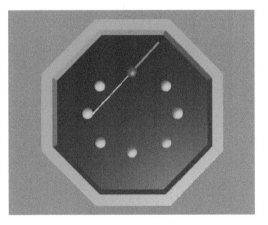

FIGURE 10.12 The Octagon during play.

This is not a complete game. There is not even a way to win or lose.

But it is fun to knock the balls around.

I could imagine several games created from this core functionality!

Select the Striker from the Hierarchy and look at its attached components in the Inspector.

FIGURE 10.13   Striker in Inspector Window.

The *LineRenderer* is used to draw a blue line from the mouse position to the red ball.

This *StrikerBehaviour* is a custom script that provides the core functionality previously described. The *pathMaterial* is set to be the yellow Material that shows where the target ball will go when hit, and the *selectionMaterial* is set to be the red Material that is applied to the target ball.

The *StrikerMat* under the script is the blue Material used to draw the line from the mouse position to the target ball.

Notice when the game is playing, one or more GameObjects appear as children of the Striker.

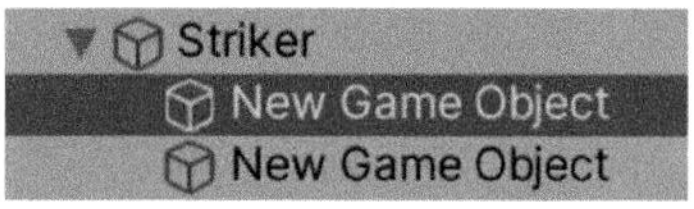

FIGURE 10.14   Children of Striker visible in Hierarchy during gameplay.

Selecting any of these GameObjects reveals that they have a LineRenderer and a Material which are used to draw the yellow path.

We will discuss why there are sometimes more than one of these objects in a moment. For now, notice that multiple objects exist when the yellow path from the target ball does not lead to another ball.

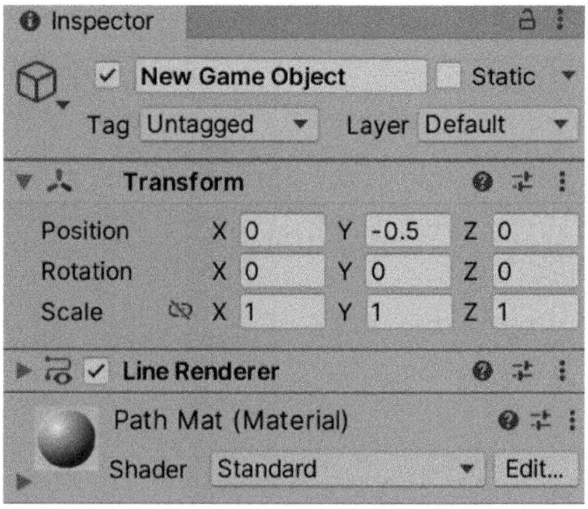

FIGURE 10.15   LineRenderer Component.

2. Become familiar with the StrikerBehaviour class.

Open the StrikerBehaviour.cs file from the Scripts folder. This is the only script in the entire project and is attached to the Striker GameObject within the scene.

First, look at the properties.

```
5   public class StrikerBehaviour : MonoBehaviour
6   {
7       LineRenderer lineRenderer;
8       public GameObject target;
9       public float pathLength = 10f;
10      public Material pathMaterial;
11      Material originalMaterial;
12      public Material selectionMaterial;
13      public float forceMultiplier = 2f;
14      public bool hidePathWhileMoving = true;
```

FIGURE 10.16   Lines 5 through 14 of the StrikerBehaviour class.

The *lineRenderer* property defined on line 7 is initialized in the Start method to reference the LineRenderer component on the Striker. This LineRenderer is used for drawing the blue line from the mouse position to the target ball.

The *target* property on line 8 is used to keep track of which ball is selected as the target. It is initialized in the Inspector.

The *pathLength* defines the maximum length of the yellow path. While it is initialized to 10f on line 9, that initial value has been changed to 16 in the Inspector. Because the table is smaller than 16 units across, you cannot see the path being restricted. However, if you temporarily change the value in the inspector to a smaller number, such as 6, you can see how this property changes the Striker behavior.

As mentioned previously, the *pathMaterial* defined on line 10 is initialized in the Inspector to a yellow Material.

Lines 11 and 12 refer to the materials that are used for the target ball. The *selectionMaterial* is initialized in the Inspector to a red material used for the currently targeted ball. The *originalMaterial* is a private property that is not visible in the Inspector. This is initialized in the *Start* and *SetTarget* methods to the original material on the newly targeted ball. By storing the original material before changing the material to the red selection material, it may be restored to the ball when it is no longer being targeted.

The *forceMultiplier* property is initialized to 2f on line 13, but this has been changed in the Inspector to 5. As you might imagine, this relates to how much force the target ball is struck with.

To better understand this, take a look at lines 58 to 62 of the Update method. This code executes when the player clicks the mouse to strike the ball.

```
58          if (Input.GetButtonDown("Fire1"))
59          {
60              lineRenderer.enabled = false;
61              Strike(endPos - startPos);
62          }
```

FIGURE 10.17   Lines 58 to 62 of StrikerBehaviour.

The *startPos* and *endPos* variables are the position vectors for the start and end points of the Striker. Subtracting the startPos from the endPos gives the vector that will be used to apply a force. This is the vector sent to the *strike* method.

The Strike method stores that vector in the *force* variable. While the vector has the correct direction, its magnitude is not sufficient for applying the desired force to the target ball.

```
void Strike(Vector3 force)
{
    Rigidbody rb = target.gameObject.GetComponent<Rigidbody>();
    rb.AddForce(force * forceMultiplier, ForceMode.Impulse);
```

FIGURE 10.18   Lines 129 through 132 of StrikerBehaviour.

To scale the force when calling the AddForce method, the force vector is multiplied by the forceMultiplier. Temporarily change the value of the forceMultiplier in the Inspector if you want to see how it affects the force in which the Striker hits the target ball.

3. Study the *DrawPath* method.

The *DrawPath* method is the only method you will need to modify to complete this activity. The goal of this method is to show the full path the target ball will take before hitting another ball, including the reflections off the sides of the table. It is not quite working yet.

The *DrawPath* method is called on line 56 from within the Update method.

```
DrawPath(target.transform.position, direction, pathLength);
```

FIGURE 10.19   Call to DrawPath method from line 56 of the StrikerBehaviour script.

Three arguments are sent to the *DrawPath* method—a vector defining the starting position for the path, a unit vector defining the direction of the path, and a scalar for the maximum length of the path.

On line 95, you can see the values sent to DrawPath are stored into three local variables. The starting position for the path is stored in *startPos*, the direction for the path is stored in the *direction*, and the maximum length of the path is stored in *length*.

```
void DrawPath(Vector3 startPos, Vector3 direction, float length)
```

FIGURE 10.20   Declaration of DrawPath method on line 95 of the StrikerBehaviour script.

We can break the discussion of the implementation of *DrawPath* into three parts.

<u>Part 1</u>: Determine if a reflection is needed.

```
97          Vector3 endPos = startPos + direction * length;
98          RaycastHit hit;
99          Ray ray = new Ray(startPos, direction);
100         bool reflectionNeeded = false;
101         if (Physics.Raycast(ray, out hit, length))
102         {
103             endPos = hit.point;
104             if(hit.transform.gameObject.tag != "Ball")
105             {
106                 reflectionNeeded = true;
107             }
108         }
```

FIGURE 10.21   Lines 97 through 108 of the StrikerBehaviour script.

The first portion of the method is primarily to determine if a reflection is needed. The path should end if it reaches the length without any collision, or if the path collides with another ball. However, if the path collides with a wall of the table, it should be reflected around the normal of that wall, continuing the path in a new direction.

Line 97 calculates a position vector *endPos* to define where the path would end assuming no collision were to occur. Checking whether a collision will occur is done through a Raycast on line 101. You can think of a Raycast as a way of firing a ray from a given point in a given direction to see what, if any, object is intercepted.

Lines 98 defines *hit* as a *RaycastHit*—an object used to store information from a Raycast including the object that is hit and the point of the hit. Line 99 defines ray as a Ray object from a starting position of *startPos* in the direction of *direction*. The *hit* and *ray* objects are used in line 101 when the Raycast is performed.

A very common practice in determining the value of a Boolean variable is to set it to either true or false, and then change it if needed based on relevant conditions. This is the programming pattern used to determine if *reflectionNeeded* should be true or false. On line 100, the variable is defined and set to the assumed value of false. Only if the Raycast collides with another object as determined from the conditional statement on line 101 and that object is not a Ball as determined from the conditional statement on line 104 will the value of *reflectionNeeded* be changed to true.

Part 2: Draw a path from the current startPos in the direction specified

```
110             GameObject line = new GameObject();
111             line.transform.parent = this.transform;
112             LineRenderer lr = line.AddComponent<LineRenderer>();
113             lr.material = pathMaterial;
114             lr.startWidth = 0.1f;
115             lr.endWidth = 0.1f;
116             lr.positionCount = 2;
117             lr.useWorldSpace = true;
118
119             lr.SetPosition(0, startPos);
120             lr.SetPosition(1, endPos);
```

FIGURE 10.22   Lines 110 through 120 of the StrikerBehaviour script.

Lines 110 and 111 create a new GameObject *line* and add it as a child to the Striker.

> In Unity, a GameObject can be made to be a child of another by setting its parent property.

On line 112, a *LineRenderer* component is created and added to the newly created GameObject.

Lines 112 through 117 define the properties of the LineRenderer. These are all properties that could be set in the Inspector if the GameObject and attached Component were not dynamically created during runtime.

Finally, on lines 119 and 120 the starting and ending position of the LineRenderer is set. The SetPosition method of the LineRenderer class requires an index for which position is being set and a position as a Vector3 object. For a simple two-position LineRenderer, the index values of 0 and 1 are used for the starting and ending positions.

Part 3: Create another path if a reflection is needed.

```
122     if(reflectionNeeded)
123     {
124         Vector3 reflectDirection = -1 * direction;
125         DrawPath(endPos, reflectDirection, length - hit.distance);
126     }
```

FIGURE 10.23   Lines 122 through 126 of the StrikerBehaviour script.

Finally, if a reflection is needed, the drawPath method needs to be called again using values that will define the new reflected path. For the first argument, the ending position of the path that was just drawn is sent as the new starting position. For the second argument, a new reflected direction calculated on the previous line is used. For the last argument, a new maximum path length is calculated by subtracting the distance of the path just drawn from the previous maximum path length.

Line 125 demonstrates a recursive call. The drawPath method is being called from within the drawPath method!

4. Identify the problem.

Based on the discussion of the code thus far, you may be wondering why you only see one yellow line when the path of the target ball hits a side wall. Recall, you do actually see a second GameObject appear under the Striker in the Hierarchy.

The reason you do not see them both on the screen is because they are drawn in the same place. That is, the line is actually not reflecting as intended but instead simply reversing direction. This should not be surprising given the calculation that was made to determine the *reflectDirection*.

```
124                          Vector3 reflectDirection = -1 * direction;
```

FIGURE 10.24 Line 124 of the StrikerBehaviour script.

Of course, multiplying a vector by a negative one results in a vector of the same magnitude in the opposite direction.

We did learn a formula in this chapter for finding a vector reflection!

5. Fix the problem

We can calculate a vector reflection $\vec{v_r}$ of a vector $\vec{v}$ around a vector $\bar{n}$.

$$\vec{v_r} = \vec{v} - 2 \cdot Proj_{\bar{n}} \vec{v}$$

Therefore, we will need to also use the formula for calculating a vector projection:

$$Proj_{\bar{n}} \vec{v} = \left(\frac{\vec{v} \cdot \bar{n}}{\| \bar{n} \|^2} \right) \cdot \bar{n}$$

Or, if the vector being projected onto is a unit vector,

$$Proj_{\hat{n}} \vec{v} = \vec{v} \cdot \hat{n} \cdot \hat{n}$$

In either case, we need to calculate the dot product of $\vec{v}$ and $\bar{n}$, which can be calculated with:

$$\vec{v} \cdot \bar{n} = v_1 n_1 + v_2 n_2 + v_3 n_3$$

And of course, we need to know v̄ and n̄.

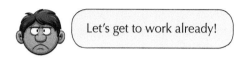
Let's get to work already!

We will first be adding code in the conditional block just before line 124.

v̄ is the vector that needs to be reflected. In our example, this is the path that was just drawn from the *startPos* to the *endPos*.

```
Vector3 path = endPos - startPos;
```

FIGURE 10.25   Vector for path calculated by subtracting startPos from endPos.

n̄ is the vector that is normal to the wall at the point the Raycast hit the wall. In our code, we have already stored the information about the RaycastHit into the *hit* property, so we can get the normal using the *normal* property of that object.

v̄ · n̄ can now be calculated.

```
float dot = path.x * hit.normal.x
          + path.y * hit.normal.y
          + path.z * hit.normal.z;
```

FIGURE 10.26   Dot product calculated from components of the path and normal vectors.

You could possibly use either of the formulas for finding the vector projection mentioned. However, the API for *normal.hit* does not specify it will always be a unit vector. Though it likely always is, using the longer formula will ensure a correct calculation.

The longer formula would be quite a bit for one line of code, so you could break it up. Already, the calculation for v̄ · n̄ was stored in *dot*. The square magnitude of n̄, $\| \bar{n} \|^2$, could also be calculated separately.

```
float magSqaured = hit.normal.magnitude * hit.normal.magnitude;
```

FIGURE 10.27   Square Magnitude of normal calculated.

The calculation for $Proj_{\bar{n}}\bar{v}$ can now be made using the *dot* and *magSquared* values.

```
Vector3 proj = (dot / magSqaured) * hit.normal;
```

FIGURE 10.28   Projection of v̄ onto n̄ calculated.

Finally, the vector projection can be used to find the reflected vector.

```
Vector3 reflectDirection = (path - 2 * proj).normalized;
```

FIGURE 10.29   Reflection of v̄ around n̄ calculated.

The full reflection is calculated within the parenthesis. However, this vector is then normalized because we are only looking for the direction of the reflection.

When complete, the code that executes when a reflection is needed should be updated to:

```
if(reflectionNeeded)
{
    Vector3 path = endPos - startPos;
    float dot = path.x * hit.normal.x
              + path.y * hit.normal.y
              + path.z * hit.normal.z;
    float magSqaured = hit.normal.magnitude * hit.normal.magnitude;
    Vector3 proj = (dot / magSqaured) * hit.normal;
    Vector3 reflectDirection = (path - 2 * proj).normalized;

    DrawPath(endPos, reflectDirection, length - hit.distance);
}
```

FIGURE 10.30   Lines 122 through 133 of the StrikeBehaviour script after updating code.

Save the updated code and run the game again to test it out.

Now you should see the initial path extending from the red ball as well as the path defined by the reflection of that vector to the normal of the wall.

Due to factors that will be discussed shortly, the ball will not follow the path exactly when hit.

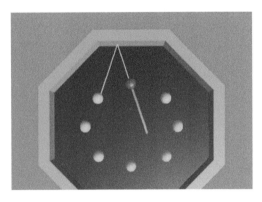

FIGURE 10.31   Reflection of the path during gameplay off one wall.

Due to the recursive nature of the code, the path will continue to extend over multiple segments until it collides with a ball, or the path reaches the maximum path length.

Remember, you can change to pathLength property in the Inspector.

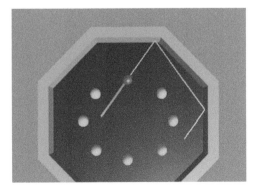

FIGURE 10.32   Reflection of the path during gameplay off two walls.

The Vector3 class provides methods that would allow us to complete the reflection with much less code. Specifically, the *dot* variable and calculation can be replaced with the *Dot* method, and the *magSquared* variable and calculation can be replaced with the *sqrMagnitude* property.

```
if(reflectionNeeded)
{
    Vector3 path = endPos - startPos;
    Vector3 proj = Vector3.Dot(path, hit.normal)
                    / hit.normal.sqrMagnitude * hit.normal;

    Vector3 reflectDirection = (path - 2 * proj).normalized;

    DrawPath(endPos, reflectDirection, length - hit.distance);
}
```

FIGURE 10.33   Simplified code using the Dot method and sqrMagnitude property.

Challenges

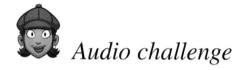 *Audio challenge*

Add an *AudioSource* Component to the Ball Prefab along with one script to play an audio file upon collision. The script should set the volume of sound based on the velocity of the ball upon collision.

Extend this challenge by playing a different audio file based on whether the ball collides with another ball or a table side.

Extend this challenge further by adding sound when a strike occurs.

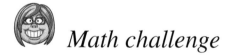 *Math challenge*

Currently, the length of the yellow path is constant, based on the initial value of *pathLength*. However, it would be nice if the length of the path related to the force in which the target ball will be hit by the Striker

Modify the code so that *pathLength* is private and continually changes value based on the distance the mouse is from the target ball (i.e., the length of the blue path). For instance, the yellow path might always be 3 times the length of the blue path. Modify this multiplier to achieve a length that feels right, and possibly make this multiplier a public property that can be modified in the Inspector.

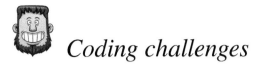

Coding challenges

1. Code improvements.

   Simplify the solution provided in the activity further by using the Reflect method of the Vector3 class.

2. Improve path prediction.

   The yellow path is a prediction of where the ball will go based on the assumption the ball will bounce off a wall in a perfect reflection. The actual path depends on factors such as the elasticity of the ball and the wall.

In the Materials folder, notice there are two *Physics Materials*—the *ballPhysicsMat* and *basePhysicsMat*.

FIGURE 10.34 Materials.

You can find these materials attached to the colliders of the GameObjects they are used on.

For example, the *ballPhysicsMat* is attached to the SphereCollider of each Ball.

FIGURE 10.35 SphereCollider of Ball with material.

Double-clicking on the *ballPhysicsMat* opens it in the Inspector.

Here you can see properties of Physics Materials that control how objects with the material are handled by the physics engine.

You could play with these properties for both the *ballPhysicsMat* and *basePhysics-Mat* to try to adjust the behavior of the balls to the predictive path.

❶ Inspector	⌂ :
🏐 **Ball Physics Mat (Physic Material)**	❷ ⇌ :
	Open

Dynamic Friction	0
Static Friction	0
Bounciness	1
Friction Combine	Average ▼
Bounce Combine	Average ▼

FIGURE 10.36   ballPhysicsMat in Inspector.

However, this has already been tuned pretty well for the desired behavior. Instead of changing the way balls move and interact with other objects in the scene, this challenge is focused on improving the prediction path itself.

The first concern is a result of using a Raycast to predict the collisions and movement of spheres.

When a ball hits a wall head on, the predicted point of collision returned from the Raycast is accurate.

FIGURE 10.37   Ball hitting the wall at 90°.

Will this be true regardless of the angle at which the ball hits the wall?

Consider a ball being hit towards a wall such that its movement vector forms a 30° angle with the wall.

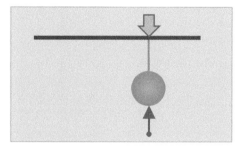

FIGURE 10.38   Ball hitting the wall at 30°.

Does a Raycast from the center of the ball still identify the point in which the ball will hit the wall?

As you can see, this is not the case. The ball will hit the wall before it reaches the end of the vector.

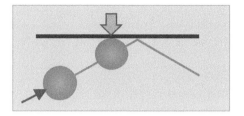

FIGURE 10.39   Offset of collision point.

If the ball hits a wall from a non-orthogonal angle, the predicted point of collision is inaccurate. The further the path is from being orthogonal and the larger the ball is, the more inaccurate the prediction point will be.

The reflection can still be made accurately if applied at the true moment of collision.

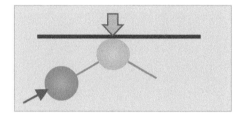

FIGURE 10.40   Reflection at offset.

This challenge requires modifying the code to achieve this. The Physics class in Unity provides a *SphereCast* method which should be quite helpful.

When complete, assuming you do not aim the ball directly at a wall, your predicted path should change direction before hitting a wall.

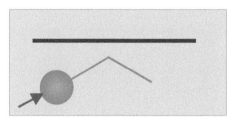

FIGURE 10.41   Path reflected before the wall.

While this will be a much better prediction of where the ball will go, it may be visually confusing to see the path change without a clear indication of the causal point of contact.

Extend this challenge by improving the visual feedback. One option is to show a partially transparent ball or circle underneath the path at each collision point.

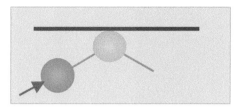

FIGURE 10.42   Partially transparent ball displayed at the point of reflection.

Using a SphereCast instead of a Raycast will also eliminate another bug.

When aiming such that the predictive path of the red ball passes closely by another ball, the current Raycast does not detect that a collision with the ball will occur.

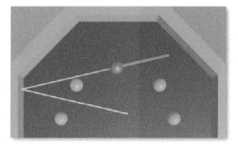

FIGURE 10.43   Path passing closely by another ball.

In such a case, the first point of collision will be with the ball, at which point the yellow path should end.

We could show the path reflected off the ball as well. This would only require removing the conditional statement related to the Ball, leaving only the assignment of *reflectionNeeded* to true.

```
//if(hit.transform.gameObject.tag != "Ball")
//{
    reflectionNeeded = true;
//}
```

FIGURE 10.44   Conditional commented out so reflectionNeeded is always true.

However, this is not advisable because after the first collision with a ball, multiple items will be in motion making further prediction quite difficult.

Achievements

In this chapter you:

- Derived a formula for finding scalar projection.
- Derived a formula for finding vector projection.
- Applied a vector reflection to create and show a predictive path.
- Learned a practical use for the concept of recursion.

Exercises

$$\text{Given}: \vec{a} = \left\langle\ 12\ \ -3\ \ 0\ \right\rangle$$

$$\vec{b} = \left\langle\ 4\ \ -5\ \ -2\ \right\rangle$$

1. Find $Proj_{\vec{a}}\vec{b}$

2. Find $Comp_{\vec{a}}\vec{b}$

3. Find $Proj_{\vec{b}}\vec{a}$

4. Find $Comp_{\vec{b}}\vec{a}$

5. Describe the relationship of the vectors.

6. Find the reflection of $\vec{a}$ around $\vec{b}$.

Conclusion

Mathematics is an essential tool for game developers. It is used in every aspect of game development, from the design of the game world to the implementation of the game mechanics. Without a strong understanding of mathematics, creating complex and engaging games would be impossible.

 Well, it's hard to do anything well without math.

In this book, we have explored some of the many ways that mathematics is used in game development. Utilizing linear algebra, calculus, geometry, and trigonometry, we have discussed how mathematical concepts are used to:

- Position game elements using various coordinate systems.
- Calculate the distance between objects.
- Implement an enemy field of view.
- Apply frame-rate independent movement to the player character and NPCs.
- Oscillate objects between two points following a sinusoidal curve.
- Use the relative directionality of objects to determine an action.
- Find perfect reflections around the normal resulting from an object colliding with a plane.

  and more!

Most importantly, we applied the mathematical concepts learned to actual games.

 In doing so, we covered many computer programming concepts—also in an applied manner.

I hope that this book has given you a better understanding of the role of mathematics in game development. If you are interested in learning more about this topic, there are many resources available online and in libraries.

 With a little effort, you can gain the mathematical skills you need to create your own amazing games.

Answers to Exercises

Chapter 3

1. B (–4, 0); C (4.5, 3); D (0, 0); E (–3, –2); F (3, –1)

2. $\overline{BC}$ = 2 units; $\overline{CD}$ = 3 units; $\overline{DO}$ = 1 unit

3. 80 units; 95 units; 260 units

4. (270, –60)

Chapter 4

1. 50 units

2. 44.72 px

3. 35.35 px

4. $\sqrt{942500}$ units, or $\approx$ 970.82 units

   Yes, the robot will detect the player.

5. $\sqrt{181}$ units, or $\approx$ 13.45 units

Chapter 5

1. $c \approx 87.17$ units, $b \approx 61.04$ units, $\alpha = 55°$

2. $\theta \approx 0.588$ rad or 33.69°, $\alpha \approx 0.983$ rad or 56.31°, $h \approx 72.11$ px

3. a. distance = $\sqrt{(\text{mouse.X} - \text{cheese.X})^2 + (\text{mouse.Y} - \text{cheese.Y})^2}$

   b. direction = $180° - \tan^{-1}(\text{mouse.Y} - \text{cheese.Y} / \text{mouse.X} - \text{cheese.X})$

4. | cat.forward – directionToMouse | < π/6

5. | cat.forward – mouse.forward | < π/6

Chapter 6

1. 1

2. 1

3. $\sqrt{3} \approx 1.732$

4. $\overrightarrow{PE} = \langle \begin{array}{ccc} 7 & 2 & -3 \end{array} \rangle$

5. $\left\langle \dfrac{7}{\sqrt{62}} \quad \dfrac{2}{\sqrt{62}} \quad \dfrac{-3}{\sqrt{62}} \right\rangle$ or $\left\langle \dfrac{7\sqrt{62}}{62} \quad \dfrac{2\sqrt{62}}{62} \quad \dfrac{-3\sqrt{62}}{62} \right\rangle$

6. $\overrightarrow{EP} = \begin{array}{ccc} -7 & -2 & 3 \end{array}$

7. $\left\langle \dfrac{-7}{\sqrt{62}} \quad \dfrac{-2}{\sqrt{62}} \quad \dfrac{3}{\sqrt{62}} \right\rangle$ or $\left\langle \dfrac{-7\sqrt{62}}{62} \quad \dfrac{-2\sqrt{62}}{62} \quad \dfrac{3\sqrt{62}}{62} \right\rangle$

8. W key: 5 meters

   D key: 5 meters

   W & D keys together: $5\sqrt{2}$ meters ≈ 7.07 meters

9. Diagonal movement will be faster.

$$\left\langle \dfrac{1}{\sqrt{2}} \quad \dfrac{1}{\sqrt{2}} \quad 0 \right\rangle \text{ or } \left\langle \dfrac{\sqrt{2}}{2} \quad \dfrac{\sqrt{2}}{2} \quad 0 \right\rangle$$

Chapter 7

1. $\sin\theta \cdot 100$ is the percentage of $\vec{v}$ in the vertical direction.

2. $\cos\theta \cdot 100$ is the percentage of $\vec{v}$ in the horizontal direction.

3. $0 < \sin\alpha < 1$, $\sin\alpha$ is between 0 and 1.

4. $-1 < \sin\alpha < 0$, $\sin\alpha$ is between -1 and 0.

5. amplitude $= 1$, median $= 0$, period $= 2\pi$, min $= -1$, max $= 1$.

6. y-intercept of sin wave $= 0$, y-intercept of cos $= 1$

7. $y = 3 \cdot \sin\left(\dfrac{\pi}{3}(x+1) \right) + 1$ or $y = 3 \cdot \cos\left(\dfrac{\pi}{3}\left(x - \dfrac{1}{2} \right) \right) + 1$

8. $x = 3 \cdot \sin(\pi \cdot time) + initPosX$

Chapter 8

1. If θ is the angle between $\langle\, 12 \quad -3 \quad 0 \,\rangle$ and $\langle\, 4 \quad -5 \quad -2 \,\rangle$,

$$\theta = \cos^{-1}\left(\frac{63}{\sqrt{6885}}\right)$$

$$\theta \approx 40.601294645°$$

2. No, the vectors are not scalar multiples and therefore not parallel.

3. Yes, the vectors are orthogonal because their dot product is zero.

4. Yes, the vectors are scalar multiples and therefore parallel.

5. No, the vectors are not perpendicular because their dot product is not zero.

6. 3

7.

    a. Angle formed is obtuse.

    b. Angle formed is acute.

    c. Vectors are orthogonal.

    d. Vectors are parallel and in the same direction.

    e. Vectors are orthogonal and in opposite directions.

Chapter 9

1. $\langle\, 3 \quad 1 \quad -4 \,\rangle, \langle\, 6 \quad 2 \quad -8 \,\rangle, \langle\, -3 \quad -1 \quad -4 \,\rangle$ etc.

2. Answers may vary depending on the point of inclusion. Example: Plane includes (0, 0, 0) and a normal of $\langle\, -24 \quad -17 \quad 11 \,\rangle$

3. ≈ 34.65 units

4. ≈ 405.79 units^2

Chapter 10

1. $\approx \langle\, 4.94 \quad -1.24 \quad 0 \,\rangle$

2. ≈ 5.09

3. $\langle\, 5.6 \quad -7 \quad -2.8 \,\rangle$

4. ≈ 9.39

5. $\bar{a}$ and $\bar{b}$ form an acute angle.

6. $\langle\, 0.8 \quad 11 \quad 5.6 \,\rangle$

Index

Note: *Italic* page numbers refer to figures.